THE IMPACT OF
CRIME

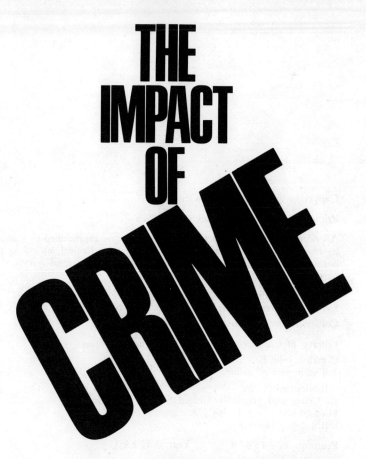

THE IMPACT OF CRIME

John E. Conklin
Department of Sociology, Tufts University

Macmillan Publishing Co., Inc.
NEW YORK

Collier Macmillan Publishers
LONDON

Macmillan Publishing Co., Inc.
866 Third Avenue, New York, New York 10022

Collier-Macmillan Canada, Ltd.

Library of Congress Cataloging in Publication Data

Conklin, John E
   The impact of crime.

   Bibliography: p.
1. Crime and criminals—United States. I. Title.
HV6791.C65   364'.973   74-4645
ISBN 0-02-324260-4

Printing: 1 2 3 4 5 6 7 8   Year: 5 6 7 8 9 0

Preface

THIS BOOK examines what people do when they are confronted, directly or indirectly, with violent crime. Crime is taken
as a given, rather than as a phenomenon to be explained. We do
not explore how the laws against murder, rape, robbery, and
assault developed nor how people label the perpetrators of such
crimes. Little use is made of labeling theory, since it emphasizes
institutional reactions to deviants rather than the way that people
alter their lives in response to crime. Also, labeling theory has
concentrated on behavior that many people feel should not be
criminal—homosexuality, drug use, and abortion.

We have sought to avoid an alarmist position on the threat of
crime to our society, favoring instead an analytical study of the
effects of crime on the social structure. We hope this book will
cast some light on the impact of crime on society and will help the
reader see the public as having an integral role in any solution
to the crime problem.

J. E. C.

**To My Parents,
Evan and Susan Conklin,
With Love and Appreciation**

Acknowledgments

I ORIGINALLY explored community response to crime in my doctoral dissertation, *Public Reactions to Crime: A Survey of Two Communities*, completed at Harvard University in the Department of Social Relations in 1969. Ruth Conklin provided invaluable aid in interviewing residents of "Port City" and "Belleville" for that study. Lloyd E. Ohlin offered encouragement and suggestions during the study, and David J. Armor advised me in the preparation of the questionnaire and in the data analysis.

The results of my doctoral research are presented in part in Chapters 2, 4, and 7 of this book. Chapter 4 is based on my paper, "Dimensions of Community Response to the Crime Problem," *Social Problems* XVIII (Winter 1971), pp. 373–385. Chapter 7 is largely drawn from another paper, "Criminal Environment and Support for the Law," *Law and Society Review* VI (November 1971), pp. 247–265. Ann Richardson made useful suggestions in the writing of each of these papers.

Contents

1 The Costs of Crime   1

2 Perceptions of Crime and Criminals   15

3 Crime and the Community: Durkheim and Capote   50

4 Crime and the Community: Port City and Belleville   73

5 Defensive Responses to Crime   105

6 Informal Social Control of Crime   131

7 Crime and Support for the Law   154

8 Collective Response to Crime: Vigilante Movements and Civilian Patrol Groups   185

9 Individual Response to Crime: Helping the Victim   214

10 Epilogue   248

Appendix A: Port City and Belleville   251

Appendix B: Statistical Tables   259

Bibliography   267

Index   279

The Costs of Crime 1

I N 1968 the National Advisory Commission on Civil Disorders observed that a sense of personal security is basic to the quality of life in a community and that personal security is affected more by crime than by anything else.[1] During the last decade, Americans have not felt that security. "The crime problem," "law and order," and "crime in the streets" are catch phrases that have been used to summarize popular fears and concerns about rising crime rates, student protests, and urban riots. These different forms of behavior are often lumped together, as when a United States Senator referred to the recent crime wave as "a riot in slow motion."[2] As campus violence and ghetto disturbances subsided, public concern with the crime issue did not abate in spite of attempts to reassure the citizenry that the streets were safer. On March 5, 1973, a front-page headline in *The New York Times* read: "Nixon Says Crisis in Cities Is Over; Cites Dip in Crime." [3] Two months later another headline stated: "Fear Persists in the Cities Despite Dip in U.S. Crime."[4]

To a significant extent, concern with crime is as much a disquietude with "improper behavior in public places" as a preoccupation with violent criminal behavior. A survey of Boston homeowners found widespread distress about "the failure of community" and the violation of "standards of right and seemly conduct" in public places.[5] Of the types of inappropriate behavior, street crime—especially violence at the hands of a stranger—elicited the strongest reaction. People were apprehensive about criminals lurking in dark alleys and behind trees, ready to strike at the first vulnerable passerby.[6] Attitudes of defensiveness and suspicion were seen as necessary adaptations to a threatening social environment. However, these responses may destroy social order even if they protect particular individuals. Roscoe Pound once said, "In civilized society men must be able to assume that those with whom they deal in the general intercourse of society will act in good faith."[7] When fear of crime is pervasive, such an assumption is often missing.

Today many people think that crime is a greater threat than ever before, that the very foundation of society is crumbling. In fact, recent studies by Presidential commissions show that the past decade has not been the most lawless or violent one in American history.[8] The nineteenth century and the early part of the twentieth century had higher rates of violent crime, and contemporary popular concerns reflected those high rates.[9] A portrait of New York in the 1850's by an Englishwoman sounds much like recent descriptions of American cities: "Probably in no city in the civilized world is life so fearfully insecure. Terrible outrages and murderous assaults are matters of such nightly occurrence as to be thought hardly worthy of notice."[10] This suggests that crime may become such a pervasive phenomenon that people accept it as an integral part of urban life, although it still evokes considerable anxiety.

Crime also elicited strong reactions from the public in early nineteenth-century Paris. In *Laboring Classes and Dangerous Classes*, Louis Chevalier pictures Paris of that period as a place where there was a great dread of crime.[11] Streets were just as "dark and deserted" as they are in large American cities today, and for much the same reasons. Parisians were alarmed at criminals' indiscriminate attacks on innocent victims. They spoke of crime in their daily conversations. Periodicals stimulated and reinforced public fascination with crime, as did the popular novels of the time. Crowds watched the pillorying and the execution of convicted offenders. Concern with crime also spurred the collection of crime statistics, which contributed to public fear by documenting the crime problem. During the nineteenth century in Paris, the popular view of crime shifted from crime as picaresque and limited to a closed society of romantic rogues to crime as an omnipresent threat to the quality of urban life.

Contemporary Americans are therefore not unique in their fear of crime. Their ancestors in this country and the residents of other nations, past and present, have felt similar concerns. The idyllic image of a crime-free past shared by many is untenable in light of historical evidence. Such an image makes contemporary fears even greater by contrast, although that image may provide a utopia toward which present solutions to the crime problem can aim.

Crime and violence, as well as public concern with crime and violence, rise and fall with regularity.[12] Crime waves are not new; they have existed throughout history. When there is a crime wave, people change their behavior to protect themselves, their families, and their property from the depredations of criminals. They feel like "hunted animals" and are "curfewed by their own fear."[13] Sometimes, "in the daily lives of many citizens the fear of crime takes an even greater toll than crime itself."[14] We can look at the toll of crime in terms of *direct* costs, attributable to the offenses themselves, and *indirect* costs, attributable to reactions to the criminal behavior.

The direct costs of crime can be measured in dollars lost, injuries suffered, and lives taken. Losses are suffered by victims of such crimes as murder, aggravated assault, rape, robbery, burglary, larceny, and auto theft—the seven crimes which comprise the Federal Bureau of Investigation's Crime Index. According to official statistics for 1972, there were 18,515 people murdered in the country; 388,650 who suffered aggravated assault (attack with intent to cause bodily injury); 46,431 women who were raped; 374,555 citizens who were robbed (had property taken with the threat of force); 2,344,991 people who had homes or businesses burglarized; 1,837,799 cases of larceny in which the loss exceeded $50; and 880,983 automobiles stolen.[15] These figures are based on reports filed by local police departments, reports that probably measure only half of the crimes that actually occur. Still, the direct loss from even these reported crimes is significant.

Direct victimization sometimes results from contributory behavior by the victim. He may precipitate his own loss through negligence, by leaving a window open through which a burglar can enter his home, or by leaving car keys in the ignition so that even an inexperienced youth can steal his car. Sometimes a victim is involved in the social dynamics that culminate in a crime, for

3

instance, by drinking in a bar and getting into an argument with someone who has a prior record of criminal violence. Such interactions occasionally produce homicides.[16] Victims may be accused of stupidity or naiveté in contributing to their own victimization, but they are generally not legally culpable. Whatever their contribution, they still incur direct losses as a result of the offender's behavior.

Crime also has indirect costs. There is the cost of maintaining the vast but undermanned criminal justice system that processes suspects. There are expenditures for the police, the courts, and the correctional institutions. Aside from these easily measured expenses, there are losses to inmates and to society from time spent in jails and prisons. Inmates working at prison jobs earn only a fraction of the money they could make in the outside world. Not only do they suffer the loss of earning power and dignity, but their families are not provided for and often require welfare assistance, an additional cost to society. Society also suffers in the incarceration of inmates because of the expense of maintaining prisons and their staffs, and because of the loss to the economy of the full productive effort of the inmates.

Not all the indirect costs of crime are related to the criminal justice system. There are also substantial costs associated with changes in the attitudes and behavior of people who are never directly involved in a crime, but who incur losses because they try to prevent their own victimization. For example, by staying home at night to avoid predators, people are unable to visit their friends or attend a movie. The costs to society of such reactions to crime may be even greater than the direct losses suffered by the victims of crime. For instance, the cost of installing burglar alarms in homes to prevent property theft may soon exceed the value of all property stolen in actual burglaries, although such target-hardening measures may have a subsidiary effect of increasing the occupants' sense of security in protected homes.

Economist Thomas C. Schelling suggests that we must look at the direct and indirect costs of crime in order to get a clear notion of what it would be worth to reduce crime and who would benefit from the reduction.[17] He argues that if we could eliminate all crime through security measures and law-enforcement practices, the direct costs of crime would be nil, but the costs of living in "an environment of potential crime" would be substantial. Since streets would be empty, there would be no street crime, but the "opportunity cost" to those who stayed indoors would be great. Schelling concludes that there is no direct relationship between the amount of actual crime and the cost of crime in a broader sense. In fact, the indirect costs may even exceed the losses directly attributable to criminal offenses.

The indirect costs of crime are not obvious or easily measurable. For example, our society suffers in many ways from the impact of crime against businesses. Industrial managers may decide that the threat of crime in a particular community is so great that locating a new plant there is impractical. They may locate in a nearby suburb or a neighboring state because they would have difficulty finding employees to work in the high crime-rate area. Executives may also fear damage to plant facilities by local vandals. As a result of a company's decision not to locate in such a community, fewer jobs will be available to local residents. This will contribute to a higher unemployment rate, which in turn might increase the crime rate because of the greater propensity of the unemployed to commit certain types of crime.

Public fear of crime in an area may reduce patronage of local businesses, especially after dark. As a result, some businessmen may close early, giving citizens fewer reasons to be on the streets and making the streets even more deserted. Some businessmen may even close down their businesses, as happened in ghettos after the riots of the 1960's.[18] This reduces the number of shopping facilities in the area and allows remaining businessmen to boost their prices. Furthermore, businessmen who suffer burglaries and larcenies may pass their losses on to customers in the form of higher prices. Some proprietors will install security devices to protect against crime, often passing the cost of such measures on to customers. Such costs can be quite substantial, as suggested by a 1969 study that estimated that businessmen spent about $3.3 billion on private crime prevention measures in one year, including $120 million on alarm systems, $123 million on armored car services, and $2.2 billion on special police and security guards.[19] Another costly measure is theft insurance, although some insurance companies refuse to sell policies to businessmen in high crime-rate areas. This may force them to close and move to another location, again reducing the supply of goods for local customers and raising the prices charged by remaining establishments.

Measuring the costs of crime against businesses is a complex undertaking. There are the direct losses to businessmen, then the costs of security measures and insurance policies, and finally the increased cost of goods and the reduced number of shopping facilities. To look only at the financial losses sustained by businessmen from the crimes themselves is clearly an oversimplification of the problem.

The indirect costs of crime also include the changes in attitude and behavior by people who fear their own victimization. They stay off the streets at night and lock their doors. If they go out, they walk only in groups and avoid certain areas of the city. They use taxis or cars to protect themselves from street crime. If they have to drive through high crime-rate areas of the city, they roll up their car windows and lock the doors. To avoid possible victimization, people do not use library and educational facilities at night, they stay away from meetings of social groups and organizations, and they keep out of parks and recreational areas. Some forfeit additional income by refusing overtime work which would force them to go home after dark. Some even carry firearms or knives. Many take security measures to protect their homes—additional locks on doors and bars on windows, brighter lights on porches and in the yards, burglar-alarm systems, and watchdogs. Judging by the types of precautions that people take, they seem to fear personal attack more than the loss of property through theft.[20] One extreme but fairly common reaction to both personal and property crimes is a desire to move, to escape from the community where crime poses such a great threat.[21]

In studying public reactions to crime, the National Crime Commission found that people feared most those crimes which occurred least often—murder, rape, and aggravated assault. Common crimes such as larceny and auto theft were less feared.[22] Even the violent crimes were dreaded less because of the injury or death involved—accidents and suicides account for more deaths than all crimes—than because such crimes were associated with strangers. Fear of crime is fear of the stranger, the unknown person who commits an unpredictable and violent attack on a vulnerable and innocent citizen who is merely going about his regular business. The stranger is seen as intending harm and as indiscriminate in his selection of a victim, making it difficult for the victim to avoid him. The popular view of the criminal is that he is a stranger or an outsider, someone different from those who fear crime. In fact, significant proportions of the most-feared crimes are committed by people with whom the victims are already acquainted—spouses, relatives, friends, and lovers.[23] However, the common view of the criminal as outsider has important effects. It enhances the fear of crime. It also makes the reintegration of the ex-convict into society difficult, pushing him back into a life of crime and increasing the threat to society.

Fear of violence from strangers is generalized to fear of the streets, especially in the high crime-rate areas of large cities. Such fear also reduces interpersonal trust and erects barriers between longtime residents of a community and newcomers to the area. Fear of the stranger diminishes social solidarity in a community. It also restricts the geographical mobility of those who fear crime in the streets. Jane Jacobs has said, "When people say that a city, or a part of it, is dangerous or is a jungle what they mean primarily is that they do not feel safe on the sidewalks."[24] Since streets are public areas, they are open to criminals as well as the general public. Fear of street crime arises largely because of this public nature of the street. One observer suggests, "The street is public, and the public display of tabooed behavior threatens to make it part of daily life. Openness gives such behavior an actuality and carries the threat of public acceptance and approval."[25] Streets where such tabooed behavior occurs become stigmatized areas. These areas become subject to "isolation, avoidance and protective encirclement" by the public, and "inhabitants of these encircled enclaves acquire a general stamp of community exclusion."[26] The tarnished image of the community reinforces the fears of residents of nearby areas, as well as the residents of the community itself. Fear of crime can thus subdivide a city into microcosmic communities with loyalty to the immediate neighborhood but hostility and distrust of other areas and their residents. This makes the formulation of social policies and the government of the city as a whole difficult, as each community seeks its own aggrandizement to the detriment of other areas with which it shares no common identity.

Crime in the streets is thus threatening because people want "unmolested privacy in public places."[27] Deviance and crime are prominent and visible in such public places, posing a threat to the existing social order. Even comparatively harmless behavior such as public drunkenness and juvenile loitering are seen as a threat to dominant social values. As Biderman et al. note, "Crimes therefore have significance in proportion to the extent to which they affront the moral sensibilities of persons. This impact is not limited to those who are victimized directly."[28] The moral significance of the act depends on a number of aspects of the crime, including the characteristics of the offender, the characteristics of the victim, the locale of the crime, the intended harm, and the strength of the norm violated by the act.

Street crime is least feared in one's immediate neighborhood. People feel safest near home; high crime rates and high risks of victimization are seen as characteristic of adjacent communities.[29] Crime is worst "just over there." Familiarity produces greater security, even though the objective risk may be inconsistent with such an optimistic assessment. There is no one-to-one relationship between actual risk and anxiety about crime. There is also no easy way to determine if fears are excessive, because we cannot say how much fear a person *should* feel when confronted with a particular probability of victimization. Fear of crime tends to be higher among blacks than among whites and higher in large cities than in suburbs and rural areas.[30] Both differences are consistent with actual crime rates, which are higher in black communities and in large cities. However, women fear crime more than men, even though rates of victimization for all crimes but rape are higher for men.[31] Clearly, factors other than objective risk play an important part in determining level of anxiety about crime.

Richard Quinney has pointed out that "the reactions that are elicited in response to crime are at the same time shaping the social reality of crime. As persons react to crime, they develop patterns for the responses of the future."[32] Durkheim claims that crime draws attention to the violated norm and in doing so helps bind people together by enhancing social solidarity. This is by no means a universal reaction to crime. In fact, crime is more likely to generate interpersonal distrust, feelings of insecurity, and dislike for one's neighborhood than to produce solidarity. This distrust and suspicion stems as much from the unpredictability of crime and the sense of invasion of private space as from the direct harm produced by offenders.[33] Fortifying homes with watchdogs, burglar alarms, locks and bars, and spotlights may minimize vulnerability to some extent, although these measures may merely shift crime onto less protected targets. These protective measures also create barriers between people and reduce social solidarity, possibly contributing to increased crime rates. Newcomers to a community are not accepted for a long time. Neighbors stay home rather than venture past a barking dog to borrow a cup of sugar. Other neighbors may be avoided as potentially dangerous because they keep a loaded shotgun in their homes.

Crime reduces trust and attachment to neighbors and to the community as a whole. By reducing solidarity, it weakens informal social control in the community, which is probably more effective in preventing crime than formal methods of social control such as the police. In a closely knit community, there is surveillance of public and private places. If surveillance is reinforced by willingness to report suspicious events to the police or by willingness to intervene in order to stop a crime, crime can be reduced by increasing the risk to the offender. One study found that aggressive violation of social norms is more common among people who feel anonymous and deindividuated.[34] This suggests that group solidarity may also reduce tendencies toward violent crime. Crime diminishes social solidarity, which in turn leads to higher crime rates. Jennie McIntyre has noted this process as follows:

As social interaction is reduced and fear of crime becomes fear of the stranger, the social order is further damaged. Not only are there fewer persons on the street and in public places than there might be, but persons who are afraid may show a lack of concern for each other.

9

The logical consequences of this reduced sociability, mutual fear, and distrust can be seen in the reported incidents of bystanders indifferent to cries for help.[35]

Evidence to be examined in a later chapter indicates that bystanders are not apathetic to cries for help from victims, even when they fail to offer assistance. The bystander often has no previous experience with crime and has little knowledge of how to react. He is faced with an event that is often ambiguous, and the victim's cries are usually not directed at him personally.

Occasionally crime elicits a collective response in the form of vigilante action or a civilian police patrol. Such groups arise to establish order in a community. They increase surveillance of the streets in much the same way that informal social bonds among residents of closely knit communities do. By strengthening social control, patrol groups may increase the risk perceived by potential criminals and thus prevent crime or at least shift crime to less protected communities. By making residents of the area see that something is being done to make the community safe from crime, they may increase the number of people who are willing to spend time on the streets. This in turn augments informal social control and may contribute to a decline in local crime rates.

One common reaction to crime is to assign full responsibility for crime prevention to the police. This reduces public willingness to report crime to the police or to help them make an arrest. If this lack of support for the law becomes known to criminals, they may be more likely to commit crime in the community because of the lower risk of apprehension. This can lead to higher crime rates, produce an even greater reliance on the police in the fight against crime, and further reduce informal social control over potential criminals.

The costs of crime are many. There are direct costs in terms of money lost and lives taken. There are indirect costs such as the expense of maintaining the criminal justice system. The impact of crime on public attitudes and behavior is also great. In fact, the influence of crime on such attitudes and behavior can actually contribute to the crime problem, as we shall see throughout the following chapters.

Footnotes

1. *Report of the National Advisory Commission on Civil Disorders.* New York: Bantam Books, Inc., 1968, p. 266.
2. Senator Robert Griffin of Michigan, as cited in "A Plan to Cut Crime," *Life* magazine LXXII (June 30, 1972), p. 52.
3. "Nixon Says Crisis in Cities Is Over; Cites Dip in Crime," *The New York Times*, March 5, 1973, pp. 1, 20.
4. Paul Delaney, "Fear Persists in the Cities Despite Dip in U.S. Crime," *The New York Times*, May 8, 1973, p. 37.
5. Concern about inappropriate behavior was greatest among females, those over 65, Catholics, and those earning less than $5,000 a year. James Q. Wilson, "The Urban Unease: Community vs. City," *The Public Interest*, No. 12 (Summer 1968), pp. 25–39.
6. In this book, we will not deal with public reaction to either white-collar crime or to government crime against private citizens. Although white-collar crime has a significant impact on society, people often find it difficult to grasp the details and implications of such offenses. Because people do not see white-collar crime as presenting a threat of direct harm to themselves, they are less apt to change their attitudes and behavior in response to such crime than in reaction to street crime. For a review of the literature on attitudes toward business-related crimes, see John E. Conklin and Erwin O. Smigel, "Norms and Attitudes toward Business-related Crimes." Paper presented at the Symposium on Studies of Public Experience, Knowledge and Opinion of Crime and Justice. Bureau of Social Science Research, Inc. Washington, D.C., March 1972. We will also not deal with government-related crimes such as drug raids on innocent citizens and political corruption, although such crimes undermine respect for the law and reduce the legitimacy of the government itself. For a study of corruption, see John A. Gardiner, *The Politics of Corruption: Organized Crime in an American City.* New York: Russell Sage Foundation, 1970.
7. Roscoe Pound, *Jurisprudence*, III. St. Paul, Minnesota: West Publishing Company, 1959, p. 10.
8. See the various volumes written by the President's Commission on Law Enforcement and Administration of Justice (the National Crime Commission) and by the National Commission on the Causes and Prevention of Violence (the Violence Commission).
9. For example, see Victor G. Strecher, *The Environment of Law Enforcement: A Community Relations Guide.* Englewood Cliffs, N.J.: Prentice-Hall, Inc., 1971, pp. 16–19; Richard Sennett, "Mid-

dle-Class Families and Urban Violence: The Experience of a Chicago Community in the Nineteenth Century," in Stephan Thernstrom and Richard Sennett, editors, *Nineteenth-Century Cities: Essays in the New Urban History*. New Haven: Yale University Press, 1969, pp. 386–420; and Andy Logan, *Against the Evidence: The Becker-Rosenthal Affair*. New York: The McCall Publishing Company, 1970.

10. Cited in Charles Lockwood, "Crime—100 Years Ago," *The New York Times*, June 5, 1972, p. 33.

11. Louis Chevalier, *Laboring Classes and Dangerous Classes in Paris During the Nineteenth Century*. Translated by Frank Jellinek. New York: Howard Fertig, 1958, 1973.

12. Similarly, government corruption and public concern with such corruption also rise and fall. See Gardiner, op. cit., passim.

13. Howard Whitman, *Terror in the Streets*. New York: The Dial Press, 1951, pp. 38, 48–49.

14. Jack Rosenthal, "The Cage of Fear in Cities Beset by Crime," *Life* magazine LXVII (July 11, 1969), p. 17.

15. Clarence M. Kelley, *Crime in the United States—1972*. Washington, D.C.: United States Government Printing Office, 1973, pp. 2–29, 61.

16. See Marvin E. Wolfgang, *Patterns in Criminal Homicide*. Philadelphia: University of Pennsylvania Press, 1958, pp. 134–167.

17. Thomas C. Schelling, "Economic Analysis and Organized Crime," in the President's Commission on Law Enforcement and Administration of Justice, *Task Force Report: Organized Crime*. Washington, D.C.: United States Government Printing Office, 1967, p. 120.

18. See Howard Aldrich and Albert J. Reiss, Jr., "The Effect of Civil Disorders on Small Business in the Inner City," *The Journal of Social Issues* XXVI (Winter 1970), pp. 195–198.

19. Cited in *Victims of Crime*, Hearing Before the Subcommittee on Criminal Laws and Procedures of the Committee on the Judiciary, United States Senate, 92nd Congress, First Session. Washington, D.C.: United States Government Printing Office, 1972, p. 381.

20. Albert D. Biderman, Louise A. Johnson, Jennie McIntyre, and Adrianne Weir, Field Surveys I of the President's Commission on Law Enforcement and Administration of Justice, *Report on a Pilot Study in the District of Columbia on Victimization and Attitudes toward Law Enforcement*. Washington, D.C.: United States Government Printing Office, 1967, pp. 129–130.

21. One survey found that between 20 and 30 per cent of the residents of high crime-rate districts wished to move. See Albert J. Reiss, Jr., Field Surveys III, Part 1, of the President's Commission on Law Enforcement and Administration of Justice, *Studies in Crime and*

Law Enforcement in Major Metropolitan Areas. Washington, D.C.: United States Government Printing Office, 1967, p. 31.

22. The President's Commission on Law Enforcement and Administration of Justice, *The Challenge of Crime in a Free Society.* Washington, D.C.: United States Government Printing Office, 1967, pp. 50–52.

23. For example, Wolfgang found that 85 per cent of murder victims had a prior relationship with their killers. See Wolfgang, op. cit., p. 207. Another study showed that about half of rape victims were previously acquainted with the rapists. See Menachem Amir, *Patterns in Forcible Rape.* Chicago: University of Chicago Press, 1971, pp. 234–235. Also, large proportions of the victims and offenders in cases of aggravated assault have prior relationships with each other. See *Report of the President's Commission on Crime in the District of Columbia.* Washington, D.C.: United States Government Printing Office, 1966, p. 66; and James Q. Wilson, *Varieties of Police Behavior: The Management of Law and Order in Eight Communities.* Cambridge: Harvard University Press, 1968, pp. 23–24. However, there is some evidence to suggest that increasing proportions of violent crimes occur between strangers rather than people who know each other. The proportion of all murders that are felony-murders (killings resulting from felonious activities) has increased from 13 per cent in 1962 to 27 per cent in 1972. Most of these murders are probably between strangers. Also, homicide data from four large cities suggest an increase in stranger-to-stranger murders. See "Murder: Chances Rise It'll Be by a Stranger," *Boston Evening Globe,* May 3, 1973, p. 2.

24. Jane Jacobs, *The Death and Life of Great American Cities.* New York: Vintage Books, 1961, p. 30.

25. William C. Rhodes, *Behavioral Threat and Community Response.* New York: Behavioral Publications, Inc., 1972, p. 36.

26. Ibid., p. 37.

27. Robert M. Cipes, *The Crime War.* New York: The New American Library, 1968, p. 41.

28. Biderman et al., op. cit., p. 164.

29. See Biderman et al., op. cit., p. 120; Reiss, op. cit., p. 28; Sarah L. Boggs, "Formal and Informal Crime Control: An Exploratory Study of Urban, Suburban, and Rural Orientations," *The Sociological Quarterly* XII (Summer 1971), pp. 320–322; and Simon Dinitz, "Progress, Crime, and the Folk Ethic: Portrait of a Small Town," *Criminology* XI (May 1973), p. 16.

30. Biderman et al., op. cit., pp. 120–126; and the President's Commission on Law Enforcement and Administration of Justice, *Task Force Report: Crime and Its Impact—An Assessment.* Washington, D.C.: United States Government Printing Office, 1967, p. 87.

31. Ibid.
32. Richard Quinney, *The Social Reality of Crime.* Boston: Little, Brown and Company, 1970, p. 278.
33. See Philip H. Ennis, Field Surveys II of the President's Commission on Law Enforcement and Administration of Justice, *Criminal Victimization in the United States: A Report of a National Survey.* Washington, D.C.: United States Government Printing Office, 1967, p. 51.
34. Philip G. Zimbardo, "The Human Choice: Individuation, Reason, and Order versus Deindividuation, Impulse, and Chaos," in William J. Arnold and David Levine, editors, *1969 Nebraska Symposium on Motivation.* Lincoln: University of Nebraska Press, 1969, pp. 263–270.
35. Jennie McIntyre, "Public Attitudes toward Crime and Law Enforcement," *The Annals of the American Academy of Political and Social Science* CCCXXIV (November 1967), p. 41.

Perceptions of Crime and Criminals 2

T H E *actual* amount of crime that occurs in our society is unknown. Crimes remain hidden from official view because they are not observed by a witness or are not reported to the police. The *recorded* amount of crime is that proportion of actual crime that is officially noted by the police. The difference between the actual amount of crime and the recorded amount of crime is often referred to as the *dark figure*, the proprotion that occurs but is not officially recorded.

To determine the magnitude of this dark figure, the National Crime Commission sponsored a nation-wide survey in 1965. Individuals from 10,000 randomly selected households were interviewed to learn the extent to which they had been victims of crime.[1] The survey showed that the dark figure was large for many of the crimes in the FBI index. The greatest discrepancy between actual (victim-reported) crime and recorded crime was for rape; the actual rate was four times the official rate. This is due to the stigma of being a rape victim and the embarrassment of having to recount the details of the crime to a male police officer. Recently the New York City Police Department created a unit of female rape investigators, hopefully reducing resistance to calling the police and providing emotional support for the victim.[2] This may even cause a rise in official rates of rape if the dark figure is reduced through better reporting.

The victimization survey also found that the actual crime rate for aggravated assault was twice the official rate, and that actual rates for individuals suffering burglaries or larcenies over $50 were more than twice the official rates. The actual robbery rate was about one and a half times the official rate; the actual rate for auto theft and murder were about the same as the official rates.[3]

There are several reasons for public unwillingness to report crime. A rape victim may feel ashamed and think there is little to gain and much to lose from reporting the crime, but the victim of an auto theft may have to report the crime to collect insurance for his loss. The major reason for failure to report crime is a belief in the ineffectiveness of the police in doing anything about the crime, such as catching the offender or recovering the stolen property. Other reasons include fear of reprisals, a feeling that the crime was a private matter, a desire to avoid entanglement with the police and the courts, ignorance of how to report a crime, and fear of increased insurance premiums if the crime were reported.[4] Generally, more serious crimes, such as those involving violence or large property losses, are reported more often than less serious offenses.[5]

Some of the discrepancy between actual crimes and official statistics cannot be accounted for by citizen failure to report crime. The police sometimes fail to record crimes that citizens report to them.[6] Also, some crimes pass unnoticed; if a loss of property is not observed or if it is attributed to personal carelessness rather than theft, no crime will be reported. Some crimes are not reported because they do not involve unwilling participants who will make a complaint to the police. Crimes without victims, such as homosexuality and drug addiction, usually produce no complainant, and thus no official report of the crime is normally made.[7]

In recent years there has been an increase in official crime rates. Some argue that this apparent change does not represent an increase in *actual* crime rates, but rather a change in the *proportion* of all crimes that are recorded by the police. Specifically, it is argued that a major reason for rising crime rates is that reporting and recording practices have been improving, thus reducing the proportion of crime that remains unknown to the police.[8] The National Crime Commission suggested that crime rates might be rising because the public is increasingly willing to report crime to the police. The Commission argued that this was especially true of the poor and the minority-group members, who became more willing to call the police as they gained a greater stake in society.[9] However, in the national victimization survey done for the Commission, blacks and whites reported crimes to the police equally often and the reasons they gave for not reporting crimes when they failed to do so were similar.[10] Whether the two groups differed in reporting practices in earlier years cannot be determined from the survey evidence. There are no solid data that show a decline in the dark figure over time as a result of greater public willingness to report crime. However, it is possible that greater police professionalism in record-keeping practices may have reduced the dark figure in recent years. Still, there are no data to show that more professional departments have experienced sharper rises in crime rates in recent years than less professional departments. Yet another possible reason that the dark figure may have declined in recent years is that increased ownership of insurance policies may have stimulated better citizen reporting of property crimes, although this would not explain the equally steep rise in violent crimes. The dark figure may indeed have fluctuated or declined in the last few years as official crime rates have increased, but there is no solid evidence that better reporting and better recording of crime have been the major reasons for rising crime rates. In fact, careful examination of official statistics shows that even if one assumes that the dark figure disappeared completely by 1972—which of course it did not—there has still been a very substantial increase in crime rates since 1965. In other words, the *official* crime rates in 1972 were generally higher than the *actual* rates (based on the victimization survey) were in 1965.[11] In spite of any changes in reporting and recording crime over this period of time, there was still a very real increase in *actual* crime rates.

Public Perception of Crime Rates

People react to their perception of social problems rather than to the problems themselves. If poverty is hidden from public view, there will be little concern with poverty and little pressure to develop programs to alleviate the condition of the poor. Similarly, if crime is not regarded as a serious problem, there will be little discussion of the issue and little pressure to reduce crime rates, even if those rates are increasing dramatically.

Perception of crime is influenced in part by officially reported crime rates. For instance, one study of eight communities found that crime was more likely to become a political issue in towns with higher-than-average crime rates than in towns with lower rates.[12] Before crime affects an individual's attitudes and behavior, it must be regarded as a personal threat. In some instances, an individual may even suffer victimization but be unaware that a crime has been committed; an example of this is attributing the loss of property to carelessness rather than theft. In such a case, the victim would not grow anxious about rising crime rates, become suspicious of strangers, or install extra locks in his home. However, this individual might perceive a great threat if he heard on the news that property crime in his city had increased substantially in recent months, even if all the increase were actually due to reports of theft from individuals who had in fact carelessly mislaid property. Perceptions of crime and even official rates of crime do not necessarily reflect the amount of crime that actually occurs.

A threat may be perceived without being real; for attitudes and behavior to change, only the perception of the threat need be real. For example, in 1969 in the French city of Orléans a story circulated that the owners of certain dress shops were drugging women and selling them into white slavery. This story had absolutely no basis in fact, not even in any problems within the dress shops and certainly not in the disapperance of any women. The rumor spread solely by word of mouth and received no support from the press. In reaction to the rumor, mothers and teachers warned girls not go into or even near the shops. These precautions added fuel to the rumor. Even after the story was shown to be untrue, women were still afraid to enter the stores without escorts. They no longer believed the story, but they nevertheless felt uneasy, as though something must have happened to have caused such a rumor in the first place.[13] Perception of crime had created substantial changes in attitudes and behavior without any offense actually being committed.

The threat of crime must be immediate and salient to elicit behavioral and attitudinal changes aimed at reducing risk. Marvin E. Wolfgang suggests some of the factors that are related to perception of such a threat:

The perspective of the potential victim is not concerned about the crime rate of *offenders*, or even the rate at which persons become victims of crime. He is concerned, rather, with the probability of becoming a victim in a given urban space, like on a certain street corner, on a given block, or near a certain place of business. The population of a neighborhood may have increased over fifteen years, the number of youths in crime-prone ages may have increased even though the crude rate of violent crime or even the rate of juvenile crime may have remained fairly steady. Since the size of the neighborhood has not increased (a street intersection retains the same square footage), the result is that the chances of a given citizen's being assaulted at that intersection have increased.[14]

When perceptions of a high threat of crime continue over a period of time and are contrasted with a lower threat in the recent past, there is a crime wave. Few sociologists have explored crime waves in a systematic way. One who has is Kai T. Erikson, who examined crime and deviance in the seventeenth-century Massachusetts Bay Colony. He suggests that whenever a community confronts a shift in the boundaries of acceptable behavior, the kinds of behavior given attention by the law will change. Behavior that was previously regarded as normal and nonthreatening is redefined as dangerous. Crime waves are characterized by publicity, excitement, and alarm over particular types of deviance, as well as by sudden shifts in community norms. A crime wave does not necessarily reflect any real change in the amount of a particular type of behavior, but may just indicate that the label *deviant* or *criminal* has been attached to that behavior.[15]

Another sociologist who has examined crime waves is Edwin M. Lemert, who employs the concept of *tolerance quotient*. The tolerance quotient is a ratio of actual criminal behavior to public attitudes toward that behavior.[16] The numerator of the ratio is an objective measure of the criminal behavior; the denominator is a subjective measure of attitudes toward the same behavior. No one has been able to express this quotient in numerical terms, primarily because of the difficulty of measuring the objective and the subjective quantities in the same units. Unless this can be done, the idea of a tolerance quotient is of little empirical value. However, the idea is conceptually useful in thinking about crime waves, since it allows us to think of a critical breaking point at which the public will no longer accept more crime. After this point is reached, people will demand official actions to reduce crime. Up to this point, they will tolerate (not necessarily approve) some crime. Lemert argues that the tolerance quotient fluctuates over time, primarily because public attitudes toward acceptable levels of crime are volatile; the actual crime rate is a more constant factor in the tolerance quotient. One value of the tolerance quotient is to compare communities with each other. The ratio may be the same in two communities which have different crime rates and different public attitudes toward acceptable amounts of crime. This would explain why people in one town become upset with a smaller increase in local crime rates than do the residents of another town. Lemert suggests that in many communities the tolerance quotient is just short of the critical point at which people become aroused.[17] If this is so, it would explain why crime waves can develop with relatively small increases in crime rates.

We can speak of the *criminal environment* of a community as consisting of the myths, legends, ideas, and views about crime in a given social setting. These views are affected by information gathered from the following sources:

> The mass media
> Statements by politicians
> Observation of the activities of the local police
> Conversations with friends
> Stories by victims of crimes
> First-hand observations of crime and criminals
> Personal victimization

The "climate of concern and worry" in a community that is generated or reinforced by information from these sources does not necessarily bear any close relationship to the objective dangers faced by the residents, but people's "criminal conceptions" do influence their attitudes and behavior.[18] Information and ideas about crime can create the impression that crime is a greater threat than it was in the past. Perception of the threat of crime is more influenced by changing crime rates than by static rates, even if those rates are high.[19] This is probably because an increase in crime rates produces a contrast with the "safer" past. Leslie T. Wilkins has noted:

If the public are continuously told that "crime is going up" it is likely that they will become anxious in terms of *what they perceive as crime;* but what they perceive as crime may be quite different from what crime in fact represents. The mere information set—"crime is going up"—might lead to the public being more suspicious of actions and persons that do not justify anxiety, and such suspicion could lead to further alienation of people who are merely "different" in a harmless way, and turn into a self-fulfilling prophecy.[20]

Since the mid-1960's there has been a widespread public view that crime rates are rising. A survey in 1967 found that nearly half of the people in the country thought that rates had increased *in the previous year;* most of the rest thought that rates had not changed much in the last year.[21] A survey in high crime-rate communities in Boston and Chicago in 1966 found that about three-fourths of the people felt that crime rates had increased in recent years, and those who did not feel that way thought that rates had remained constant.[22] In a study carried out by this author in 1968 in two communities in the Boston area—one with a low crime rate (the suburb of "Belleville") and the other with a relatively high crime rate (the urban community of "Port City")*—71 per cent of the residents of the low-crime area and 82 per cent of those in the high-crime area thought that crime rates had increased in the previous twenty years. Only one in twenty thought that rates had declined, the remainder thinking that rates had stayed the same.[23] In fact, there has been an increase in official (as well as actual) crime rates in the last two decades, whether one looks at statistics for the nation or statistics for the two communities where residents were interviewed. However, the fact that more of those in the high-crime area perceived an increase in crime rates suggests that perceptions of crime are influenced by more than just a change in officially reported crime rates.

*See Appendix A for a more detailed description of these two communities.

Comparatively little is known of exactly how people receive their impressions of crime rates. Ramsey Clark has said, "Most lives in America are unmarred by serious crime. The only meaningful impression such people can have about the incidence of crime is made from the press, other communications media and the police. As crime becomes more topical, the tendency of distorted impressions to mislead increases."[24] Little research has been directed at sorting out the relative impact of various factors on people's impressions of crime, but it does seem clear that the mass media have a major effect. Facts that once were never known to the public or were treated briefly in newspapers are now reported swiftly on television and radio, in daily newspapers, and in weekly magazines. Even in communities with no real crime problem, residents are aware that crime in the streets is a serious problem in this country.[25]

The total flow of information is greater today than a few decades ago. People are now aware of the news more quickly, which makes them better informed but also more apprehensive about events such as crimes and riots. The media have increased the number of threat messages through the reporting of crime and violence. They usually report only the most dramatic, hence the most threatening crimes. This gives people an unbalanced picture of crime. When a mass murder or a rape is reported, neither media spokesmen nor media viewers stop to examine the present rate of murders or rapes per 100,000 people and compare those rates with rates in the past. In this way, the media increase public fear unintentionally. There is a larger pool of crimes to be reported today than in the past simply because the population of the nation has increased. Even if the *rate* of certain crimes had remained the same over time, there would still be more crimes to report.[26] Reporting crimes without mentioning their frequency in comparison to the number of people in the nation creates the impression that crime is a greater threat in comparison with the past than it really is. Media reporting of crime is immediate, dramatic, and free of historical perspective and therefore leads to exaggerated public fear of crime.

The media can create crime waves through the reporting of crime news. Newspapers sometimes try to increase circulation through front-page stories about sensational crimes. In fact, the British police for a time thought that the 1969 kidnapping of the wife of a newspaper executive was an attempt to create a front-page story that would increase the paper's circulation. Reluctance to believe that the abduction was real delayed police efforts to solve the crime, possibly contributing to the woman's death.[27] Lincoln Steffens has recounted an instance in American history in which newspapers that were engaged in a competition for readers created a crime wave through their attention to spectacular crimes.[28] Such reporting techniques can enhance public fears. They also create a public demand for additional, perhaps reassuring information about crime. Media reporting can also stimulate the police to give fuller and more accurate accountings of crime, which in turn can reinforce public anxiety and generate a demand for additional news from the media.[29] Crime reporting can fulfill the public demand for information about crime, but crime reporting can also produce this demand in the first place.[30]

American newspapers have typically paid somewhat more attention to crime news than the press in other nations. Although foreign newspapers also engage in yellow journalism, they generally act with greater overall restraint in their reporting of crime news.[31] Variation in styles of reporting crime news involves such factors as the amount of space given a story, the nature of the motivations attributed to the offender (trivial motives being more threatening than "rational" motives), and follow-up reporting on the type of punishment meted out to the offender.

A study in Colorado discovered that crime rates were not related to the amount of crime news in the papers.[32] Percentage changes in crime rates were not in line with percentage changes in reported crime news. In fact, over certain periods of time, official crime rates even changed in the direction *opposite* to changes in the amount of crime news. Crime waves are probably created more easily by fluctuations in newspaper reporting of crime than by changes in official crime rates, since people have greater familiarity with and access to what they read in the papers than what appears in the annual FBI reports. In fact, interviews with Colorado residents showed that people's opinions about crime more closely reflected changes in the amount of crime reported in local newspapers than changes in official crime rates. People were especially sensitive to the types of crime that were most personally threatening. For example, women made larger estimates of increases in crime rates than men, the discrepancy being particularly great for the crime of rape. Other surveys have found that women feel more vulnerable to crime than men, even though men have higher rates of victimization for most crimes.[33]

Not only does the amount and quality of newspaper reporting of crime influence public perceptions of crime, but the newspaper one reads also makes a difference, since papers differ in their reporting practices. One study found that over a three-month period of time the New York *Daily News* presented twice as many stories about juvenile delinquency as *The New York Times*. The stories in the *Daily News* were also more apt to appear on the front page and to be written in emotionally charged language.[34] We might infer that readers of the two papers would differ in their perception of crime, but we have no direct evidence of this. However, it might also be true that readers are drawn to a particular newspaper because they are concerned about crime and know that a particular paper is likely to provide them with more information about the problem.

One of the few studies to deal with the sources of public perception of crime was done for the National Crime Commission. No close relationship was found between anxiety about crime and exposure to crime.[35] The measure of exposure to crime included personal victimization, acquaintance with someone who had suffered a violent crime, and witnessing a crime. The Commission concluded that anxiety was probably more influenced by information from news reports and conversations than it was by exposure to crime. The only direct support for this conclusion appears in one of the Commission's reports:

After they were asked for their estimates of an increase or decrease [in crime, the respondents] were asked where they had obtained their information on this subject. A preponderant majority either said they got their information from the news media or from what they heard people say.[36]

The survey conducted by this author in Belleville and Port City found that neither perception of local crime rates nor feelings of personal safety were related to overall exposure to either television news or news in the daily papers.[37]

After spending much money and effort to collect data on public attitudes toward crime, the Crime Commission was only able to state that "we need many more intensive studies to determine what it is that most influences people's views and feelings about crime."[38] The Commission's warning that media responsibility in the interpretation of crime news is needed in order to prevent public hysteria is good advice, but it offers little guidance as to what constitutes responsible reporting, since it gives no clear picture of exactly how the public's perception of crime is formed.[39]

At this point we cannot precisely identify the sources of people's perception of crime. Probably certain types of information are given more weight than others by people in different communities. For example, news of a gangland slaying may elicit a different amount of fear in an area where there is widespread gambling than in an area where there is none. Selective perception and assimilation of crime news is probably influenced by a person's prior experiences, his social background, the nature of the criminal environment in which he lives, his willingness to believe the source of information, and a number of other factors. Still, little of a concrete nature can be said about how long impressions of crime will last and under what circumstances they will produce changes in attitudes and behavior.

If the media can influence public perception of crime, so too can the political use of the crime issue. Crime has been effectively employed by politicians—including a number of ex-policemen—to gain public support, although no politician has yet gone on record as being in favor of crime. Deep-seated fears and concerns are aroused by crime, and the promise to reestablish law and order and to make the streets safe is an effective way to mobilize support. Crime is an even better target than Communism because it affects everyone.[40] It is both a realistic threat and a symbol of the breakdown of the social order. However, these scare tactics make crime, which is the product of such social problems as poverty and discrimination, stand for these social ills, when the emphasis should be on the causes of crime. Crime becomes the problem to which people demand immediate response by political leaders. Long-run solutions to the social problems that underlie crime are eschewed for tough talk and repressive social control.

When street crime was limited to communities of the lower class, the disenfranchised, and the ethnic minorities, it was not as effective a political issue. When it spread to middle-class communities and claimed middle-class victims, it caused greater fear and concern.[41] Because the middle class is highly property-conscious and because the threat of victimization contrasts with a comparatively crime-free past, it is more concerned with the crime issue than the lower class, the group that actually suffers the highest rate of victimization. Middle-class concern with crime is reinforced by the perception that crime is a lower-class black phenomenon that threatens the white middle class. This view augments white middle-class support for law-and-order candidates. Lower-class people and black people have the greatest *fear* of crime because they face the highest risk of victimization and face it every day in their neighborhoods, but *concern* with crime as a political issue is concentrated in the middle class.[42]

Crime in recent years has been an issue used for political purposes more by politicians of the right than by those of the left. Walter B. Miller looks at the assumptions and crusading issues of the right and the left with regard to the crime issue and finds that the right assumes individual responsibility for personal behavior (as opposed to placing the blame on social conditions); proclaims the need for a strong moral order based on familial and religious values (as opposed to seeing the current moral order as poorly adapted to existing social conditions); stresses security of person and property (as opposed to emphasizing the injustices of the distribution of wealth and power in society); asserts the need for conformity to legitimate authorities (instead of saying that the authorities should be more responsive to the needs of the socially disadvantaged); and emphasizes divisions within society by various social groupings (rather than pointing to the need for a more open society that provides everyone with greater opportunities).[43] These assumptions about individuals and the social order differentiate the crusading issues of the right from those of the left. The right stresses the excessively lenient treatment of criminals by the legal system, the impropriety of favoring the rights of defendants over the rights of victims, the erosion of discipline and respect for authority, the great costs of crime, and the permissiveness of society. These issues are often lumped together under the phrase *law and order*. In contrast, the crusading issues of the left include overcriminalization of behavior by the law, the stigmatization of offenders, excessive reliance on the institutionalization of offenders, the overcentralization of correctional and law-enforcement agencies, and discrimination in the criminal justice system. Miller states that a person's position on the crime issue—whether on the right or on the left—often becomes "infused with deeply felt, quasi-religious significance."[44]

Crime in the streets was the major domestic issue in the 1968 Presidential election, with Richard Nixon effectively adopting the law-and-order stance and Hubert Humphrey being forced on the defensive.[45] This issue was of somewhat less significance in the elections of 1970 and 1972, although one survey found that in the 1972 Presidential election the issue of personal safety caused a large number of blue-collar workers who had traditionally voted Democratic to shift to President Nixon.[46] Concern with personal security was also responsible for the increase in public support for the death penalty that followed the Supreme Court's 1972 decision that execution was unconstitutional under most circumstances.[47] Support for the death penalty has become an additional plank in the law-and-order candidate's platform.

The political use of the crime issue is not limited to the United States. Law and order has been an issue of political significance in West Germany in recent years.[48] In Italy, public reactions to robberies and violence have in recent years threatened to create a backlash favoring the Neo-Fascists. As a result, the ruling party has sought to gain political support by taking measures to reduce crime, including overtime work for policemen just before election day.[49] Even in nations without free elections, such as the Soviet Union, crime and "hooliganism" have been used by the government and the press to rally public support for measures designed to induce conformity to official morality.

The crime issue has also been used for political ends in developing nations. One reason given for the 1971 coup d'état in Uganda was public fear of crime, "the frequent loss of life and property arising from almost daily cases of robbery with violence and kondoism [a violent form of armed robbery by gangs] without strong measures being taken to stop them."[50] Another instance of the political use of the crime issue arose in Iraq in 1973. After a series of brutal murders, the government imposed a curfew in Baghdad, banned flights out of the country, and closed the borders. It also began a security dragnet to apprehend those responsible for the violence. Because of the recent execution of the national director of security for his part in an attempted coup d'état, the government argued that "[t]he latest crimes are not the work of a sadist, as some may imagine, but are crimes committed by agents and traitors who have sold themselves to foreigners."[51] The curfew was ended a day later, after thousands had been arrested in raids and searches and after industry and commerce had been paralyzed.[52] Murders that may or may not have been politically motivated were used to arrest those who posed a political threat to the rulers.

A dilemma that confronts an incumbent who has used the crime issue to gain victory in the past is that, in seeking reelection, crime and the breakdown of social order can no longer be attributed to the opposition, but to be used as an issue it must still be maintained that crime is a problem. One solution is that adopted by President Nixon in 1972, to argue that crime rates are still rising but at a slower rate than before he took office. Significantly, he was unable to point convincingly to the ways in which the rise had been curbed, if indeed it had. Cities with declining official crime rates were pointed to as models of successful efforts to reduce crime, although the role of the federal government in crime prevention in most of those cities was minimal. Recently it has been argued that crime rates are actually declining. Still, public perception of high crime rates has not changed much. One reason is that overall crime rates may drop because of a reduction in the number of such common crimes as larceny and auto theft, while rates continue to rise for the violent crimes that elicit the greatest fear.

Politicians may exert pressure on police chiefs to show a reduction in crime rates. The police commissioners then pass the word to their subordinates that rewards and promotions will be based on "effectiveness in reducing crime." Crime is then "reduced" by not recording certain crimes or by downgrading the classification of a crime, such as calling a robbery a petty larceny. The commissioner then rewards the "effective" subordinates and takes the crime report to the media, asserting that the hard work of his men had finally paid off in safer streets for the public. Few people ask exactly *how* the reduction was achieved, and few are convinced that their safety has been significantly improved.

A clear example of this occurred in 1972 in New York City. The Police Commissioner released police statistics that he said showed that "people are definitely safer in the streets of New York than they were a year ago."[53] Although rates of some index crimes had increased, the robbery rate had declined. This is often a stranger-to-stranger crime, and it involves violence used to steal property. Consequently, it elicits great fear from the public. Because of this, the Commissioner had promised when he came to his post that he would reward precinct captains who reduced robbery rates. When he presented the data showing such a reduction at a later time, he reiterated the special attention his department had given the crime of robbery. The next day a newspaper article suggested that the type of "attention" that robbery had been receiving was not what many people thought. A Vassar College freshman had tried to report that she had been assaulted and robbed of her purse. The desk officer wanted to record the crime as a larceny. The student later returned to get the crime recorded as a robbery, this time with a concealed tape recorder. The following exchange occurred:

Policeman: Over here we're considered a Harlem precinct . . . and that's a very bad connotation. So as a result, what they try to do is knock down everything they can. Like if you were robbed and there was no force involved, they make it grand larceny.

Student: I see.

Policeman: Because of the fact that this way the number of robberies looks very bad for this area. . . . So, like say that your bag was snatched, then they try to make it "loss of property" just to knock everything down. Because at the end of the year the Commissioner comes out with this thing about we knocked down crime.[54]

This exchange makes more comprehensible the way in which robberies were reduced in number while other serious crimes increased. Many robberies were reclassified to lesser offenses; some were not even recorded at all. The Vassar student probably felt no safer knowing that she had officially suffered a "larceny" rather than a "robbery."

Occasionally, the FBI will uncover systematic practices of this sort and attempt to pressure local police departments to correct the situation by refusing to publish their "official" statistics in the annual Uniform Crime Report. This occurred in 1949 in the New York City Police Department, with one official later saying:

The unwritten law was that you were supposed to make things look good. You weren't supposed to report all the crime that actually took place in your precinct—and, if you did, it could be your neck. I know captains who actually lost their commands because they turned in honest crime reports.[55]

Such pressures to underreport crime exist wherever it is politically expedient to show reduced crime rates. Few local police commissioners have the influence that J. Edgar Hoover demonstrated in being able to convert increases in crime rates into successful requests for greater Congressional appropriations for the FBI.

Criminals as Outsiders

So far we have looked at public perception of crime and crime rates. People also react to criminals as people. They hold ideas of the typical offender, ideas which overlook the great diversity of criminals. They also have stereotypes of various subcategories of typical offenders, such as muggers, sex criminals, and gangsters. They associate certain traits with various types of offenders, reacting to them as though their deviant behavior "is only the tip of an iceberg."[56] Specific behavior is linked to a broader cluster of behavioral characteristics; the deviant becomes "associated with fear of multi-faceted evil."[57] The label of deviant or criminal becomes a master trait that conveys much more information than a mere description of a particular action.

Stereotypes of criminals are probably most likely to develop in the absence of first-hand experience with offenders. For example, a study of homosexuality discovered that imprisoned homosexuals made fine distinctions among the acts for which they were sentenced, one important distinction being between paedophiliacs (child molesters) and adult-seeking homosexuals.[58] The author of the study suggested that Parliament and other authorities were less able to make such distinctions because they viewed homosexuality as a general type of behavior. Stereotypes of offenders are probably cruder as the social distance between the offender and the person holding the stereotype increases.

A common attitude toward the criminal is that he is an outsider to society. The National Crime Commission noted this in its conclusion that fear of crime is basically fear of the stranger.[59] The stranger is an outsider. People attribute local crime to outsiders and suspect the motives of strangers in the community. Views of the criminal as an outsider and the outsider as a criminal reinforce each other.[60]

In a study by this author, residents of a high crime-rate area (Port City) and a low crime-rate area (Belleville) were asked where they thought people who committed crime in their community resided. People in the high-crime area were more apt than those in the low-crime area to attribute local crime to residents of the town. In Port City, 32 per cent felt that most people who committed crime there also lived there, but only 20 per cent of the Belleville residents thought that most local crime was attributable to insiders. This statistically significant difference may reflect accurate assessments by each group, since Port City is an area that is nearly isolated by water from surrounding communities, meaning that a nonresident criminal would have to use a car or public transportation to reach his target. On the other hand, access to the suburb of Belleville would also require a trip by car or bus in most cases, since most targets in the town are not within easy walking distance to outsiders. The proportion of crimes committed by outsiders may be as high as the residents of the two communities believe, but a study of Westchester County, New York, found that, contrary to local opinion, most felonies committed in the county were by local residents rather than outsiders. Seventy-eight per cent of all arrests (and more than nine of every ten juvenile arrests) were of local residents.[61]

Seeing crime as coming from within one's own community might make it more threatening, since it has to be faced on a daily basis. On the other hand, crime might be more threatening if it is attributed to outsiders, since people fear the unknown and do not know what to expect from strangers. The Crime Commission suggests that the latter interpretation is correct, that fear of crime is intense because strangers and outsiders arouse greatest anxiety.

A survey of two Boston communities—Roxbury and Dorchester —for the Crime Commission asked residents where they thought people who committed crimes in the area lived. In spite of different crime rates in the two areas, similar responses were obtained in each area. In each community, about one respondent in eight said that most criminals lived in the area, two-fifths said that they lived elsewhere, one in eight felt it was about half local residents and half outsiders, and the rest did not know.[62] Again we find much attribution of local crime to outsiders, making it possible for residents to feel more secure than if they thought their neighbors were preying on them. In both of these communities, fewer residents attributed local crime to insiders than was true in Port City, another Boston community. This may be because the isolated nature of Port City makes it more difficult for residents to attribute crime to outsiders. With no clear physical boundaries between communities, it is easy to say that local crimes are committed by people who live "just over there."

In none of the four Boston-area communities do a majority of the residents attribute local crime to insiders. These views may be correct, although the data from Westchester County suggest otherwise. Also, a study of alcoholism found that although local residents felt that the typical chronic drunk arrested by the police in their community was a resident of another city or state who had migrated there during his wanderings, most of the alcoholics were in fact longtime residents of the city rather than outsiders.[63] Another study found that although residents of a housing project blamed crime on recently arrived tenants, offenders did not differ from nonoffenders in their length of residence in the project.[64] What little evidence we have suggests that people tend to blame crime in their area on outsiders even when much of the crime is being perpetrated by their neighbors.

In blaming outsiders for crime, people are able to dissociate themselves from the offenders. This removes the problem from the immediate vicinity, since the criminal is seen as a person who lives elsewhere, journeys to the community, commits a crime, and then returns home. A view of the criminal as a mysterious, unknown predator may increase anxiety about crime, but it also makes continued residence in the community psychologically possible. Denying the indigenous origin of the offender by invoking a we-they dichotomy permits people to condemn offenders more harshly, since they are not then condemning an important part of their own lives, the community in which they live. This permits them to maintain a more positive image of their community. Even where there is little crime, as in one Ohio town studied by Simon Dinitz, the we-they distinction may be used to prevent crime from being imported to the community.[65] "We" form a peaceful, homogeneous community; "they" will bring crime and violence to the area if they are not excluded.

Negative identification with or dissociation from the criminal allows people to see offenders as completely different from themselves. Two dimensions of identification between the public and offenders are empathy (the imagining of oneself in the offender's position) and sympathy (the capactiy to understand and even experience the offender's emotions). Research shows that these two dimensions are not closely related to each other and that the ability of college students, at least, to identify with delinquents and adult offenders is slight.[66] This creates a gulf between offenders and the public that makes it difficult to reintegrate an individual into society once he has been convicted of a crime.

One aspect of negative identification with the offender is class antagonism, a hostile attitude by the middle and upper classes toward the working and lower classes, from which most imprisoned criminals are drawn. Offenders are seen as a threat to certain dominant values such as private property; linking those offenders to a broader social class often produces class antagonism.[67] Gerald D. Suttles has suggested that stereotypes of the poor in the United States are tied to the suspicion that they are criminal or potentially criminal.[68] These class stereotypes are reinforced by racial and ethnic prejudices, strengthening views of criminal-as-outsider and outsider-as-criminal. When crime is associated with the lower class or with a racial or ethnic minority, fear of crime can contribute to segregation of that group in housing and education.[69]

Another example of class antagonism being tied to the perception of criminals is reported by Louis Chevalier in his study of nineteenth-century Paris. He found that over time the popular image of the criminal changed from a romantic one in which he was seen as a rogue who was part of a closed society to one in which he was seen as typical of the "dangerous classes," which involved both the lower classes and the working classes. The view that criminals were outsiders in terms of social class was reinforced by the notion that there were certain criminal occupations, trades that included a disproportionately large number of offenders.[70] There was also a widespread belief that criminals were recent immigrants to Paris from the countryside, making the offenders outsiders in geographical terms as well. In eighteenth- and nineteenth-century French cities, the police and the public commonly focused on outsiders as the perpetrators of local murders, helping to "exculpate one's own people by incriminating the 'stranger.' "[71] Some murders were in fact committed by people who had migrated from other areas, but most were done by local residents who had previously known their victims.[72]

Another case of recently arrived immigrants being blamed for crime and violence occurred in Chicago in the nineteenth century. Following the bombing of Haymarket Square in 1886, the native-born residents of a lower-middle-class community blamed the immigrant poor for the violence. This happened in spite of evidence that the bombing had not been done by members of the lowest social classes. Nevertheless, Sennett notes that a communal force led people to "an immediately shared interpretation of what objectively was a confused event."[73] The bombing was seen as part of a broader effort by the lower class to destroy middle-class security. Fear of anarchism and hostility toward the foreign-born were enhanced by rumors, and things colored red were cut from street advertisements to prevent the excitement of radical tendencies. Sennett attributes this strong response, as well as the community's reaction to a series of burglaries and robberies two years later, to the workers' desire to achieve success in the city being in conflict with their desire to shelter themselves and their families from the harsh life of the city. Ambivalence toward urban life produced "a hysterical belief in hidden, unknown threats ready to strike at man at almost any time."[74] Fear of the unknown was projected onto supposed enemies, foreigners who were a threat to dominant values. This prevented the assimilation of the immigrants, strengthening the solidarity of the lower-middle-class community but dividing the city into ethnic and class enclaves.

The insider versus outsider issue was also a part of the rumor of white slave traffic in Orléans, France. Although all the shop-keepers about whom rumors were spread were Jewish, Edgar Morin argues that anti-Semitism was not an initiating force in the rumor that women had been abducted from the shops; instead this element was added to the story after the rumor began.[75] People sought someone to blame, preferably an outsider. Historically the Jew has been discriminated against and seen as different. However, the Jewish shopkeepers in Orléans who were the focus of attention were neither visible nor traditional in their ways. Still, by emphasizing their ethnicity, other residents of the town could disidentify with the Jewish shopkeepers and blame them for the alleged crimes. Morin points out that the significance of ethnicity was shown by the fact that the rumors were not passed to local Jews who were not shopkeepers, since the non-Jews saw them as "latent accessories" to the supposed crimes.[76] Even after the rumor was quashed, there remained a sense of distance between Jews and the rest of the townspeople.

Anti-Semitism also played a role in the Leo Frank case in Georgia in 1913.[77] The murder of a thirteen-year-old working girl in his factory led the public to believe that Leo Frank, a Jewish industrialist from the North, had committed the crime. Frank was an outsider in place of origin as well as ethnicity and religion. Anti-Semitic stereotypes such as the strange customs of the Jewish religion and the control of international finance by

35

Jews contributed to the selection of Frank as the target of public wrath. The fact that he employed young girls also challenged the traditional Southern idealization of women. Many members of Atlanta's working class had recently migrated there from the countryside, and they were ambivalent or hostile toward the city and its large factories.[78] An industrialist was thus an apt person to blame for the murder. Because Frank was an immigrant to the South, it was even easier to blame him for the murder. He represented a threat to traditional values of community, family, and religion. Public hostility toward Frank, who was probably innocent of the crime, was shown in the public celebration that followed his conviction. His death penalty was commuted by the governor, even though it meant his political ruin, but Frank was taken from prison and hanged by a lynch mob.

Public fear of outsiders often victimizes minority-group members in this way. For example, the search for the killer in the Jack the Ripper murders in London in 1888 elicited hostility toward Jews and foreigners, as well as strangers in general.[79]

When a criminal is of the same racial or ethnic group as those who fear the crime, other characteristics may be used to explain how the offender differs from law-abiding citizens. For instance, a black politician, in referring to local black criminals, said, "We don't consider criminals to be a brother. We consider them to be an enemy and they will be dealt with as such." [80] He thus argued that blacks needed to close ranks to protect themselves from outside oppression, but that those blacks who preyed from within the community would be regarded as part of the oppressor class. Here members of the community were redefined as outsiders because they committed crimes, rather than because of any characteristic that distinguished them from other residents of the area.

An apparent exception to blaming outsiders for local crime problems is the recent experience with welfare hotels in New York City. Formerly exclusive but now run-down, these hotels have been used to house welfare recipients, including many drug addicts and ex-convicts as well as the elderly and the disabled. Many residents of the communities where there are welfare hotels have complained that these hotels are crime centers which house criminals who have caused increasing crime rates and have destroyed the quality of the neighborhood. Residents say that some of those who live in the hotels go out to the streets, rob and assault innocent people, and then return to their apartments, areas of privacy to which the police cannot easily gain access.[81] Even within the hotels there is a serious crime problem, since potential offenders have a highly vulnerable population—the elderly and the handicapped—on which to prey.

People who live in areas where there are welfare hotels have changed their attitudes and behavior—they stay off the streets and out of the buildings' corridors, they adopt security measures to keep intruders out of their apartments, they form discussion groups and tenant patrols. They have called on the police to stop the crime wave, but they have generally been dissatisfied with police response.[82] Local residents despise the welfare hotels. They see criminals living *within* their own community, across the block or down the street in many cases. However, they vociferously claim that the people who are committing crime in the area are really *outsiders*, transients who have been assigned rooms in their neighborhood by the welfare agency. The hotels are lightning rods for the fears and anxieties of the local residents; they are seen as places from which dangerous offenders who have been thrust into their midst can prey upon the community. The immediate presence of these threatening outsiders creates even more fear of crime than would be the case in a community where people thought that criminals struck from the outside but then returned home.

One way that distance is placed between the general public and criminals is by the establishment of social agencies that take responsibility for the offenders. Public concern with deviants is alleviated if people are assured that the deviants are under professional care or are institutionalized. These buffers or social protectors include professional specialists who interpret and treat the threatening behavior and institutions such as mental hospitals and prisons that isolate the threatening individual.[83] Although public fear may be reduced by placing deviants under the care of someone or some institution, this also reinforces the stereotype of criminal-as-outsider and outsider-as-criminal.

37

Systematic exclusion of deviants can generate or reinforce stereotypes of typical deviants if the characteristics of those who are officially stigmatized become generalized as deviant traits. For example, Arnold S. Linsky examined the characteristics of people who were involuntarily committed to state mental hospitals. He found a tendency to commit nonwhites more than whites, the less educated more than the better educated, those residing in non-family situations more than those living with families, those who were not in the labor force more than the employed, and men more than women. Generally, the socially marginal and those with weaker social ties were most apt to be committed.[84] Over time, the "typical" mental patient may be stereotyped by the traits of those who have in fact been committed; he will be seen as a nonwhite, poorly educated, unemployed male who is not living in a family setting. Such a stereotype may create distrust and suspicion of people with these traits, whether or not they have any mental problems. In this way, the formal mechanism of excluding people and labeling them as deviant may produce a certain image of the deviant. Kai T. Erikson found this tendency among the Puritans in seventeenth-century Massachusetts. The Puritans saw deviance as "the special property of a particular class of people who were more or less frozen into deviant attitudes."[85] This made reform and reintegration difficult, since deviants were locked into their roles by public attitudes.

People apparently find it easier to attribute crime and deviance to personal failings rather than to underlying social causes. If they blame crime on the nature of criminals, they are more easily absolved of responsibility for the "sick" individuals who commit offenses, whereas they might feel more responsibility for "sick" social conditions if they were viewed as the primary cause of crime.[86] However, people will not always take responsibility for deficient social conditions, since they may think that poverty or dissatisfaction with the income distribution will always be present. Viewing criminals as sick individuals also makes it easier for people to see themselves as good and unlikely to ever commit such heinous acts. Such a view also justifies imprisonment or hospitalization of deviants rather than expensive social programs to eradicate the causes of crime.

Excluding the criminal makes it difficult to reintegrate him when he returns to society, pushing him back into a life of crime and perpetuating the crime problem. Training an inmate in prison is of little use if no one will hire him when he is released. One study found that a person with a criminal record, even an acquittal in court, has a more difficult time finding a job than a person with no record.[87] Research in Denmark showed that people of higher socioeconomic status were more reluctant than people of lower status to work with ex-convicts or to have social contact with them.[88] This is important because those who are least accepting of the ex-convicts are in the best position to help them readjust to society and escape from the criminal life. In this country, most employment agencies will not handle people who have an arrest record, probably because firms will not hire such people.[89] Many agencies even turn down job applicants who have been acquitted, reasoning that the arrest itself suggests guilt.[90] If an ex-convict can find a job, he is usually limited in the type of job he is given and in his opportunity for advancement.[91]

Perceptions of ex-convicts are sometimes grounded in reality. For example, the commutation of a convicted murderer's life sentence, which made him eligible for parole, elicited a strong reaction from one of the women who had been involved in his crime. She said to those who had commuted the sentence, "I want to stay alive and you can't guarantee my life will be safe if he is let out."[92] In this case, there was a legitimate fear of future victimization. However, the public's fear of ex-convicts is usually more vague than this, a sense that someone who has done something wrong will do it again. This expectation may become self-fulfilling, since ex-convicts who cannot find jobs often return to crime in order to survive.

Societal reaction to convicted offenders often reinforces the popular view of criminals as outsiders. Society has elaborate rituals for moving offenders *out* of society but has no rituals for reintegrating them.[93] Many penal institutions are located far from population centers, although there has recently been a trend toward community-based correctional facilities. There is a common fear that a community will be stigmatized and endangered by the presence of a correctional institution, whether a prison or a halfway house. People feel that the presence of the institution will increase the risk of escape and further crimes. Sometimes the institution may indeed have a negative impact on the community. One town with a nearby state prison found that the safety of the townspeople was sometimes threatened because the ambulance and the fire department personnel were often occupied at the institution and were unavailable when needed by the townspeople.[94] Locating institutions in rural communities means that inmates from large cities are separated from their families and friends. This leads to prisonization of the inmates, immersing them in a subculture that teaches and reinforces criminal behavior. Geographical isolation also increases the possibility that there will be significant demographic differences between inmates (young, black, urban) and guards (older, white, rural).[95] Also, in rural areas there is a smaller and probably less well-trained population from which to draw administrative, treatment, and custodial personnel. There are fewer opportunities for inmates to work in such settings, limiting work-release programs and increasing isolation from the outside world. The kinds of work that would be available in such communities even if work-release programs were possible would not provide marketable skills for inmates returning to urban homes.

Attributing crime to people vastly different from the average citizen can undermine programs to rehabilitate and reintegrate offenders. In a number of communities, hostility on the part of local residents has arisen in response to proposals to establish methadone clinics for the treatment of drug addicts. The addicts are seen as outsiders, as dangerous and different people who will bring crime to the area. In many instances, the addicts are actually local residents who are more apt to commit crime in the community to support their heroin habits than they would be if they were under treatment.

An example of how a realistic view that crime is being committed by local residents can lead to productive crime-reduction programs involves an organization of black businessmen in a Pittsburgh community. The leader said that while many blacks felt that whites were their greatest enemy, "I say that the greatest menace to the blacks in Manchester are blacks who prey upon other blacks. We are not being menaced from the outside; we are being menaced from within. We are not being menaced by the so-called enemy—'whitey.' "[96] While whites have been responsible for creating the social system that systematically discriminates against blacks and perpetuates the social conditions that lead to crime, it is also true that the immediate threat to blacks in terms of crime comes from other blacks. The crimes that people most fear, with the exception of robbery, are usually committed by a member of one race against another member of the same race.[97] Also, most black robbery victims are probably held up by other blacks, although many white victims are also robbed by black offenders.[98] A long-run program to reduce crime must get at the roots of crime, but short-run protection can be achieved if efforts are directed against those offenders who actually prey upon the community. The Pittsburgh group of black businessmen pressured the city police department to provide more officers for their community and managed to get a drug rehabilitation program established in the community. Although the effects of those changes are not clear, the businessmen's realistic view that insiders were committing crimes in the area allowed them to direct efforts at indigenous offenders rather than try to exclude outsiders from the community.

One way that the perception of criminals as outsiders often hinders the development of correctional programs is to create resistance to the establishment of halfway houses. A national survey found that four-fifths of the people favored the idea of a halfway house, but that only half favored the idea if it involved setting one up in their own neighborhood. Only one in five said that most people in their neighborhood would favor the establishment of a halfway house in the area; three of every five felt that their neighbors would oppose the idea.[99] Disapproval of halfway houses stemmed from the ideas that the offenders would cause trouble in the area, be a bad influence on local youths, or would make the area less safe.[100] Respondents realized that ex-convicts face great problems after their release from prison, but many still said they would feel uneasy working with ex-convicts. Contrary to the Denmark study already mentioned, uneasiness was concentrated among the disadvantaged in this survey. Those with low income, those with little education, and blacks were least accepting of ex-convicts. Those people with whom the ex-convicts were most likely to have social and on-the-job contacts, those with social characteristics similar to their own, were most hostile toward the ex-convicts. Obviously this makes the process of reintegrating the offender a difficult one.

A study of community resistance to halfway houses in Massachusetts found that people opposed such institutions in their own community because they feared the area's image would be tarnished, they thought property values would drop, they were afraid that offenders would commit crimes in the area, and they were apprehensive that the offenders would influence their children.[101] In order to neutralize community resistance to halfway houses for juveniles, Coates and Miller suggest a strategy that includes having the house represented by house parents rather than a governmental agency, getting the juveniles to renovate the home and thus increase its value, using staff and peer pressure to prevent crime, getting acquainted with local people in various ways, and reducing barriers to social interaction by having the juveniles look acceptable to the townspeople. These measures can be supplemented by using a low-profile approach in introducing the house to the community, by discussing the house with a few important political leaders in the area, and by a campaign in the community. The particular strategy that will be most effective will depend on the type of community to which the halfway house is being introduced.

Measures that make offenders seem human to the general public and that demonstrate how continued exclusion and rejection of ex-convicts only perpetuate the crime problem can ease the reintegration of offenders. In this way, not only will the lives of the ex-convicts be made more satisfying and productive, but crime rates will be reduced and the direct and indirect costs of crime will be minimized.

Footnotes

1. Philip H. Ennis, Field Surveys II of the President's Commission on Law Enforcement and Administration of Justice, *Criminal*

Victimization in the United States: A Report of a National Survey. Washington, D.C.: United States Government Printing Office, 1967.

2. Michael Knight, "Police Give Rape Victims a Special Phone Number," *The New York Times*, March 22, 1973, p. 47; Grace Lichtenstein, "Rape Squad," *The New York Times Magazine*, March 3, 1974, pp. 10–11, 61–65.

3. These differences are based on crimes reported for all members of a household by one respondent in the household, divided by the number of members in the household. Because respondents often remembered their own victimization better than others' misfortunes, the actual rates of victimization are considerably higher if one divides crimes in which respondents were involved by the number of respondents. Looking at actual crime rates in this way, for certain offenses and certain cities, the actual rates are sometimes three to ten times as high as the official rates. See the President's Commission on Law Enforcement and Administration of Justice, *Task Force Report: Crime and Its Impact—An Assessment.* Washington, D.C.: United States Government Printing Office, 1967, pp. 17–18.

4. Ibid., p. 18.

5. Ennis, op. cit., pp. 41–42.

6. Albert D. Biderman, Louise A. Johnson, Jennie McIntyre, and Adrianne Weir, Field Surveys I of the President's Commission on Law Enforcement and Administration of Justice, *Report on a Pilot Study in the District of Columbia on Victimization and Attitudes toward Law Enforcement.* Washington, D.C.: United States Government Printing Office, 1967, p. 118.

7. Edwin M. Schur, *Crimes without Victims: Deviant Behavior and Public Policy.* Englewood Cliffs, N.J.: Prentice-Hall, Inc., 1965.

8. The President's Commission, *Crime and Its Impact*, p. 22.

9. The President's Commission on Law Enforcement and Administration of Justice, *The Challenge of Crime in a Free Society.* Washington, D.C.: United States Government Printing Office, 1967, p. 25.

10. Ennis, op. cit., p. 47.

11. For example, the official FBI rate of robbery in 1965 was 61 per 100,000 people in the country, and the rate calculated from the national victimization survey was 94 per 100,000. In other words, two-thirds of the actual robberies were reported, and the remaining one-third constituted the dark figure. Now if *all* robberies were reported, the official rate could only rise to 94 per 100,000 without some *real* increase in actual robberies occurring. In fact, by 1972 the official robbery rate was 180 per 100,000, twice the actual (victim-reported) rate in 1965. Clearly a significant in-

crease in robberies had occurred, aside from any changes in reporting or recording practices.

12. James Q. Wilson, *Varieties of Police Behavior: The Management of Law and Order in Eight Communities.* Cambridge: Harvard University Press, 1968, p. 95.

13. Edgar Morin, *Rumour in Orléans,* translated by Peter Green. New York: Pantheon Books, 1969, 1971.

14. Marvin E. Wolfgang, "Urban Crime," in James Q. Wilson, editor, *The Metropolitan Enigma.* Garden City, N.Y.: Doubleday & Co., Inc., 1970, p. 293.

15. Kai T. Erikson, *Wayward Puritans: A Study in the Sociology of Deviance.* New York: John Wiley & Sons, Inc., 1966, pp. 3–29.

16. Edwin M. Lemert, *Social Pathology: A Systematic Approach to the Theory of Sociopathic Behavior.* New York: McGraw-Hill Book Company, Inc., 1951, pp. 57–58.

17. Ibid., pp. 60–61.

18. "Climate of concern and worry" is a phrase used in Biderman et al., op. cit., p. 126; "criminal conceptions" are discussed in Richard Quinney, *The Social Reality of Crime.* Boston: Little, Brown and Company, 1970, p. 277.

19. See M. K. Block and G. J. Long, "Subjective Probability of Victimization and Crime Levels: An Econometric Approach," *Criminology* XI (May 1973), p. 91.

20. Leslie T. Wilkins, *Social Deviance: Social Policy, Action, and Research.* Englewood Cliffs, N.J.: Prentice-Hall, Inc., 1965, p. 142.

21. Joint Commission on Correctional Manpower and Training, *The Public Looks at Crime and Corrections.* Washington, D.C.: Joint Commission on Correctional Manpower and Training, 1968, p. 4.

22. This survey also found that whites, males, and the better educated were more likely to feel that crime rates had increased than were blacks, females, and the less educated. See Albert J. Reiss, Jr., Field Surveys III, Part 1, of the President's Commission on Law Enforcement and Administration of Justice, *Studies in Crime and Law Enforcement in Major Metropolitan Areas.* Washington, D.C.: United States Government Printing Office, 1967, pp. 36–37, 95.

23. Although these data were collected during a time of much public discussion of the crime issue—the summer of 1968—it is likely that the proportion who would say that rates are higher now than in the past would not be much different if the respondents were questioned again today.

24. Ramsey Clark, *Crime in America: Observations on Its Nature, Causes, Prevention and Control.* New York: Simon and Schuster, 1970, p. 45.

25. Simon Dinitz, "Progress, Crime, and the Folk Ethic: Portrait of a Small Town," *Criminology* XI (May 1973), p. 17.
26. The President's Commission, *Crime and Its Impact*, p. 85.
27. Peter Deeley and Christopher Walker, *Murder in the Fourth Estate*. New York: McGraw-Hill Company, Inc., 1973.
28. Lincoln Steffens, *The Autobiography of Lincoln Steffens*. New York: Harcourt, Brace, and Co., 1931, pp. 285–291.
29. Biderman et al., op. cit., p. 112.
30. For example, see Louis Chevalier, *Laboring Classes and Dangerous Classes in Paris During the Nineteenth Century*. Translated by Frank Jellinek. New York: Howard Fertig, 1958, 1973, pp. 8, 29–58. Chevalier found that in nineteenth-century Paris, the media and popular novels aroused public interest in crime while they fulfilled the public's demand for information about crime. This interest led to the collection of official crime statistics, which in turn fed public fears of crime.
31. For an examination of legal issues related to the press in the United States, see Alfred Friendly and Ronald L. Goldfarb, *Crime and Publicity: The Impact of News on the Administration of Justice*. New York: The Twentieth Century Fund, 1967.
32. F. James Davis, "Crime News in Colorado Newspapers," *American Journal of Sociology* LVII (January 1952), pp. 325–330.
33. For example, see the President's Commission, *The Challenge of Crime in a Free Society*, pp. 50–51.
34. Rita Bachmuth, S. M. Miller, and Linda Rosen, "Juvenile Delinquency in the Daily Press," *Alpha Kappa Delta* XXX (Spring 1960), pp. 47–51.
35. Anxiety about crime was related to personal victimization among black males, but not among other groups. Biderman et al., op. cit., pp. 126–127; the President's Commission, *Crime and Its Impact*, p. 87. Another study found that victims perceive high crime rates more often than nonvictims. Paula H. Kleinman and Deborah S. David, "Victimization and Perception of Crime in a Ghetto Community," *Criminology* XI (November 1973), p. 328.
36. Biderman et al., op. cit., p. 128.
37. The measures of exposure to the news were not measures of exposure to *crime* news specifically, but rather measures of the frequency with which people watched television news and the frequency with which they read daily newspapers. The assumption was that the greater the individual's exposure to news in general, the more news of crime he would encounter.
38. The President's Commission, *Crime and Its Impact*, p. 87.
39. Ibid.
40. Richard Harris, "The New Justice," *The New Yorker*, XLIX (March 28, 1973), p. 44.

41. *Fear* of victimization is highest in areas with high crime rates, but *concern* with the crime issue is concentrated in low crime-rate areas. Still, the level of fear of crime is higher today in low crime-rate communities than it was in the past. For an examination of fear of victimization and concern with the crime issue, see Frank F. Furstenberg, Jr., "Public Reaction to Crime in the Streets," *The American Scholar* XL (Autumn 1971), pp. 601–610.

42. Ibid.

43. Walter B. Miller, "Ideology and Criminal Justice Policy: Some Current Issues," *The Journal of Criminal Law and Criminology* LXIV (June 1973), pp. 141–162.

44. Ibid. p. 151.

45. Concentration on the issue of crime in the streets may reduce the attention given to the problem of organized crime. See Ralph Salerno and John S. Tompkins, *The Crime Confederation*. New York: Popular Library, 1969, pp. 266–268. They argue that the Johnson administration focused more energy on street crime than on organized crime because people were more easily aroused by the threat of violence by strangers than they were by the many costs of organized crime. Also, an attack on organized crime might have revealed that in some large cities there were close ties between organized crime and the local Democratic party. However, the Nixon Administration also concentrated on street crime rather than organized crime. In a system of privately financed political campaigns, no party may be willing to attack gangsters, who directly or indirectly are able to supply campaign funds to politicians, particularly at the local level. Street criminals are more vulnerable and have little to offer those seeking political power, other than to act as a target for hostility.

46. George Gallup, "Safety Fears Swelled Nixon Vote," *Boston Globe*, November 11, 1972, p. 7.

47. "57% in Poll Back a Death Penalty," *The New York Times*, November 23, 1972, p. 18.

48. David Binder, "A Wave of Violent Crime Stirs West German Debate," *The New York Times*, January 21, 1972, p. 2.

49. Paul Hofmann, "Crime Wave an Election Issue in Italy," *The New York Times*, May 24, 1971, p. 12; Paul Hofmann, "Italy Is Aroused by Rise in Crime," *The New York Times*, February 27, 1972, p. 7; Paul Hofmann, "Italy Battles Political Violence and Crime," *The New York Times*, March 13, 1972, pp. 1, 3.

50. Marshall B. Clinard and Daniel J. Abbott, *Crime in Developing Countries: A Comparative Perspective*. New York: John Wiley & Sons, 1973, p. 20.

51. Cited in Juan de Onis, "8 Murders in Baghdad Bring Curfew and

Security Dragnet," *The New York Times*, September 29, 1973, p. 6.

52. "Iraq Ends Curfew, Lifts Flights Ban," *The New York Times*, September 30, 1973, p. 7.

53. Cited in "Street Crime off, Murphy Declares," *The New York Times*, November 22, 1972, p. 44.

54. Cited in John Sibley, "Student Says a Policeman Tried to Falsify Her Report of Holdup," *The New York Times*, November 23, 1972, pp. 1, 40.

55. Cited in Fred J. Cook, "There's Always a Crime Wave," in Donald R. Cressey, editor, *Crime and Criminal Justice*. Chicago: Quadrangle Books, 1971, p. 27.

56. Ralph H. Turner, "Deviance Avowal as Neutralization of Commitment," *Social Problems* XIX (Winter 1972), p. 310.

57. Ibid., p. 311.

58. Michael Schofield, *Sociological Aspects of Homosexuality: A Comparative Study of Three Types of Homosexuals*. Boston: Little, Brown and Company, 1965, p. 39.

59. The President's Commission, *The Challenge of Crime in a Free Society*, p. 52.

60. The Crime Commission found that fear of the strange and the unknown was also characteristic of people's attitudes toward different areas of the city. They felt most comfortable nearest home and least comfortable in strange parts of the city, even if the crime rate was higher near their own home. See ibid., p. 50.

61. Paul L. Montgomery, "Its Crime Indigenous to Westchester," *The New York Times*, May 13, 1973, p. 43.

62. Reiss, op. cit., pp. 31, 34–35.

63. David J. Pittman and C. Wayne Gordon, *Revolving Door: A Study of the Chronic Police Case Inebriate*. Glencoe, Illinois: The Free Press, 1958, pp. 27–29.

64. Oscar Newman, *Architectural Design for Crime Prevention*. Washington, D.C.: United States Government Printing Office, 1973, pp. 105, 107.

65. Dinitz, op. cit., p. 19.

66. Thomas E. Dow, Jr., "The Role of Identification in Conditioning Public Attitude toward the Offender," *Journal of Criminal Law, Criminology and Police Science*, LVIII (March 1967), pp. 75–79.

67. Dennis Chapman, *Sociology and the Stereotype of the Criminal*. London: Tavistock Publications, 1968, pp. 26–27.

68. Gerald D. Suttles, *The Social Construction of Communities*. Chicago: The University of Chicago Press, 1972, pp. 192–193.

69. For an example of this process, see Nathan Glazer, "When the Melting Pot Doesn't Melt," *The New York Times Magazine*, January 2, 1972, pp. 12–13, 27–31.

70. Chevalier, op. cit., passim.
71. Richard Cobb, *The Police and the People: French Popular Protest 1789–1820.* London: Oxford University Press, 1970, p. 32.
72. Ibid, pp. 32–34.
73. Richard Sennett, "Middle-Class Families and Urban Violence: The Experience of a Chicago Community in the Nineteenth Century," in Stephan Thernstrom and Richard Sennett, editors, *Nineteenth-Century Cities: Essays in the New Urban History.* New Haven: Yale University Press, 1969, p. 394.
74. Ibid., p. 413.
75. Morin, op. cit., pp. 55–66.
76. Ibid., p. 63.
77. See Leonard Dinnerstein, *The Leo Frank Case.* New York: Columbia University Press, 1968.
78. This is similar to the situation in Chicago in 1886 that is reported in Sennett, op. cit.
79. Tom A. Cullen, *When London Walked in Terror.* New York: Avon Books, 1965, pp. 63–64.
80. Cited in Christopher Wallace, "Atkins Announces Drive against Black-Area Crime," *Boston Globe,* August 19, 1971, p. 3.
81. Max H. Seigel, "Welfare Hotel Crime Is a Local Problem," *The New York Times,* November 19, 1972, p. 62; Max Seigel, "Wide Community Crime Traced to 'Singles' in Welfare Hotels," *The New York Times,* November 16, 1972, pp. 1, 52; Paul L. Montgomery, "A Welfare Hotel Where Gaiety Is Just a Memory," *The New York Times,* November 27, 1972, p. 39.
82. Some have suggested that welfare hotels could be legally declared criminal nuisances by showing that such places produce high amounts of crime and high arrest rates. They could then be closed. However, this would just shift crime and criminals to other parts of the city rather than reducing crime rates.
83. William C. Rhodes, *Behavioral Threat and Community Response.* New York: Behavioral Publications, Inc., pp. 15, 21.
84. Arnold S. Linsky, "Who Shall Be Excluded: The Influence of Personal Attributes in Community Reaction to the Mentally Ill," *Social Psychiatry* V (July 1970), pp. 166–171.
85. Erikson, op. cit., p. 196.
86. Philip G. Zimbardo, "Vandalism: An Act in Search of a Cause," unpublished manuscript, p. 8.
87. Richard D. Schwartz and Jerome H. Skolnick, "Two Studies of Legal Stigma," in Richard D. Schwartz and Jerome H. Skolnick, editors, *Society and the Legal Order: Cases and Materials in the Sociology of Law.* New York: Basic Books, Inc., 1970, pp. 568–579.
88. Berl Kutschinsky, "Knowledge and Attitudes Regarding Legal

Phenomena in Denmark," in Nils Christie, editor, *Scandinavian Studies in Criminology, Volume 2: Aspects of Social Control in Welfare States.* London: Tavistock Publications, 1968, pp. 152–153.

89. Fred P. Graham, "F.B.I.: When Should Its Arrest Records Be Expunged?" *The New York Times,* December 6, 1970, p. 8.

90. Ibid.

91. Ronald L. Goldfarb and Linda R. Singer, *After Conviction: A Review of the American Correction System.* New York: Simon and Schuster, 1973, pp. 642–643.

92. Cited in James Ayres, "Life Term of Slayer Commuted," *Boston Globe,* November 23, 1972.

93. Erikson, op. cit., pp. 15–16.

94. Andrew Carron, "Norfolk Worried by Prison Security," *Boston Globe,* September 4, 1972, p. 54.

95. For example, see *The Official Report of the New York State Special Commission on Attica.* New York: Bantam Books, Inc., 1972, pp. 24–31.

96. Cited in "Pittsburgh Striving to Reduce Crimes by Black against Black," *The New York Times,* August 18, 1972, p. 37.

97. See Marvin E. Wolfgang, *Patterns in Criminal Homicide.* Philadelphia: University of Pennsylvania Press, 1958; and Menachem Amir, *Patterns in Forcible Rape.* Chicago: University of Chicago Press, 1971.

98. Data on the race of victims and offenders were not included in John E. Conklin, *Robbery and the Criminal Justice System.* Philadelphia: J. B. Lippincott Company, 1972. The reason is that data on the race of both parties to the robbery were available in only one-third of the cases drawn from 1968 and in even fewer of the 1964 cases. However, looking at the race of the victim and the race of the offender for those 1968 cases for which data were available, we find that 90 per cent (47 of 52 cases) of the black victims were robbed by black offenders and that 81 per cent (175 of 216 cases) of the white victims were held up by black offenders. However, these data are not necessarily representative of the larger sample of robberies, since these robberies may differ in some significant way from the two-thirds of the cases in which information on race was missing.

99. Joint Commission on Correctional Manpower and Training, op. cit., pp. 13–17.

100. Ibid.

101. Robert B. Coates and Alden D. Miller, "Neutralization of Community Resistance to Group Homes," in Yitzhak Bakal, editor, *Closing Correctional Institutions.* Lexington, Mass.: D. C. Heath and Company, 1973.

3 Crime and the Community: Durkheim and Capote

W E have seen that one effect of crime is to decrease the mental well-being of the residents of a community. Fear of crime leads them to change their behavior in an attempt to minimize vulnerability. It enhances their suspicion of strangers, and it undermines the social fabric of community life. Contrasted with this view of the impact of crime is that of the French sociologist, Emile Durkheim. In this chapter, we explore some of his ideas about crime and its impact on society and then look at some examples of public reaction to crime. In the next chapter, we investigate more systematically the relationship between perception of crime and attitudes toward other people and toward the community in which one lives. In Chapter 6, we examine the possibility that decreased social interaction and attenuated social bonds may produce higher crime rates by reducing informal social controls in a community.

Durkheim: The Impact of Crime on the Community

Emile Durkheim claims that crime is positively functional for a society because it provides an occasion for people to unite against a common enemy—the law-violator. In *The Rules of Sociological Method* (1895), he writes:

To classify crime among the phenomena of normal sociology is not to say merely that it is an inevitable, although regrettable phenomenon, due to the incorrigible wickedness of men; it is to affirm that it is a factor in public health, an integral part of all healthy societies.[1]

Durkheim defines crime by the effect that certain behavior has on individual consciences—it shocks the sentiments found in all "healthy" consciences.[2] These sentiments are of high intensity and are strongly held, are specific to particular types of behavior, and are written in the society's criminal code.[3] Crime is thus defined by its impact on the *collective conscience*, the communal sense of what is valued and worth pursuing. Durkheim suggests that reactions to crime are more intense and more apt to promote social solidarity if the communal spirit is stronger, because crime then poses a greater threat to social norms and values. Punishment is seen as a passionate reaction to the offending act, any vengeance that is involved being a cruelty that is necessary to defend society and regulate social behavior.[4] Durkheim never makes clear just how such vengeance protects society and its members.

We can summarize Durkheim's views on the social effects of crime with the following quotations from *The Division of Labor in Society* (1893):

Crime brings together upright consciences and concentrates them. We have only to notice what happens, particularly in a small town, when some moral scandal has just been committed. [People] stop each other on the street, they visit each other, they seek to come together to talk of the event and to wax indignant in common.[5]

[If the offended sentiment] is strong, if the offense is serious, the whole group attacked masses itself in the face of the danger and unites, so to speak, in itself.[6]

As soon as the news of a crime gets abroad, the people unite, and although the punishment may not be predetermined, the reaction is unified.[7]

Durkheim thus suggests that people react to crime by increasing their social contacts and pulling together, thereby enhancing the solidarity of the community.

Kai T. Erikson builds on some of these ideas. He argues that crime may fuse individuals into one entity by focusing group feelings and drawing attention to the values of the collective conscience.[8] Crime also defines and maintains boundaries of acceptable social behavior. "Deviant forms of behavior, by marking the outer edges of group life, give the inner structure its special character and thus supply the framework within which the people of the group develop an orderly sense of *their own cultural identity*." [9] Reactions are sometimes more intense than would be expected by the actual harm done or by the small number of deviant individuals; people react to "a threat beyond the bounds of reality." [10] This intense reaction stems from a perceived threat to the status quo, rather than from the specific harm done by the deviant. In Durkheim's view, "[p]unishment is thus a kind of declaration that 'you are either with us or against us,' and tends to mobilize the sentiments of solidarity with the group in the interest of continuing conformity. A good deal of it therefore is not directed at the criminal himself, but at the others who potentially might become criminals." [11] For instance, the historical custom of hanging criminals in public produced "outbursts of collective madness" which reinforced the violated laws and stimulated conformity by onlookers.[12] In this way punishment unified the community in condemnation of the hanged man and his crime.

Durkheim's views on crime are similar to Georg Simmel's notion that conflict between an in-group and an out-group "pulls the members so tightly together and subjects them to such uniform impulse that they *either* must get completely along with, *or* completely repel, one another." [13] Lewis Coser also argues that conflict may integrate a group and clarify group norms, although the group may be divided rather than unified by the conflict if consensus is not strong prior to the conflict.[14] The reaction of a community to crime is a type of social conflict, one in which the enemy is internal to the group but is defined as an outsider after the commission of a crime. The community may sometimes unite against the offender, especially if he is apprehended, convicted of violating a strongly-held norm, publicly confesses to his wrongdoing, and no longer constitutes a threat to society. Also, if collective action can be taken to reduce the risk of future depredations, people may be drawn together by a crime. However, when such conditions are absent, crime may generate distrust, suspicion, and a breakdown in social solidarity.

One instance of an alleged crime unifying members of a community is the white slavery abductions in Orléans, France. Morin suggests that one reason for the rumor that young women were being sold into prostitution by shopkeepers was that the traditional culture of adults was being threatened by the *yeye* or mod culture of the young. Dress shops were a natural focus, since clothing styles were symbolic of the gap between the two cultures.[15] The rumor of the kidnappings united old and young and created an opportunity for parents and teachers to tell the young of the dangers of the dress shops.[16] However, community solidarity across the generation gap faded as the story of the kidnappings was shown to be a rumor. If there had been evidence that actual harm had been done, the townspeople probably would have not been drawn together to the same extent. Distrust would have developed, strangers would have been suspected of wicked intentions, and security precautions would have been taken. These changes did occur to some degree, but they might have been more widespread if solid evidence of the "crimes" had been produced.

John Barron Mays claims that Durkheim's idea that crime is socially integrative is generally unfounded. He suggests that crimes such as bank robberies and forgeries serve no useful purpose and do not knit a community together; instead, they make people fearful and suspicious of each other.[17] Even when crime does unite most members of the community, it still divides the society by separating the criminal from the rest of the people. Mays suggests that even if crime does integrate a society under certain conditions, this function is better served by other means.

George Herbert Mead made a similar point in 1918, stating that whatever the positive functions of punitive justice for society, crime in its attack on social values places people in a posture of defense.[18] Sometimes crime increases community solidarity and inhibits criminal tendencies in members of the community. However, Mead points out that although the group may be unified, it is unified in a *negative* way. The concentration of public hostility on the offender often paralyzes any effort to conceive of the violated norm in a positive way. Such a hostile attitude educes attitudes of retribution, repression, and exclusion, but it provides no way to eradicate the causes of criminal behavior and no way to return the criminal to normal social relations after he has been punished.[19] A society can reduce crime by instituting a rigid system of formal and informal social controls, but in doing so it may also stamp out individuality and creativity, since fear will be implanted in anyone who wishes to act in an unusual way.

Capote: Mass Murder in a Kansas Town

In November 1959, a family of four was found shot to death in their home in the small town of Holcomb, Kansas. Eventually the story was pieced together of how two ex-convicts entered the Clutters' home to steal money from a nonexistent safe. Public reaction to this crime is carefully reconstructed in Truman Capote's *In Cold Blood*.[20] Durkheim would have suggested that in such a small town, a crime which violates the deeply-held value of human life would lead people to "wax indignant in common," unite as a group, and come together to talk of the crime. Let us look at how the townspeople reacted to the four murders.

A common initial response was disbelief, followed by an attempt to learn more about the murders. When one woman was told of the crime by Myrt Clare, the postmistress of Holcomb, she responded: "Myrt—don't say things like that. Who shot them?"[21] She sought information to make the crime more comprehensible; knowing who committed the crime would help explain why they had done it. Knowing the reason for the crime might make this woman feel more secure herself, at least if she felt that she would never have been involved in the situation that culminated in the murders.

Myrt Clare tried to provide this woman with an answer to her question. Myrt—a public character because of her regular contacts with the townspeople[22]—responded in a revealing way: "The man in the airplane. The one Herb sued for crashing into his fruit trees. If it wasn't him, maybe it was you. Or somebody across the street. All the neighbors are rattlesnakes. Varmints looking for a chance to slam the door in your face. It's the same the whole world over. You know that."[23] Later, she said, "If there's somebody loose around here that wants to cut my throat, I wish him luck. What difference does it make? It's all the same in eternity."[24] Capote notes that her extreme reaction was not typical of the townspeople; most of them initially responded with "amazement, shading into dismay; a shallow horror sensation that cold springs of personal fear swiftly deepened." [25]

However, Mrs. Clare's distrust of her neighbors was fairly typical of townspeople's reactions. According to the woman who owned the local cafe:

One old man sitting here that Sunday, he put his finger right on it, the reason nobody can sleep; he said, "All we've got out here are our friends. There isn't anything else." In a way, that's the worst part of the crime. What a terrible thing when neighbors can't look at each other without kind of wondering! Yes, it's a hard fact to live with, but if they ever do find out who done it, I'm sure it'll be a bigger surprise than the murders themselves.[26]

Thus another public character also felt suspicious of her neighbors. She "waxed indignant," but more so *against* her neighbors and their possible criminal behavior than *with* her neighbors against the violation of the law by an outsider.

A few days after the murders, with no arrest in sight, distrust of neighbors was still widespread. Capote writes that one reason for so much fear,

the simplest, the ugliest [reason], was that this hitherto peaceful congregation of neighbors and old friends had suddenly to endure the unique experience of distrusting each other; understandably, they believed that the murderer was among themselves, and, to the last man, endorsed an opinion advanced by Arthur Clutter, a brother of the deceased, who, while talking to journalists in the lobby of a Garden City hotel on November 17, had said, "When this is cleared up, I'll wager whoever did it was someone within ten miles of where we now stand." [27]

The inclination was to feel that an insider was the murderer, contrary to the tendency noted earlier for people to attribute local crime to outsiders. In Chapter 2, we saw that residents of the comparatively isolated Port City were most apt to attribute local crime to insiders, probably because they knew that outsiders would have to exercise some effort to enter their community. Similarly, Holcomb residents probably attributed the murders to an insider because the town was geographically isolated. The lack of any apparent motive made it unclear why anyone would travel to Holcomb to kill the Clutters. People thought that someone would have to bear a grudge against the family to murder them; the only people likely to hold such a grudge would be those who knew the family and thus lived nearby. Fear of crime seemed to be less a fear of the stranger than a fear that those nearby might harbor grievances.

Distrust in Holcomb reached the point that two families moved from the town. One man said that neither he nor his wife could get any sleep because they feared repetition of the murders; they moved to Colorado. The other family had considered moving before the crime, but finally decided to leave after the murders because the wife consented to her husband's desire to move since she could not stop thinking about the crime. Distrust became so great that the woman who owned the local cafe said, "Myself, I don't want to hear another word. I told them, We can't go on like this. Distrusting everybody, scaring each other to death. What I say is, if you want to talk about it, stay out of my place." [28] She saw that talk was reinforcing distrust and creating rumors, destroying any vestige of community solidarity that still remained; she thus sought to stop such discussions.

At dawn a few days after the murders

a carload of pheasant hunters from Colorado—strangers, ignorant of the local disaster—were startled by what they saw as they crossed the prairies and passed through Holcomb: windows ablaze, almost every window in almost every house, and, in the brightly lit rooms, fully clothed people, even entire families, who had sat the whole night wide awake, watchful, listening. Of what were they frightened? "It might happen again." That, with variations, was the customary response. However, one woman, a schoolteacher, observed, "Feeling wouldn't run half so high if this had happened to anyone *except* the Clutters. Anyone *less* admired. Prosperous. Secure. But that family represented everything people hereabouts really value and respect, and that such a thing could happen to them—well, it's like being told there is no God. It makes life seem pointless. I don't think people are so much frightened as they are deeply depressed." [29]

This reflects what Durkheim would have called a violation of the community's collective conscience. The Clutters represented the dominant values of the townspeople, and their murder was a sharp attack on those values. When people appear to be protected from crime by their wealth, age, sex, social status, or physical strength, their victimization enhances others' sense of vulnerability; it seems that no one is safe from such depredations. Still, there is no real evidence in Capote's account that the people of Holcomb united as a community or had their values reinforced in any way by the murders. Most people reacted by trying to provide greater security for themselves, their families, and their homes; there were few collective efforts to protect the community. The proprietor of a local hardware store said that "locks and bolts are the fastest-going item. Folks ain't particular what brand they buy; they just want them to *hold*."[30] This sounds more like a high crime-rate area in a large city than a small town where everyone was acquainted and had lived with each other for years.

Eventually the two murderers were arrested. The reaction of the townspeople when they heard that two suspects had been apprehended was somewhat unexpected. Most people felt relief and a few wept in a release of tension. However, a number continued to keep their doors and windows locked, feeling that others might have been involved. Capote writes that

the majority of Holcomb's population, having lived for seven weeks amid unwholesome rumors, general mistrust, and suspicion, appeared to feel disappointed at being told that the murderer was not someone among themselves. Indeed, a sizable faction refused to accept the fact that two unknown men, two thieving strangers, were solely responsible. As Mrs. Clare now remarked, "Maybe they did it, these fellows. But there's more to it than that. Wait. Some day they'll get to the bottom, and when they do they'll find the one behind it. The one wanted Clutter out of the way. The *brains*." [31]

For nearly two months, the people of Holcomb had tried to guess who among them had committed the murders. The only possible suspects they knew were those who lived nearby. When two strangers were arrested, their theories were proved wrong. They naturally found it difficult, perhaps even embarrassing and guilt-producing, to accept the fact that their distrust of their neighbors had been unwarranted. It is also possible that if they had to admit to themselves that two strangers came to town one night and murdered four of their neighbors, continued residence in Holcomb would have been difficult. In the city, most people one sees on the street are strangers or people with whom one has limited contact. Strangers are suspected of crimes because little is known of them and they are convenient scapegoats. In small towns such as Holcomb, few strangers are encountered. Most contacts are with people one knows intimately. When a crime occurs, it makes little sense to blame a stranger, since there are few around. People then turn to those they know and begin to suspect them, although they do not necessarily make open accusations. Social solidarity may be great in small homogeneous communities, as Durkheim claims, but the reaction of the Holcomb residents suggests that this solidarity is fragile and likely to be broken or weakened rather than strengthened by crime.

When the two murderers were brought to jail, some townspeople were gathered there. On seeing the culprits, they did not shout abuse or show anger, nor engage in violence, but rather fell silent, "as though amazed to find them humanly shaped."[32] The objects of all their fears and suspicions looked like anyone else. The crowd then dispersed.

A change of venue[33] for the trial was considered, but the idea was dropped because there were few places in Kansas where people did not know of the murders. However, intense reactions soon subsided; an editorial in the newspaper of a nearby town later stated:

Even a hundred miles west of here in Colorado few persons are even acquainted with the case—other than just remembering some members of a prominent family were slain. This is a sad commentary on the state of crime in our nation. Since the four members of the Clutter family were killed last fall, several other such multiple murders have occurred in various parts of the country. Just during the few days leading up to this trial at least three mass murder cases broke into the headlines. As a result, this crime and trial are just one of many such cases people have read about and forgotten.[34]

Six years after the murders, the two killers were hung, among the last Americans to have been executed.

People in Holcomb initially disbelieved the horrendous crime. Then they tried to figure out who had committed the murders; suspicions turned toward their neighbors when no one was apprehended and few strangers were visible. Defensive measures such as the purchase of firearms, the installation of locks on doors and windows, and keeping lights on at night were taken to prevent recurrence of the crime. When the suspects were caught, anxiety did not immediately diminish to the zero-point, but rather subsided gradually as people realized that they had been mistaken in suspecting their longtime friends of the brutal murders. Daily life eventually returned to normal, although there probably remained a residue of distrust of others and guilt at having accused one's friends. Recurrence of such crimes may quickly build up distrust and suspicion and produce a disorganized community in which people feel little solidarity with their neighbors.

Community Reaction to Crime: Some Additional Examples

Violent crimes such as the murders in Holcomb, Kansas, evoke especially intense reactions. After Charles Starkweather's murders in Nebraska in 1958, people kept their children off the streets and out of school, notified neighbors when they left home, and sought information and reassurance to the extent that Lincoln's telephone system was paralyzed. District court sessions were recessed, downtown businesses booked hotel rooms for late-working employees so that they would not have to travel home after dark, and the National Guard was stationed at a local bank to prevent a rumored robbery.[35]

Following the brutal murder of a ten-year-old boy in New York City, parents grew panicky when their children strayed out of sight or were late coming home from school. More than a month after the crime, the fear persisted that the offender was still in the neighborhood. Police questioning of residents enhanced this fear. Children were anxious; one kept a knife under his pillow at night.

Schools showed a videotape to teach students such safety precautions as avoiding strangers. One teacher asked, "Can someone tell me why it's not safe to leave the school yard by yourself?" A student replied, "Because someone might kill you." Other students nodded in agreement. Suspicion of others was heightened by the crime, although there was some pulling together of the community in response to the crime. Block-watchers were organized to protect school children; mothers accompanied children everywhere. Community residents collected money for the boy's funeral and for his family's trip back to Puerto Rico, where they resettled.[36] This collective effort to help the boy's family did unite the community to some extent, but the family's resettlement divided rather than united the community. The overall effect of the crime on the community was negative.

Under certain conditions, people may mobilize to demand passage of a law to punish the violation of social norms in a harsh way. An example is the development of sexual psychopath laws that provide for the detention and treatment of certain types of sex offenders in state hospitals.[37] Such laws developed in response to public outcry for action after a series of sex offenses. As Sutherland points out:

The hysteria produced by child murders is due in part to the fact that the ordinary citizen cannot understand a sex attack on a child. The ordinary citizen can understand fornication or even forcible rape of a woman, but he concludes that a sexual attack on an infant or a girl of six years must be the act of a fiend or maniac. Fear is the greater because the behavior is so incomprehensible.[38]

Even if such a strongly-held norm is violated, the norm may not be transformed into a law. The public must first see the possibility of legal action, mobilize, and apply pressure for the new legislation. If new laws are passed, they may not be enforced unless public pressure is sustained over time. Sexual psychopath laws now exist in many states but are rarely used in most places.

So far, our examples all involve violent crimes in which no offender was immediately apprehended. It could be argued that Durkheim did not necessarily have such dramatic crimes in mind when he suggested that crime served positive functions for the community. We do have a piece of research by Tony G. Poveda which explores a small town's reaction to a less threatening type of criminal behavior, adolescent drug use.[39] Revelation of drug use by the local newspaper created a shocked reaction among the residents that "crime in the streets" had spread to their formerly peaceful community. Local crime could no longer be attributed to a few outsiders or to a small number of deviants in the town, since newspaper reports indicated that marijuana was used freely and openly by local teenagers.

One immediate response to these reports was the formation of discussion groups to try to better understand the youthful deviance. A mass meeting was held; after a panel discussion on drug use, many felt that drug education was the solution to the problem. A drug information center was set up, educational programs dealing with drugs were started in the schools, and the police became involved in drug education (although they became more aggressive in their enforcement of drug laws at the same time). A halfway house for drug rehabilitation was established. Unlike Holcomb residents, most of whom engaged in protective measures on an individual basis, the residents of this small town engaged in collective action to fight the problem, much as Durkheim would have predicted. The youthfulness of the "offenders" and the absence of any threat of harm minimized fears that risks were entailed in working to eliminate drug use by local teenagers.[40]

Community recognition of adolescent drug use also resulted in greater sensitivity to other types of crime in the community. Interest in violence increased. Local newspapers devoted more space to crimes that occurred in the vicinity. An apparent kidnap-murder reported in the paper produced widespread suspicion of men driving cars near local schools. "One policeman reported that while cruising the streets at a low speed, and wearing sunglasses, many mothers gave him a distrustful look as though he were the guilty party." [41] The alleged kidnap-murder caused adults to set up safety islands where their children could stop on their way to and from school if they encountered a suspicious stranger. We wonder how children in this community, or those in the New York City neighborhood mentioned earlier, will regard other people when they grow up, having been taught that any unknown male who approaches them may intend to kill them. Short-run protective measures may in the long run undermine interpersonal trust and weaken social solidarity in the community.

In sum, reaction to adolescent drug use in this town was one of "uncertainty and anxiety," as well as sensitization to other kinds of crime. Marijuana use created suspicion of adolescents, dividing the community by generations at the same time that some residents united to fight drug abuse. The perceived challenge to the dominant life style did draw certain members of the community together as Durkheim suggests. However, this crime did not threaten direct harm nor was much risk entailed in holding a discussion group or establishing a drug education program. In a small Missouri town where three "straight" people were killed by a "hippie," the use of violence by someone with a greatly different life style provoked deep fears. Straights saw a conspiracy to undermine the community. A near-vigilante group developed, but no lethal violence was used against the youths. The community was divided, and few constructive measures followed the murders.[42]

John Gerassi's *The Boys of Boise* provides another example of response to a type of deviance that does not involve violence—homosexual relations between adults and teenagers.[43] At first there was little concrete information available; this led to questions, rumors, and suspicion of all single men. The local newspaper expressed alarm over the revelations of homosexuality in the community; its readers concluded that there must be some cause for alarm. The major issue fastened upon was the corruption of youth, the contamination of the innocent by older men.[44] Fears were generalized to strangers, bachelors, and homosexuals who had never had sexual contacts with teenagers. One homosexual left the community after a "crush the monster" campaign was initiated. Reaction to the stories about homosexual behavior in the community was strong, although not necessarily consistent with the private behavior of the condemners. One local physician said:

Like every narrow-minded, proper town, Boise had its Peyton Place aspects, but oh my God, if anyone dared to say so publicly . . . I think the greatest characteristic of towns like Boise is their hypocrisy. Everybody goes to church, sends their kids to Sunday School, and all that, and of course violently condemns any and all aberrations or deviations from the norms, but then, when they can get away with it, they tend to practice what they do not preach as much as people anywhere else.[45]

By reacting very negatively, people were able to show others that they were not at all like the deviants. One Boise resident said that the night with the boys disappeared, that "[y]ou never saw so many men going out to the bars at night with their wives and girl friends."[46]

Cries were heard for community action to fight homosexuality and to provide help for the adolescents who had been involved with the older men. Although an organization was set up to help the boys by giving them jobs (since monetary gain had been a reason for their involvement in homosexual relations), the program was ineffective. No other constructive programs emerged from a meeting of law enforcement agents, lawyers, doctors, youth agency employees, parent-teacher association members, and other Boise residents. The overall effect of the scandal on the community was divisive. Single men were stigmatized and suspect, the police were blamed for their ineffectiveness in dealing with the problem, and some teenagers were labeled as corrupted if not actually deviant. Gerassi suggests that this harsh reaction may have been due to the traditional and conservative setting, a community that was moralistic and intolerant of behavioral diversity. He suggests that such a community is more likely to explode when norms are challenged than is a more diversified community,[47] a conclusion opposite to Durkheim's argument that reaction to crime and deviance will be intense but unifying in small and homogeneous communities.

Crimes such as the theft of property have recently spread to small homogeneous communities that were once relatively crime-free. Reaction to crime in such communities has been much like reactions in the high crime-rate areas of large cities. For instance, a story in *The New York Times* under the headline "Rural Crime Spreads Fear and Distrust" begins:

Perry, Iowa, Jan. 15—There was a time when the Durwood Scheibs left the front door of their farm home unlocked day and night and offered a steamy cup of coffee and a cherry "Hello, there!" to any stranger coming up their muddy lane to break their isolation.

No more.

Today, the big, windowless door stays solidly bolted shut round the clock and strangers are inspected cynically through a peephole, then greeted over an intercom with a cold, metallic: "Who are you and what do you want?"

The Scheibs have transformed their once-peaceful country home into a fortified camp because of a sharp increase in crime in rural America. It is not just an increase in such routine rural crime as cattle rustling and grain stealing but one in more fearful things like robbery, burglary and assault.

In fact, it is so serious that farm folk everywhere are abandoning traditionally trusting ways and adopting the fears, suspicions and protective measures most often associated with their city cousins.[48]

The Scheibs and a number of their neighbors had suffered robberies and burglaries. As a result, they installed vapor lamps, bought watchdogs, and avoided strangers. The aura of suspicion was so pervasive that the local deputy sheriff said, "It's gotten so serious that whenever I drive up to a farm home at night, I turn on my red roof flashers at the bottom of the lane, just so everybody will know who I am."[49] The social fabric of this community was greatly weakened by the fear of crime. People distrusted strangers and were even suspicious of their neighbors and local policemen. Some even moved away. Durkheim's picture of small towns and rural communities banding together against violations of the collective conscience is not reflected in this report from rural Iowa.

Community Reaction to Crime: The Effect of Race Relations

If Durkheim is correct that crime unites people, we might expect that it would bring together urban residents who daily face the common threat of crime. However, we have seen that even relatively homogeneous communities are divided by crime. This tendency is exacerbated in communities that are comprised of various racial and ethnic groups. The fear of strangers and the perception of outsiders as criminals are reinforced by racial and ethnic prejudices. "Crime is continuing to drive a wedge between disadvantaged blacks and other minorities who provide a disproportionate share of the prison population and middle-class whites who in fear set themselves up in enclaves." [50]

This is especially true after an interracial crime in which the members of the ethnic group to which the victim belongs unify among themselves but in strong opposition to the group to which the offender belongs. The victim symbolizes the threat to his group by the offender's group. Ethnic group solidarity is enhanced, but it is a negative and destructive form of unity rather than one which is functional for the community as a whole. Violence may break out between the groups, either for retaliation or for self-protection. This kind of reaction was common in the South when black men were lynched after allegedly committing crimes against whites. It is also seen in the reaction to a New York City policeman's killing of a ten-year-old black boy as he fled from a car that he had allegedly stolen. Blacks in the community were outraged, both because of the racial issue and because lethal force had been used against someone so young. Local black youths reacted with violence against whites. Two whites were beaten unconscious. One young black said, "Anything white that came down Jersey Street was bombed." [51] The black youths may have grown closer together as a result of the slaying, but their solidarity was based on hostility toward whites; it was divisive of the larger community.

A similar incident in New York City involved a teller who was chasing a bank robber. The offender was black; the teller was Puerto Rican. When the teller finally caught the robber and pinned him against the wall of a building to hold him for the police, he found that none of the bystanders in the community would help him hold the offender or call the police, just as no one had helped him chase the thief. The offender yelled that he had no money, and a crowd of blacks gathered and demanded that the teller release the youth. Fearing violence from the crowds, the teller let the thief go and returned to the bank. A black teller pursuing a white offender in a white community would probably have met with a similar response.[52]

The murder of a Jewish woman in New York City also fueled inter-ethnic antagonisms.[53] Jewish residents of the community attributed much of the recent violence in their neighborhood to blacks. Crime had heightened tensions between the growing black population and the declining Jewish population. The local Jewish Defense League had organized an escort system to protect elderly shoppers and had distributed pamphlets urging Jews to protect themselves, suggesting "Every Jew a .22." Jews were made more conscious of themselves as a separate group facing a great threat, but they also became more hostile toward blacks. The community as a whole was not unified.

A nearby community was also undergoing change from an all-white population to one of mixed racial composition. Although many local whites were reluctant to *directly* blame the new residents for the rising crime rates, their major complaint about the community was its changing racial composition and their second major complaint was the increasing threat of crime. The two were linked together in the minds of many of the whites. One said that criminals entered the community from outside because they knew they could expect protection from the law by local blacks. This person refused to admit that criminals lived in his neighborhood, but he did think that local crime was stimulated by those who lived there.[54] Again, members of different ethnic groups were divided rather than united by crime.

When people feel that the distinction between criminals and law-abiding citizens overlaps with racial or ethnic group differences, suspicion and hostility will divide a community. Group consciousness is enhanced, but the community as a whole suffers. In such a situation, the response of the dominant ethnic group is sometimes called racist.[55] Examining the Forest Hills, New York, housing dispute in which a group of middle-class Jews opposed the construction of low-income housing in their community, Nathan Glazer argues that the Jews were responding more to the fear of crime than to the fact that many of the new residents of the community would be black.[56] He states that a major reason that the middle-class Jews had originally moved to the area was to escape areas where schools were dangerous and stores were robbed or vandalized. Their past experiences led them to believe that neighborhood safety would decline if poor blacks entered the community. Whether or not these perceptions were correct is not of major concern here; what is important is that the fear of crime, reinforced by the association of crime with a particular racial group, drove two groups apart. Blacks who would have moved into the community also sought to escape crime, but mutual condemnation of crime did not draw the Jews and the blacks together. Blacks in the United States do commit a comparatively high percentage of the crimes that elicit the greatest fear—murder, rape, and robbery.[57] However, whites often generalize from these cross-racial differences in crime rates to the entire racial group, so that fear of crime and prejudice against blacks reinforce each other and divide communities. The perception of high crime rates for blacks becomes a self-fulfilling prophecy as this group is confined to poor housing, low-paying jobs, and inadequate schools, some of the causes of crime itself.

The strength of ethnic-group ties is illustrated by an unusual crime that occurred in Tennessee. Jesse Hill Ford, a white novelist who had written critically about race relations in his town, shot and killed a black man near his home. At first, whites felt hostility toward Ford, not because of his crime but because he had been critical of local mores. Antagonism toward Ford continued, but many whites were happy when he was acquitted of the murder charge. One author attributed this response to "a white communal instinct older and larger than Ford himself."[58] A local white man said, "I never have liked Jesse Hill Ford worth a damn, and I *still* don't. But I sure as hell liked that verdict."[59]

Under certain circumstances, members of previously hostile racial and ethnic groups may come together in reaction to crime. This can happen if the groups share a common goal such as the reduction of local crime rates and if they can unite in a cooperative effort to reach that goal. For instance, in some housing projects members of different ethnic groups have united to form tenant patrols and discussion groups to fight crime.[60] If a common goal is defined and clear means to reach that goal are found and are acceptable to all, and if people can cooperate in a noncompetitive way in accordance with the law, groups that otherwise might be antagonistic toward each other may be united by the common threat of crime.[61]

However, Durkheim's idea that crime brings people together does not seem generally valid. Crime may augment social interaction under certain circumstances and in limited ways, but this is usually for mutual self-protection rather than because people feel closer to others with whom they share the violated norms. Durkheim argues that the basis of increased solidarity following a crime is *normative*, that people interact more intensively because they have been made more acutely aware of the norms and values that they share with each other. It is probably a more accurate conclusion that, to the extent that social solidarity is enhanced by crime, the basis will be *functional* rather than normative; that is, people may come together to protect themselves and to make sense of a confusing event. However, as we have seen throughout this chapter, crime often drives people apart by creating distrust and suspicion, even in small and homogeneous communities with little history of crime.

Footnotes

1. Emile Durkheim, *The Rules of Sociological Method*, translated by Sarah A. Solovay and John H. Mueller and edited by George E. G. Catlin. New York: The Free Press, 1938, p. 67.
2. Emile Durkheim, *The Division of Labor in Society*, translated by George Simpson. Glencoe, Ill.: The Free Press, 1933, p. 73. Durkheim's point of view leaves unexplained the origin of "unhealthy" consciences in society.
3. Ibid., p. 79.
4. Ibid. p. 87. Paul Fauconnet has suggested that in preliterate societies, the attachment of the sanction to the *crime* may be close, but the attachment of the sanction to the *criminal* may not be close. There is a need to reestablish the moral order and restore confidence in the norms of society by applying a sanction. If the crime is punished, even if the actual offender is not the object of the punishment, dominant values will be reaffirmed. This process also occurs in more advanced societies; for example, in the South any con-

venient young black male was often lynched after the rape of a white woman in order to reaffirm "the regional mores of the 'untouchability' of white women by Negroes." Robert Cooley Angell, *Free Society and Moral Crisis.* Ann Arbor: The University of Michigan Press, 1958, pp. 117–118.

5. Durkheim, *The Division of Labor in Society,* p. 102.
6. Ibid., p. 103.
7. Ibid., p. 104.
8. Kai T. Erikson, *Wayward Puritans: A Study in the Sociology of Deviance.* New York: John Wiley & Sons, Inc., 1966, p. 4.
9. Ibid., p. 13. Emphasis added here.
10. Terence Morris, "The Social Toleration of Crime," in Hugh J. Klare, editor, *Changing Concepts of Crime and Its Treatment.* Oxford: Pergamon Press, 1966, p. 14.
11. Talcott Parsons, *The Social System.* Glencoe, Ill.: The Free Press, 1951, p. 310.
12. Arthur Koestler, *Reflections on Hanging.* New York: Macmillan Publishing Co., Inc., 1957, p. 8.
13. Cited in Lewis Coser, *The Functions of Social Conflict.* Glencoe, Ill.: The Free Press, 1956, p. 87. Emphasis added here.
14. Ibid., pp. 87–95.
15. Another instance of styles of dress eliciting a sharp reaction occurred in the Soviet Union.

> A sports fan in the Ukraine was so indignant he could hardly bear to watch television. A Leningrad student was disgusted. A Moscow school teacher pleaded for help from movie-makers. The newspaper Sovetsky Sport insisted that referees blow the whistle at once.
>
> The problem: Long hair, sloppy socks, dirty slacks or rumpled jeans and generally hippie fashions not only among ordinary Soviet youth but also among some of its most vaunted soccer stars during nationally televised games.

Hedrick Smith, "Long Hair, Sloppy Socks Offend Soviet Sports Fans," *The New York Times,* June 4, 1972, pp. 1, 12.
16. Edgar Morin, *Rumour in Orléans,* translated by Peter Green. New York: Pantheon Books, 1969, 1971, pp. 69–79.
17. John Barron Mays, *Crime and the Social Structure.* London: Faber and Faber Ltd., 1963, pp. 69–78.
18. George Herbert Mead, "The Psychology of Punitive Justice," *American Journal of Sociology* XXIII (March 1918), pp. 577–602.
19. In fact, exclusion of the criminal may even push him into a more

69

organized group of criminals. Edwin H. Sutherland and Donald R. Cressey, *Criminology*, eighth edition. Philadelphia: J. B. Lippincott Company, 1970, p. 23.

20. Truman Capote, *In Cold Blood: A True Account of a Multiple Murder and Its Consequences.* New York: Random House, 1965. Copyright © 1965 by Truman Capote.
21. Cited in ibid., p. 69. A similar search for further information followed the "Moors Murders" in England. People took transistor radios to work to hear any recent news that might tell them something about the crimes or the criminals. Emlyn Williams, *Beyond Belief: A Chronicle of Murder and Its Detection.* New York: Random House, 1967, p. 326.
22. Jane Jacobs, *The Death and Life of Great American Cities.* New York: Vintage Books, 1961, p. 68.
23. Cited in Capote, op. cit., p. 69.
24. Cited in ibid., p. 69.
25. Ibid., p. 70.
26. Cited in ibid., p. 70.
27. Ibid. p. 88.
28. Cited in ibid, p. 191.
29. Ibid., p. 88. Following the assassination of President John F. Kennedy, many people wondered "if anybody could really be safe in this country these days, when the President himself can get shot." Paul B. Sheatsley and Jacob J. Feldman, "The Assassination of President Kennedy: A Preliminary Report on Public Reactions and Behavior," *Public Opinion Quarterly* XXVIII (Summer 1964), p. 197.
30. Cited in Capote, op. cit., p. 88.
31. Ibid., p. 231.
32. Ibid., p. 248.
33. Change of venue is the legal term for a change in the location of a trial.
34. Cited in Capote, op. cit., pp. 271–272.
35. "Even with the World," *Time* LXXI (February 10, 1958), pp. 21–22; "Behind a Week of Terror, One Boy's History," *U.S. News & World Report* XLIV (February 7, 1958), p. 15; "Eleven Lay Dead," *Newsweek* LI (February 10, 1958), p. 42.
36. Deirdre Carmody, "Fear Holds in Hunt for Boy's Slayer," *The New York Times*, April 17, 1973, pp. 37, 70.
37. Edwin H. Sutherland, "The Sexual Psychopath Laws," in Albert Cohen, Alfred Lindesmith, and Karl Schuessler, editors, *The Sutherland Papers*. Bloomington, Ind.: Indiana University Press, 1956, pp. 185–199.
38. Edwin H. Sutherland, "The Diffusion of Sexual Psychopath Laws,"

in William J. Chambliss, editor, *Crime and the Legal Process*. New York: McGraw-Hill Book Company, 1969, p. 75.

39. Tony G. Poveda, "The Fear of Crime in a Small Town," *Crime and Delinquency* XVIII (April 1972), p. 149.

40. For an example of public reaction to violence by youths, see Joe Eszterhas, *Charlie Simpson's Apocalypse*. New York: Random House, 1973.

41. Cited in Poveda, op. cit., p. 152.

42. See Eszterhas, op. cit.

43. John Gerassi, *The Boys of Boise: Furor, Vice and Folly in an American City*. New York: Macmillan Publishing Co., Inc., 1966.

44. Ibid., p. 13.

45. Cited in ibid, p. 29.

46. Cited in ibid., p. 48.

47. Ibid., pp. 147–150.

48. B. Drummond Ayres, Jr., "Rural Crime Spreads Fear and Distrust," *The New York Times*, January 16, 1972, pp. 1, 46.

49. Cited in ibid., p. 46.

50. John Herbers, "The Bid for the Law and Order Vote," *The New York Times*, October 22, 1972, Section 4, p. 3. This process also occurred after a white woman was doused with gasoline and burned to death by six black youths in Boston in the fall of 1973. The media gave this crime much attention, and talk of a race war was heard. This murder was committed in a community that had been only 3 per cent nonwhite in 1960 but was 33 per cent nonwhite in 1970. Racial tensions over the integration of schools and the changing composition of the community gave the murders symbolic importance. Whites charged blacks with violence and crime; blacks called whites "racist" for characterizing all blacks by the actions of a very few.

51. Cited in Ronald Smothers, "Police Issue New Restrictions on Use of Firearms After the Shooting of 10-Year-Old Boy," *The New York Times*, August 18, 1972, p. 62.

52. James M. Markham, "42d Street Crowd Helps Robber Flee," *The New York Times*, January 5, 1972, pp. 1, 41.

53. Ralph Blumenthal, "Woman's Death Heightens Fear Stalking Rockaways," *The New York Times*, January 6, 1972, p. 28.

54. Lesley Oelsner, "Terrified East Flatbush Little Stirred by Slaying," *The New York Times*, August 26, 1971, p. 75.

55. In fact, similar responses to crime by whites and by blacks are sometimes interpreted in different ways. Whites who move from high crime-rate areas where there are many blacks may be called racists. Blacks who seek to escape from the same high crime areas may be seen as ambitious and desirous of improving their position,

    although they may also be criticized for deserting their people rather than trying to improve the community.

56. Nathan Glazer, "When the Melting Pot Doesn't Melt," *The New York Times Magazine*, January 2, 1972, pp. 12–13, 27–31.

57. See Marvin E. Wolfgang, *Patterns in Criminal Homicide*. Philadelphia: University of Pennsylvania Press, 1958; Menachem Amir, *Patterns in Forcible Rape*. Chicago: University of Chicago Press, 1971; John E. Conklin, *Robbery and the Criminal Justice System*. Philadelphia: J. B. Lippincott Company, 1972; and Clarence M. Kelley, *Crime in the United States—1972*. Washington, D.C.: United States Government Printing Office, 1973.

58. Marshall Frady, "The Continuing Trial of Jesse Hill Ford," *Life* magazine LXXI (October 29, 1971), p. 68.

59. Cited in ibid., p. 68.

60. Lesley Oelsner, "Rising Crime Stirs Fear on the Lower East Side," *The New York Times*, September 22, 1971, p. 51.

61. For a discussion of the effects of intergroup contact on the alleviation of racial hostilities, see Gordon W. Allport, *The Nature of Prejudice*. Garden City, N.Y.: Doubleday & Company, Inc., 1958, pp. 250–268.

Crime and the Community: Port City and Belleville*

A L T H O U G H there are some American communities where crime has had no impact on daily life, these places are becoming increasingly rare.[1] Throughout the country, people avoid strangers and neighbors. They stay home at night rather than use the streets or the parks. They do not visit friends and they warn friends not to visit them. Businesses rearrange their work schedules to allow employees to go home before dark; some companies even provide escorts and recommend safe routes of travel. Downtown areas become so deserted that in some cities merchants hold downtown discovery tours to attract suburbanites back to the city.[2]

With people "afraid to come downtown," the very basis for the existence of cities is undercut, this basis being the enrichment of life in economic, social, educational, and cultural terms through increased opportunities afforded by specialization and other means supposedly inherent in, and facilitated by, an urban setting.[3]

Fear divides suburb from central city and neighborhood from neighborhood. If an area acquires a reputation as a dangerous place, human traffic there will diminish. Business will decline, and tourism may suffer.[4] For example, after a series of murders on one of the Virgin Islands, one observer said, "Tourists have begun to bypass the island [St. Croix]. Shops and restaurants are empty and hotels have begun to close. Many properties that were in great demand just a few years ago are now up for sale at greatly reduced prices."[5]

*Portions of this chapter originally appeared in John E. Conklin, "Dimensions of Community Response to the Crime Problem," *Social Problems* XVIII (Winter 1971), pp. 373–385. Used with the permission of The Society for the Study of Social Problems.

Single events sometimes evoke great fear among the public, as we saw in the previous chapter. Personal victimization can also heighten fear, although the National Crime Commission found that victims did not differ much from nonvictims in their anxiety about crime. A reanalysis of some of the Commission's data concluded that "there appears to be a significant positive relationship between crime levels and subjective evaluations of potential victimization. There appears to be no systematic relationship between specific victimization and specific subjective probability." [6] In other words, people's fears of victimization are affected by their perception of crime in general, but their fears of being a victim of a specific crime are not affected by having been a victim of that crime in the past.

Still, victimization does have a major impact on the individual. The lone survivor of Richard Speck's murder of eight Chicago nurses said years after the crime that her fear persisted, that she could not be alone in a room and hear a knock on the door without becoming anxious.[7] The victim of a robbery described his reaction as follows: "Immediately after the mugging, I experienced (so my wife tells me), a large, and I think necessary, anger. . . . I hated everybody regardless of race, creed, color or national origin—without fear or favor. . . . "[8] People do respond to their victimization, at least in those crimes that evoke the greatest public concern. If the crime seems motiveless and likely to be repeated, and if no offender is arrested, their response is intensified.[9]

The initial reaction of many robbery victims to being held up is surprise and bewilderment.[10] Many also express fright, indignation, and resignation. At first, many misperceive the cues that they are being robbed, since the event is unusual, unexpected, and difficult to interpret; this is especially true if the robber says nothing to explain his actions. This reaction of disbelief is fairly common among robbery victims; as we shall see in a later chapter, it is also a frequent reaction to seeing another person victimized. Some robbery victims think it is a joke, others a solicitation, and still others harassment or a mistake. Most victims cooperate with the offender in order to avoid harm, but some resist by fighting back, running away, or holding on to their money. Victims find it difficult to relate the crime to their past experiences and to their definitions of normal street behavior. Most had felt relatively free of danger before the crime; many revise their assumptions after the crime. Areas of the city toward which they had felt positively are redefined as high-risk places. In cases where the robber is well dressed, the apparent discrepancy between dress and demeanor angers some victims, increasing their sense of vulnerability and their distrust of strangers. After the crime, many victims talk about the crime to others, much as Durkheim suggests people will "wax indignant in common" after a challenge to their shared values. However, the victims probably talk more to reduce inner tensions and to share their experience than to reinforce the violated norm. Talk helps them place the traumatic experience in perspective and restore a damaged social reality. The victim also has something of a star quality about him after the crime. Other people are interested in his first-hand account of a crime that they themselves greatly fear.

Women who are raped initially react with "shock, disbelief, dismay, and emotional breakdown." At first, they deny the reality of the crime and have trouble speaking of it. Later they experience "outward or pseudo-adjustment" in an effort to overcome their anxiety and fear. In a third phase, they show "depression and the need to talk" and are obsessed with their experience.[11] Although the emotional trauma is greater in rape cases, victims react in some of the same ways that robbery victims do—with disbelief, anxiety, and a need to talk.

Personal victimization in dramatic crimes does affect victims' attitudes and behavior, at least in the short run. One reason the Crime Commission probably found little relationship between actual victimization and attitudes toward crime was that most of the crimes people suffer are trivial in nature, such as the theft of a small sum of money. Reaction to such crimes is minimal, even in the short run. Also, reaction to even the more serious crimes of robbery and rape is apt to diminish over time; a sense of invulnerability returns after a period during which no additional crimes occur.

More than just *direct* victimization produces public fear of crime. In the previous chapter, we saw that the victimization of others in a dramatic crime can have a major effect on attitudes and behavior. In the first two chapters, we saw that newspaper reporting of crimes, political use of the crime issue, and crime statistics also influence public attitudes and behavior. In this chapter, we look at the impact of people's perceptions of crime on their attitudes and behavior in a high crime-rate area (the urban community of Port City) and in a low crime-rate area (the suburb of Belleville). Since people must perceive crime before they react to it, we first examine perceptions of crime in each community. Then we look at how these perceptions are related to feelings of personal safety, interpersonal trust, and attitudes toward the community itself. We do not present a rigorous testing of Durkheim's ideas about the impact of crime on the community, but the material does bear directly on his argument that crime enhances social solidarity.

Perceptions of Crime

Nationally, crime has been considered a major social problem for a number of years. In 1965, Americans ranked crime as the second most important domestic social problem after race relations.[12] At other times during the last decade, they have ranked crime first. Such rankings will vary with the condition of the economy and the society, as well as with perception of the crime problem itself. As unemployment rises and inflation increases, these issues will become of greater relative importance in comparison to crime, although people may not feel any less worried about crime in an absolute sense.

Using data from Baltimore, Frank F. Furstenberg, Jr. found that concern with the crime problem varied *inversely* with the official crime rate of a community; that is, there was most concern with crime in areas with the lowest crime rates. In low crime areas, 34 per cent of the people thought that crime was the most important domestic social problem on a list of ten problems; 29 per cent in medium crime areas and 26 per cent in high crime areas thought crime was the most serious problem.[13] These differences, though not large in percentage terms, are statistically significant. Concern with crime as a social problem was greatest in low crime areas because crime was seen as a threat to the existing social order. People who disapproved of changes in race relations were most apt to be concerned with the crime issue. Residents of high crime areas were more likely to be concerned with such social problems as race relations, unemployment, and education, although *fear of victimization* was higher in their communities than it was where rates were lower.

We asked the residents of Port City and Belleville to choose the social problem of greatest importance to themselves from a list of seven problems: poverty, rising prices, the Vietnam war, education, crime, race relations, and unemployment. Belleville residents ranked crime first in 9 per cent of the cases, second in 16 per cent of the cases, and third in 19 per cent of the cases. Residents of Port City ranked crime of greatest significance in 13 per cent of the cases, second in 24 per cent of the cases, and third in 14 per cent of the cases. Thus, more residents of the high crime rate area ranked crime as a problem of great personal concern. This finding is opposite to the one reported by Furstenberg for Baltimore. The reasons are not clear. Possibly, none of the areas in Baltimore in which interviews were conducted was similar to Belleville, a suburb a few miles outside the city with a very low official crime rate. It is also possible that the racial issue influenced answers more in Baltimore than in Boston. In 1970 the population of Baltimore was 46 per cent black; in the same year, the population of Boston was only 16 per cent black. Since concern with crime was closely related to opposition to racial change in Baltimore, the residents of the low crime communities in that city might have expressed greater concern with crime because of their racial fears. In Boston where blacks constitute a much smaller part of the population, concern with crime may reflect concern more with the actual threat of victimization than with possible changes in race relations.

We asked the residents of Port City and Belleville which *types* of crime were of greatest concern to them. In Port City, the

77

most commonly mentioned offense was drug abuse; 65 per cent of the respondents cited this as the most serious local crime problem. Official police records do show that the arrest rate for narcotics violations was higher in Port City in the years immediately preceding the interviews than in any other area of the city. Some Port City residents also attributed other crimes with which they were concerned (such as burglary) to addicts who were trying to get money to support their habits. Respondents knew of specific streetcorners where addicts bought and used drugs. In contrast to the large proportion of residents who felt that drug abuse was the major local crime problem, only 9 per cent cited burglary as the most serious offense and only 3 per cent mentioned juvenile delinquency.

Forty-two per cent of the residents of the suburb felt that the most serious local crime problem was juvenile delinquency.[14] By juvenile delinquency they meant such activities as vandalism, underage drinking, general rowdyism, and loitering. About one-fourth of the Belleville residents (28 per cent) thought burglary was the community's most serious crime problem; in fact, burglaries constitute half of the index offenses in Belleville (see Appendix A, Table A-1).[15] Still, the official per capita burglary rate in Belleville was only two-thirds as high as the rate in Port City. Burglary is a *relatively* greater problem in the suburb because of the absence of other kinds of crime there, even though it is less common than in the urban community.

Generally, the residents of Port City were more concerned with "serious" crimes than the Belleville residents. If serious crimes are defined as the seven offenses in the FBI crime index plus arson, loan sharking, and narcotics abuse, 96 per cent of the crimes mentioned as causing the greatest concern for the Port City residents are serious crimes, whereas only 44 per cent of the offenses mentioned by the Belleville respondents would be classified that way. When Port City residents say they are concerned with crime as a social issue, the crimes of which they speak are of a relatively serious nature; many of the crimes of greatest concern to the Belleville residents pose little real threat to person or property.[16]

Residents of Port City and Belleville were asked to compare the crime rate in their community with the crime rates in the nation and in the Boston metropolitan area.[17] They were also asked to describe the local crime rate as high, average, or low.[18] When asked to compare the crime rate in their own community with the rate in the Boston area, 83 per cent of the suburban residents and only 39 per cent of the urban residents said that the rate in their area was lower. Ninety-one per cent of the Belleville residents felt that the rate in their community was lower than the nation's rate, but only 57 per cent of the Port City residents felt that way. Whereas 87 per cent of the residents of Belleville described the local crime rate as low, only 53 per cent of the Port City respondents described the local crime rate that way. The differences between communities on these three questions were all greater than would be expected by chance;[19] in all instances there was a greater perception of crime in Port City, a finding that corresponds to the difference in the official crime rates of the two areas (see Appendix A). Because these three questions were correlated with each other, they were added together to form a perception of crime scale. There was a statistically significant difference between communities, with Belleville residents perceiving considerably less local crime than the Port City residents.

Because of differences in the social characteristics of the populations of the two communities (see Appendix A), the difference in perception of crime could be due to the type of people who live in each area rather than to the different criminal environments of the two towns. For example, if low-income people feel more insecure than high-income people about their property, possibly because they are closer to a subsistence level, we would expect a community with relatively more low-income residents to have a higher average perception of crime. We can determine if income and other social characteristics cause the difference in perception of crime in Port City and Belleville by looking at the scores on the perception of crime scale for high- and low-income residents of each community. The mean values on the perception of crime scale, which ranges from one to three with the higher scores representing a perception of more crime in the community,[20] and the number of respondents in each income category for each community are:

	Belleville	Port City
Low income (under $6,000)	1.16 (30)	1.58 (39)
Medium income ($6,000–$10,000)	1.09 (26)	1.56 (39)
High income (over $10,000)	1.18 (54)	1.85 (18)

Within each community, there is little variation in perception of crime by income. In Belleville those at different income levels perceive about the same amount of crime. In Port City, the averages for the two lower income groups are almost the same; those few (18) residents with higher incomes perceive more crime. Within each sample, income does not influence perception of crime very much. Other background variables were examined in this way, with the same general conclusion: *Perception of crime within each community was not affected very much by the personal characteristics of the respondents.* The interested reader can turn to Appendix B, Table B-1, for data that show that the following characteristics have minimal effects on perception of crime: sex, age, ethnic group, religion, education, income, prestige of occupation, self-designated class, and father's occupation. Some minor differences do exist, but they are neither consistent nor large. The data suggest that it is the criminal environment in which people live, rather than their personal and background traits, which affects the way they perceive local crime rates.

The above figures can be examined in another way, comparing people of the same income level in each community in terms of their perceptions of crime. For example, low-income residents of Port City perceive more crime on the average (1.58) than low-income residents of Belleville (1.16). This difference also holds for the other two income levels. In other words, residents of Port City perceive more crime in their community than residents of Belleville, even if people earning the same incomes are compared. Similar conclusions emerge from an examination of Table B-1 in Appendix B for other social characteristics. In sum, *differences between communities in perception of crime hold even when people of similar characteristics are compared,* again suggesting that a unique criminal environment exists in each community.[21]

Feelings of Personal Safety

Perceptions of crime do not necessarily correspond to the objective risk of victimization faced by the residents of a community. People, especially in high crime-rate areas, often underestimate the risk of crime in their community. To admit that they are living in a highly dangerous environment would make it difficult to continue to live there; the real risk may be denied to preserve a sense of security. For instance, a survey of two Boston communities, Dorchester (a racially mixed but predominantly white community with a high crime rate) and Roxbury (a predominantly black community with an even higher crime rate) found that residents of both areas downplayed the risk of victimization in their community. In Dorchester, 80 per cent said that their neighborhood was very safe or average in safety; only 16 per cent admitted that the area was unsafe. In Roxbury, where there was an even greater objective risk, 53 per cent said the area was very safe or average in safety and 42 per cent said it was unsafe. People underestimated the lack of safety in their neighborhood, thereby maintaining the peace of mind that was necessary to continue to live there. Interestingly, this same survey also found that many residents of the two communities made numerous changes in their daily behavior patterns because of crime.[22] They learned to live with crime by adjusting to it in a self-protective way, but they were unwilling to characterize their neighborhood as unsafe.

The original analysis of the Baltimore study of public response to crime concluded that "people *least* in danger are *most* afraid."[23] Rosenthal suggested that this might be because the better-educated know of more crimes because of exposure to the news, because they remembered items better, or because they talked more of crime. Also, crime may have been more noticeable to them because it contrasted with their relatively crime-free lives. However, Furstenberg's reanalysis of the same data showed that a distinction had to be made between *fear of victimization* and *concern with crime* as a social issue. Concern with crime was indeed greatest where rates were lowest, as we saw earlier. However, *fear* of criminal victimization was highest in communities with higher crime rates; in high crime communities, 47 per cent expressed much fear of victimization, compared to 30 per cent in medium crime areas and only 19 per cent in low crime areas.[24] Fear of victimization was not related to opposition to social change, as was concern with the crime issue. Fear of crime was greatest among those who thought that their neighborhood was least safe, and these feelings of safety were closely tied to official community crime rates.

To measure feelings of personal safety in Port City and Belleville, respondents were asked a series of questions. They were asked: "Is there any area around here—that is, within a mile—where you would be afraid to walk alone at night?" Thirty-one per cent of a national sample answered affirmatively to the same question, about the same proportion as the 33 per cent who answered this way in Belleville. In contrast, 52 per cent of the Port City residents expressed such a fear; this was a significantly larger proportion than in the suburban sample. Even though many people feel unsafe walking alone in their neghborhood at night, many do use the streets after dark fairly often; many also feel safe on those same streets during the day.[25]

A second question we asked the residents of Port City and Belleville was: "Have there been any times recently when you wanted to go out somewhere in your neighborhood, but stayed home instead because you thought it would be unsafe to go there?" In a national survey 13 per cent of the sample said yes, greater than the 9 per cent who said yes in Belleville but less than the 21 per cent who answered affirmatively in Port City.[26] Again we find a large discrepancy between the two communities, with greater fear in the high crime-rate community. Greater insecurity in Port City also turned up in response to the following: "Do you make sure that all of the doors in your home are locked when you leave for even a few minutes?" In Belleville, 56 per cent did so; in Port City the proportion was 86 per cent.

Three other questions asked of a national sample in another survey were asked of residents of the two Boston-area communities. One was: "Some people worry a great deal about having their house broken into, and other people are not as concerned. Are you very concerned, somewhat concerned, or not at all concerned about this?" Nationally, 50 per cent expressed some concern, about the same as the 49 per cent who did so in Belleville.[27] More residents of Port City—64 per cent—felt concerned about the possibility of a burglary in their home. Another question was: "How safe do you feel walking alone in your neighborhood when it's dark?" Nationally, 30 per cent felt unsafe; 14 per cent of the Belleville residents and 37 per cent of those in Port City felt unsafe.[28] The final question about safety was: "How likely is it that a person walking around here at night will be held up or attacked?" The national study found that 21 per cent felt such an attack was likely.[29] In Belleville, only 15 per cent answered that way, but in Port City 34 per cent did.

On all six questions about safety, the Port City residents felt significantly less safe than the Belleville residents. Belleville residents felt about as safe or somewhat safer than people throughout the nation, but Port City residents consistently felt less safe than the national sample. Males expressed considerably less fear for their safety than females, both in the national study and in our survey. The difference may be due to cultural norms that men must assert their masculinity and be brave, whereas women are freer to express their anxieties about crime. Women may also feel more defenseless than men and fear victimization more because they are physically smaller, because they are less apt to be armed, and because they have reason to fear sexual assaults. This suggests that the attitudes of women might be a more sensitive indicator of the criminal environment of a community than the attitudes of the entire population of the area. Blacks and whites could not be compared in our samples because both Port City and Belleville were almost all white. Nationally, blacks expressed somewhat more fear for their safety than whites, probably because they were more likely to live in high crime-rate communities.

Because of the moderate but statistically significant correlations among the six questions about personal safety, they were added together to form a safety scale. The scale showed that Belleville residents felt significantly more safe than Port City residents.

Generally, this difference between communities is not related to the social background characteristics of the residents. Within each sample, there are only small differences in how safe various types of people feel. Between samples there is still a large difference in feelings of safety when people of similar characteristics are compared. These conclusions are true for the traits of sex, age, ethnic group, religion, education, income, prestige of occupation, self-designated class, and father's occupation. The largest difference *within* samples is for sex: males feel considerably safer than females in each sample. The mean scores for each sex in each community on the safety scale, which ranges from one to three with a higher score representing greater perceived safety, and the number of respondents in each category are as follows:

	Belleville	Port City
Male	2.51 (64)	2.16 (62)
Female	2.28 (72)	1.87 (66)

These differences between sexes within each sample are not as large as the difference between males in each sample and the difference between females in each sample, although they are fairly sizable and are larger than the within-sample differences for any other characteristic. The elderly in both communities are also somewhat more apt to feel unsafe than the young or the middle-aged. Aside from differences by age and sex, no large within-sample differences exist. Scores on the safety scale are presented in Appendix B, Table B-2.

For these two Boston-area communities, residents in the one where more crime is perceived express greater fear for their safety than those who live in the area where less crime is perceived. Looking at the relationship between perception of crime and sense of personal safety *within* each sample, we find that the correlation of the perception of crime scale and the safety scale is near zero in Belleville, but moderate ($r = -.29$) and statistically significant in Port City. The fact that perception of crime and feelings of safety are unrelated in Belleville, but related in Port City—those who perceive more crime feeling less safe—

suggests that a *threshold effect* is operating. In other words, the *relationship* between perception of crime and feelings of safety emerges only when the actual crime rate of the community passes a certain critical level. Crime may not be common enough or serious enough in Belleville for perceptions of local rates to significantly affect feelings of safety. A person living in a low crime-rate community may say that he feels there is much crime in his neighborhood, but by "much" he may mean less than is necessary to make him feel unsafe. As we saw earlier, most residents of the low crime area were concerned with relatively harmless types of crime.

We can summarize the relationship between sense of safety and perception of crime as follows: In comparison with residents of the low crime-rate suburb, more residents of the high crime-rate urban area *perceive* high crime rates in the area and more residents of the urban area *feel unsafe* there. Within the low crime-rate suburb, sense of safety and perception of crime are not related to each other, but within the high crime-rate community those who perceive more crime feel less safe. The feeling that one is not safe is important in itself, since it diminishes the quality of life in a community. Feelings of insecurity can also generate distrust of strangers and neighbors and lead to detachment from the community itself.

Interpersonal Trust

In the previous chapter we saw that one reaction to the Clutter murders was an increase in interpersonal distrust. Even long-term acquaintances were viewed with suspicion. Such distrust weakens the social order. One author concluded from a national survey on criminal victimization that

it is not the seriousness of the crime but rather the unpredictability and the sense of invasion by unknown strangers that engenders this mistrust and hostility. Given these strong feelings and the lack of knowledge of the offenders, victimization could very well exacerbate the prejudices against the variety of groups typically blamed for social disorder and crime.[30]

Distrust of others has a number of ramifications for life in communities where the fear of crime exists. Suspicion may reach the point where even honest people are viewed as potential criminals. For example, a man was observed on a grille outside a sixth-floor apartment in a building where residents were very apprehensive of crime. Someone called the police to report a potential intruder, but investigation showed that the man was a painter who was preparing the surface of the building.[31] People's perceptions were so clouded with distrust that the house painter was seen as a burglar. However, as we shall see later, such distrust can be functional if it leads people to report suspicious behavior to the police.

The perception of honest and helpful citizens as potential criminals may damage the fabric of social life in a community. Reactions sometimes even produce harm to innocent people or nearly lead to such harm. For instance, a young man walked into a California police station with a grenade. Aware of recent violence by young radicals, the woman at the desk yelled, "Get out of here!" An officer drew his pistol, and two others grabbed the young man. Fortunately, he had time to explain that he had found the grenade and thought he should give it to the police to be defused so that there would not be an accident.[32] He was acting as a public-spirited citizen but was perceived (not without some justification) as a criminal who was intent on blowing up the police station. Reactions to strangers are based on probabilities that often have an empirical basis; there is good reason to doubt the motives of a person carrying a grenade into a police station. However, people may overreact to stereotypes of "typical" behavior to be expected from a particular individual in a particular situation. Assessments of the probability of dangerous behavior by others can drive a wedge between people, especially during crime waves when potential crime situations encompass a wider range of human behavior than when there is less fear of crime.

Whereas the young man with the grenade narrowly avoided harm, a boy in Virginia was less fortunate. An eighteen-year-old car-owner, said by his friends to be very protective of his car and to be suspicious of anyone who came near it, awoke at five o'clock one morning and saw a "prowler" near his car. He fired a shotgun at the "prowler" and killed the newspaper delivery boy. Townspeople later spoke of "the mood of hostility, suspicion and violence" in contemporary America. One recent college graduate thought that "people won't take the time to find out what's going on," adding that "[t]hey do something like this when they're the least bit suspicious." [33]

A similar incident involves the murder in which Jesse Hill Ford shot a black man near his home, a case mentioned in the preceding chapter. Threats against his son by local blacks made Ford suspicious one night when he saw a car pull into his driveway and then out again to a spot a short distance from his home. Thinking that the driver intended to ambush his son when he returned home, Ford took his rifle and demanded that the driver get out of the car and wait for the police to arrive. The man began to drive off. Ford fired what he later described as a warning shot and killed the driver.[34] Ford's suspicion was reasonable given the threats against his son's life, but his suspicion led to an overreaction that had disastrous consequences. Suspicion that was initially fed by fear of crime actually produced a crime.

Suspicion of others rarely has such violent results, but it does increase anxiety and weaken relationships among people. A series of abductions and murders of young children in Hamden, Connecticut, generated suspicion of all unknown men driving cars in the town. One police lieutenant said, "If a car goes up a street twice, we get a call." [35] Children were instructed to avoid strangers and to turn down rides from them. Parents' sensitivity is suggested by the following:

Outside Central Elementary, as a reporter and a photographer stopped to talk to one mother, she shouted at them and called to a friend to write down the license number of the photographer's car. Within a minute, two policemen were on the scene questioning the reporter and the photographer, but both had already identified themselves at the police station.

"The switchboard lit up like a Christmas tree as soon as you two walked toward the schoolyard," a policeman said.[36]

Violent crime often creates the feeling that all strangers have evil intentions. However, sensitivity to strangers' actions can also strengthen informal social controls that minimize the amount of crime in a community, as we shall see in Chapter 6. Even nonviolent crimes can reduce an individual's trust of his fellow man. Imagine the attitude toward strangers that the motorist must hold after the following experience:

A motorist pulled his car off the highway in Queens, New York, to fix a flat tire. He jacked up his car and, while removing the tire was startled to see his hood being opened and a stranger starting to lift out his battery. The motorist began yelling, but the stranger tried to mollify his assumed car stripping colleague by offering, "Take it easy buddy, you can have the tires, all I want is the battery."[37]

The stranger simply assumed the driver was another thief, not even considering the possibility that he was repairing a tire. Undoubtedly, the faith of that driver in his fellow man was substantially reduced after his experience, but probably not as much as the trust felt by the couple in the following incident:

It was in Briarcliffe, N.Y., where a young couple went to dinner one evening at a local restaurant, and returned to find their car apparently stolen. After reporting it to the local police, they returned to their home and the next morning were surprised to see the car in the driveway, with an envelope on the windshield.

"There was an emergency and we had to borrow the car," the note read. "Please excuse the inconvenience, but perhaps these two theater tickets will make up for it." The couple, surprised but pleased, told the police that their car had been returned, and the next Saturday used the theater tickets.

When they returned that night, they found that their house had been completely looted.[38]

Trust of others can be dysfunctional if criminals use it to their advantage, as they did in this burglary. Such experiences quickly reduce interpersonal trust to the vanishing point. However, distrust can also be functional for individuals who seek to minimize their risk of victimization in the short run. For example, robbery victims who become more suspicious of strangers and try to avoid them may indeed reduce the likelihood of their being held up again, since most robberies are stranger-to-stranger crimes.[39] Still, such distrust will weaken social solidarity in the community, for many friendly strangers will be avoided for each one who is a potential offender.

How is distrust related to perception of crime and feeling of personal safety? We asked the residents of Port City and Belleville to agree or disagree with four statements about interpersonal trust. On each item the Belleville residents expressed considerably more trust than the Port City residents. For example, 88 per cent of the Belleville sample and 67 per cent of the Port City sample agreed with the following: "Most people in this neighborhood can be trusted." In response to the item, "Most people in this neighborhood are truthful and dependable," [40] 84 per cent of the suburbanites and 65 per cent of the urbanites agreed. Another statement was, "Nice as it may be to have faith in your fellow man, it seldom pays off." Seventy-one per cent of the Belleville sample disagreed with this, compared to 47 per cent of the Port City sample. The final item was, "The world is full of people who will take advantage of you if you give them the slightest opportunity"; 38 per cent of the Belleville residents and only 16 per cent of the Port City residents disagreed with this. Disagreement on these last two items indicates greater trust of others, so that on all four items Belleville residents expressed significantly more interpersonal trust than the Port City residents. This is interesting in light of the greater homogeneity of Port City's population, particularly in terms of ethnicity (see Appendix A), and in light of the fact that most Port City residents have lived in their community much longer than the residents of Belleville have lived there.

Because the four trust items were intercorrelated, they were added together to form a scale of interpersonal trust. On this scale, the suburban residents expressed significantly more trust than the urban residents. The difference between samples remains large when people who have the same characteristics are compared across samples; for example, men in Belleville are more trusting than men in Port City, and the same is true of women in the two communities. The difference between samples on the trust scale is not due to the population composition of the two communities, but rather reflects a real difference in attitudes. Within each sample, trust was somewhat influenced by certain characteristics. Trust was somewhat greater among the better-educated, those with higher incomes, and those with occupations of higher prestige. In other words, within each community those of higher status were more trusting of others than were those of lower status. This may be because the higher-status individuals live in the more crime-free areas of the town and thus have less to fear, or it may be because they are better able to buy protection from victimization with their higher incomes (for example, by the installation of burglar alarms). The mean values on the trust scale for persons of different background characteristics are presented in Appendix B, Table B-3.

The exact relationship between interpersonal trust and perception of crime is probably quite complicated. People who distrust others may also be more apt to perceive high crime rates, that is, to be more sensitive to crime in the community. However, those who realistically perceive high crime rates may be more apt to distrust others, whom they regard as potential criminals. In Belleville, there was a near-zero correlation of the trust scale and the perception of crime scale—trust of others did not vary with how much crime a person perceived in his community. Variations in interpersonal trust did exist in the suburban community, but they were not related to how much crime a person perceived. However, in Port City the correlation of trust and perception of crime was moderate ($r = -.23$) and statistically significant. Those who felt least trusting perceived the highest crime rates in the community. These findings again suggest a threshold effect. A relationship between perception of crime and interpersonal trust emerges only when the local crime rate passes a certain threshold; below that threshold, perception of crime is not related to trust.

We might expect interpersonal trust to be related to feelings of personal safety. Again, the relationship was not present in Belleville, but it was present in Port City, although the correlation was only .19, a small but statistically significant correlation. In Port City, those who felt least safe were also least apt to trust others; safety and trust were unrelated in the suburb. Once again we see the threshold effect operating.

Briefly, there was less interpersonal trust in the high crime-rate area than in the low crime-rate area. In the suburb, no relationships existed between trust and perception of crime or between trust and feelings of safety. However, in the high crime-rate urban community, those who felt less trust of others perceived more crime and felt less safe than those who were more trusting of others.

Affect for the Community

Crime may generate a distaste for a community because of feelings of insecurity and vulnerability in the area. Residents may view their community as unworthy, immoral, or disorderly. This threatens their self-esteem, makes daily life unpleasant, and may even inhibit upward mobility.[41] The criminal environment of a community may also influence other people's decisions to move to the area. Although it is difficult to separate fear of crime from the numerous other factors that determine selection of a place of residence, one study did conclude that liking a community depended more on the "obvious convenience features of landscape and daily life" than on the moral qualities or extent of crime in the community.[42] However, another study determined that in choosing a place to live, a majority of a sample of Washington, D.C., residents who lived in high crime-rate areas placed more emphasis on the "safety and moral atmosphere of the neighborhood" than on such factors as access to jobs and schools or the aesthetic qualities of the area.[43] If this latter interpretation is correct, we would expect people to leave or want to leave high crime-rate areas for safer places. Survey evidence does indicate that in high crime-rate areas as many as 30 per cent of the residents do wish to move.[44] Recent years have seen a migration to the suburbs (along with increased crime rates in the suburbs); some have described this process more as a push from the cities than a pull to the suburbs.[45] In other words, people are leaving the cities because of negative aspects of life there (such as crime), rather than because they are strongly attracted to the suburbs. This leaves the city economically and racially unbalanced, since those who have the money and encounter no discrimination can more easily move from the city. In the long run, the migration to the suburbs may increase both urban crime rates and suburban crime rates.[46]

We use the term *affect for the community* to refer to people's feelings about how good their community is as a place to live. Four questions were used to measure affect for the community. In response to the question, "Would you someday like to move to another neighborhood?", 55 per cent of the Belleville residents and 38 per cent of the Port City residents responded negatively. In response to the query, "Do you think that [Port City, Belleville] is a good place to bring up children?", 95 per cent of the Belleville residents but only 48 per cent of the Port City residents thought so. Asked, "On the whole, do you like living in [Port City, Belleville] or not?", 96 per cent in the suburb and only 62 per cent in the urban community said they did. The final item measuring affect for the community was, "How would you describe the attitudes of your neighbors toward strangers from outside the neighborhood?" The proportion who said that their neighbors were friendly was the same in each community, 52 per cent; however, 20 per cent of the Port City sample and only 10 per cent of the Belleville sample described their neighbors as unfriendly. On all four questions, those who live in Port City expressed less positive feelings for their community than the residents of Belleville, although there was little difference in views of how friendly their neighbors were.

Adding the four items together to form a scale measuring affect for the community, we find that the difference between samples on the scale is statistically significant; the urban residents are less favorably disposed toward their community than the suburban residents. When various social characteristics are controlled, the difference between people of similar characteristics in the two communities still exists. Within each sample, the only characteristic that is related to affect for the community is age: younger residents in each community like their town less than those who are middle-aged, and both of these groups like the area less than older residents. This difference may be related to length of residence in the community, with older people liking the area better because of greater familiarity, or it may be due to lack of involvement in the community by younger residents—for example, less participation in community organizations and less concern with local schools because they have no school-age children.

Affect for the community was not significantly related to perception of crime in the suburb ($r = -.14$); in the urban community the correlation between the two scales was moderate ($r = -.32$) and statistically significant, those who perceived the most crime liking the area least. Again, we find a threshold effect, with perception of crime being related to attitudes (that is, affect for the community) in the high crime-rate community of Port City, but being unrelated to the same attitude in the low crime-rate suburb of Belleville.

In Belleville affect was not significantly related to feelings of personal safety. The relationship was barely significant in Port City, with residents who felt most safe liking the community most. Affect for the community was not related to interpersonal trust in the suburb, but in the urban area there was a significant tendency for those who were most trusting of others to express the most positive affect for the community. These relationships again suggest a threshold effect, with affect being tied to trust and to safety in Port City but not in Belleville.

In summary, there is less positive feeling for the community among the Port City residents than among the Belleville residents. In the suburb, perception of crime, feelings of safety, and trust of others are not related to affect for the community. In the urban community, those who like the community most also perceive least crime in the area, feel most safe there, and trust others most. Although our data are not longitudinal, they indirectly suggest that a high crime rate over the long run may cause a serious deterioration in a community's solidarity. We saw such a short-run change in reaction to the Clutter murders in Holcomb, Kansas. Over time, the repetition of fear-producing crimes can generate feelings of insecurity, distrust of others, and dislike for one's community.

Social Interaction

If people feel that their neighborhood is unsafe, they may try to minimize their vulnerability to crime. Anticipatory victimization may lead to various protective measures.[47] Some of these measures involve *target hardening*, such as the installation of burglar alarms, bars on windows, and locks on doors. We look at these measures in the following chapter; here we will be concerned with another type of protective measure, the avoidance of strangers and neighbors.

Furstenberg found that *avoidance techniques* are most common in high crime-rate communities, a finding consistent with the difference in interpersonal trust between Port City and Belleville residents. In fact, the Baltimore data reveal that avoidance *behavior* was most common among those with an *attitude* of distrust of others.[48] Through such avoidance techniques as ignoring strangers, keeping doors and windows locked, and staying home, people insulate themselves from others in order to reduce their vulnerability. These avoidance measures are more common than *mobilization measures*, security precautions such as alarms and weapons. Furstenberg suggests this is because avoidance measures cost less money and require smaller adjustments in daily life than do mobilization measures. Also, people may not feel that security measures are needed in their own community—we have already seen that people often view their own neighborhood as safer than other areas—but they may still take measures to avoid strangers.[49] The survey of Baltimore residents found no relationship between taking avoidance measures and taking mobilization measures.[50]

Residents of the high crime areas in Baltimore were most apt to engage in avoidance behavior; nearly half of those living in high crime areas were ranked high on avoidance behavior, but only about a quarter of those in low crime areas were ranked that way. Avoidance behavior was thus tied to the objective risk faced by residents of a community. However, within communities, avoidance behavior was not related to whether or not an individual himself had suffered criminal victimization.[51] Avoidance behavior was closely tied to anxiety about the crime problem; people who were more anxious were more apt to avoid strangers. Such behavior was more common among those who thought that the crime rate in their neighborhood had been increasing and among those who felt that their neighborhood was unsafe in comparison to other neighborhoods. Avoidance behavior was not related to concern with crime as a social issue, since such concern is more a political attitude than a perception of risk of victimization. Overall, subjective risk was more important than objective risk in producing risk-avoiding behavior, but there was still a strong relationship between avoidance behavior and a community's crime rate.

Women expressed somewhat more fear than men, but they were *much* more likely to engage in avoidance behavior. Furstenberg suggests that men may find it more difficult to change their behavior because the roles in which they are engaged (for instance, the role of worker) take them outside the home more often than is true for women. In fact, working women did take avoidance measures less often than nonworking women, suggesting that working outside the home does influence changes one makes in daily behavior in response to the threat of crime.[52] People expect men and women to react differently to crime; "[t]hese expectations may, in fact, help explain why victimization rates are higher for males than for females as men are more willing to expose themselves to risk." [53]

Both men and women were more apt to engage in avoidance behavior if they were older. The difference by age was not due to a difference in fear of crime by the young and the old, since levels of fear were about the same for people of different ages. The difference in avoidance behavior stemmed instead from unwillingness by the young to alter their behavior in response to their fears. Younger people preferred to run risks rather than change; young blacks were more unlikely to change their behavior than young whites. Unwillingness to change behavior in the face of high risks may help explain high rates of victimization, since people who do not make changes expose themselves to victimization.[54] Blacks, the poorly educated, and the less affluent were especially likely to engage in avoidance behavior, mainly because they were more apt to live in high crime areas than were whites, the well educated and the more affluent. Avoidance behavior was not influenced by length of residence in a community, nor was it affected by marital status or by number of children. Avoidance behavior was also unrelated to being liberal or conservative politically, favoring or opposing law and order, and holding racial prejudices or not.[55]

A study of robbery victims found that about one in four (23 of 90) made no change in daily behavior after the crime. The rest made at least one change. Twenty-two became more suspicious of strangers and groups of people on the streets and tried to avoid such potential dangers. Fourteen said they never went out alone at night. Twelve avoided the area where they were robbed; those who continued to go to the area did so with greater caution. Ten victims found new jobs or sold their businesses as a result of the robbery. A substantial number of victims thus made changes to avoid risks and reduce social interaction. Strangers were ignored and friends were not seen because people stayed home at night or avoided certain parts of the city.[56]

Direct evidence of the way that social interaction is influenced by fear of criminal victimization is difficult to obtain, since many factors affect the amount and quality of interaction in a community. Length of residence and homogeneity of population are probably related to social interaction in a community, as are local traditions of group life (such as the storefront men's clubs in Boston's North End). One direct effect of the fear of crime on social interaction that has occurred with increasing frequency in recent years is the rescheduling of meetings and events from nighttime to daytime.[57] Such changes reduce vulnerability, but they also diminish social interaction because many people work during the day and only seek the company of others at night. Public places where social interaction might occur are also used less at night, as people avoid parks and local libraries where they would see friends or make new ones.

Lee Rainwater has found that for the poor this threat of crime even extends to their own housing. To protect themselves from perceived dangers in and around their homes, they become suspicious of strangers and neighbors and seek to avoid them. Rainwater traces this distrust to the nature of the housing in which the poor live,[58] giving as an example of the way that housing may reduce interpersonal contact the following: "Where, as in St. Louis, the laundry rooms seem unsafe places, tenants tend to prefer to do their laundry in their homes, sacrificing the possibility of neighborly interactions to gain a greater sense of security of person and property."[59] Changes in architectural design can help alleviate such problems and increase social interaction, as we shall see in Chapter 6.

Another example of how fear of crime can reduce social interaction is seen in the reaction of many Boston-area university students to a series of murders of young women. One female student said, "One floor [in the dormitory] made out a code where if you don't call out your name when you knock on someone's door, she won't even acknowledge she's there." [60] This reduces social interaction, especially among people who are not yet well acquainted. Some students did band together for mutual self-protection after the murders, but the overall effect of the crimes was to increase suspicion and to reduce contacts between people.

Unfortunately, we do not have any good measures of the extent of social interaction in Belleville and Port City. There was a substantial difference in the proportion of people in each community who had ever stayed home because of fear of crime—9 per cent in Belleville and 21 per cent in Port City. However, this is not direct evidence on the degree of social interaction in each area. A measure of *how often* residents of the two towns walked alone in their neighborhoods after dark provided the following results:

	Belleville	Port City
Every day	9%	20%
A few times a week	15%	12%
A few times a month	18%	16%
Less often than a few times a month	20%	14%
Never	38%	38%

These figures suggest that on the average the residents of Port City walk in their community more often than people who live in Belleville, the major difference being in the proportion who walk in their neighborhood every day. However, this measure is not a very good index of social interaction. Since Port City residents are considerably less wealthy than those who live in Belleville, they are probably less apt to own cars. Many who do own cars still take the subway to and from work and walk to a corner store for groceries. In the suburb, with greater distances between home and job and between home and shopping districts, and with less convenient access to mass transportation, people

rely more on their cars. Since cars can be parked in one's driveway and near jobs and stores, there is less reason to walk in the
neighborhood. Thus, the extent of walking in a neighborhood
reflects more than just the impact of crime on daily behavior.

One possible difference between the two communities that
might be related to fear of crime is the extent of participation in
local organizations, clubs, and social groups, although such participation is influenced by many factors other than perception of
crime. In Port City, 72 per cent of the respondents belonged to no
local group or organization, 22 per cent belonged to one, and 6
per cent belonged to two or more. In Belleville, 56 per cent
belonged to none, 25 per cent to one, and 19 per cent to two or
more. There was thus greater participation in social groups in the
suburb, but we cannot attribute this solely to the lesser fear of
crime there. In fact, in neither Belleville nor Port City was the
extent of group participation related to the perception of crime
scale, suggesting that factors other than fear of victimization (such
as social class or education) affected involvement in organizations.

Likewise, our attempt to measure social interaction by asking
people how many of their three best friends lived in the town
proved inconclusive. Only 21 per cent of the suburbanites, but 54
per cent of the urban residents, said that all three of their best
friends lived in the area; whereas 41 per cent of those in Belleville
and only 21 per cent of those in Port City said that none of their
best friends lived in the same community. Responses to this question were not related to perception of crime in the community.
Probably this rather large difference between communities is due
to the greater homogeneity of Port City and its physical isolation
from the rest of the city. Also, the more educated and professional
residents of Belleville may have a more cosmopolitan orientation
toward the world, in contrast to the more local orientation of the
Port City residents.[61]

One impressionistic piece of evidence suggests that Port City
residents may engage in more social interaction of one particular
type. During warm weather, people in that community, especially
young males, congregate on streetcorners to talk with each other.
Older people sometimes sit on their front porches or door stoops
and talk with neighbors. However, when dark comes the older

people go inside. The youths often stay on the street after dark, with little fear of others. As Furstenberg found, the young are unwilling to take avoidance measures to reduce their risk of victimization. Social gatherings on streetcorners probably reduce risks anyway, because the presence of many people inhibits the criminal tendencies of others. However, under certain conditions, interactions on the street may lead to crime. Arguments may begin and lead to assaults or even murders. Rivalries over girlfriends may sometimes have such an effect. On a dare or as relief from boredom, someone may steal an item from a nearby store.

Aside from a few streetcorners, there is little on-the-street inter-action in Port City after dark, largely because residents fear victimization. The streets of Belleville are not used much for social interaction, less because of fear of crime than because backyards or air-conditioned living rooms are preferred to streetcorners. In the suburb there is little on most streetcorners to attract people, but in the city a grocery store often acts as a focus of interaction. There is more interaction on the streets of Port City, but the extent and type of interaction in Belleville is probably less influenced by fear of crime than is true in Port City. People in the suburb choose places other than the street to interact; those in the urban community congregate on streetcorners or talk with neighbors in front of their homes until dark, but then they move inside to a haven of safety.

Little of the material we have examined in this chapter suggests that Durkheim was correct in arguing that crime brings people together and strengthens social bonds. Instead, crime produces insecurity, distrust, and a negative view of the community. Although we lack conclusive evidence, crime also seems to reduce social interaction as fear and suspicion drive people apart. This produces a disorganized community that is unable to exercise informal social control over deviant behavior.

Footnotes

1. For a study of one town where fear of crime is minimal, see Simon Dinitz, "Progress, Crime, and the Folk Ethic: Portrait of a Small Town," *Criminology* XI (May 1973), pp. 3–21.

2. Jack Rosenthal, "The Cage of Fear in Cities Beset by Crime," *Life* magazine LXVII (July 11, 1969), p. 17.

3. Chamber of Commerce of the United States, *Marshaling Citizen Power against Crime*. Washington, D.C.: Chamber of Commerce of the United States, 1970, p. 5.

4. For examples of the effect of fear on tourism, see "A French View of New York: Perilous City to Visit," *The New York Times*, January 24, 1972, p. 1; Jon Nordheimer, "Golf Club Slayings and Other Murders in Virgin Islands Raise Fears and Demands for Law and Order," *The New York Times*, December 10, 1972, p. 41; J. Anthony Lukas, "Murder in Paradise: The Case of St. Croix," *The New York Times*, February 10, 1974, Section 10, pp. 1, 16–17; and Paul Delaney, "Washington Losing 'Crime Capital' Image," *The New York Times*, March 28, 1973, p. 26.

5. Earl Caldwell, "Virgin Island Governor Says Press Overplays Racial Role in Killings," *The New York Times*, October 16, 1973, p. 22.

6. M. K. Block and G. J. Long, "Subjective Probability of Victimization and Crime Levels: An Econometric Approach," *Criminology* XI (May 1973), pp. 87–93.

7. "Names, Faces in the News," *Boston Globe*, October 17, 1972, p. 2.

8. Richard R. Lingeman, "Writer Is Mugged, Denies Being 'Victim,'" *The New York Times Magazine*, October 22, 1972, p. 20.

9. Gangland violence often evokes no loud public outcry because it appears to be patterned and nonthreatening to the general public. However, when such crime spills over and affects innocent members of the general public, the reaction is often one of extreme anger and demand for official action. See John E. Conklin, editor, *The Crime Establishment: Organized Crime and American Society*. Englewood Cliffs, N.J.: Prentice-Hall, Inc., 1973, p. 2.

10. This discussion of the reaction of robbery victims is drawn from John E. Conklin, *Robbery and the Criminal Justice System*. Philadelphia: J. B. Lippincott Company, 1972; and from Robert Lejeune and Nicholas Alex, "On Being Mugged: The Event and Its Aftermath," paper presented at the Twenty-third Annual Meeting of the Society for the Study of Social Problems, New York City, August 1973.

11. Sandra Sutherland and Donald J. Scherl, cited in Kurt Weis and Sandra S. Borges, "Victimology and Rape: The Case of the Legitimate Victim," *Issues in Criminology* VIII (Fall 1973), pp. 100–101.

12. The President's Commission on Law Enforcement and Administration of Justice, *Crime and Its Impact—An Assessment*. Washington, D.C.: United States Government Printing Office, 1967, pp. 85–86.

13. Frank F. Furstenberg, Jr., "Public Reaction to Crime in the Streets," *The American Scholar* XL (Autumn 1971), p. 604.

14. In Dinitz's study of a small Ohio town with a very low crime rate, vandalism and juvenile delinquency were also the most commonly mentioned "serious" crimes in the community. See Dinitz, op. cit., p. 12.

15. For a study of suburban burglary, see John E. Conklin and Egon Bittner, "Burglary in a Suburb," *Criminology* XI (August 1973), pp. 206–232.

16. Although few people mentioned the subject in either community, another aspect of the criminal environment is organized crime. No one in Belleville referred to organized crime or offered any information about gangsters, bookmakers, loan sharks, or "fences" in the community; a few people in Port City did know of such people in their community. No specific questions were asked about organized crime, but the issue did arise spontaneously at various points in the interviews. A few people knew that the victim of a gangland slaying had been found in Port City shortly before the interviews were conducted. A number mentioned that a well-known leader in organized crime lived in Port City and frequented a particular bar there. A police detective in Port City said that many organized criminals lived in the community, but that their activities seldom came to public attention because local residents "kept it to themselves." Two heroin addicts said that they had always found it easy to fence stolen goods in Port City, often to people linked to organized gambling activities. Indirect evidence thus suggests that organized crime was a salient aspect of the criminal environment in Port City, but was almost completely absent from Belleville.

17. Another method that has been used to gauge individual perception of crime is to ask people to make a numerical estimate of crime in their community. For example, in a survey for the National Crime Commission, residents of Boston and Chicago were asked: "About how many people would you guess are murdered in [city] each year?" One quarter of the people who were asked this question could not even make a guess. Most who did said the number was nine or less, and a few estimated the number at more than 30. However, some guessed that more than 90 were killed in their city each month. Albert J. Reiss, Jr., Field Surveys III, Part 1, of the President's Commission on Law Enforcement and Administration of Justice, *Studies in Crime and Law Enforcement in Major Metropolitan Areas*. Washington, D.C.: United States Government Printing Office, 1967, p. 96. Another study that found that such an estimation procedure posed a difficult problem for respondents was done by F. James Davis in Colorado. He found that many people could not answer the following: "If Colorado had 100 crimes of all types in a certain period back in 1948, how

many crimes would you guess we have in the same period now [1952]?" Not only did people have a difficult time guessing numbers, but many who did took meaningless stabs at a correct figure. F. James Davis, "Crime News in Colorado Newspapers," *American Journal of Sociology* LVII (January 1952), p. 326. Responses to questions such as these probably reflect little about an individual's perception of the threat of crime or the relative rate of crime in his neighborhood.

18. The problem that exists with this type of question is that what is a high crime rate to one individual may be an average crime rate to another.

19. Here and in all later references to statistically significant differences, we shall use the .05 level of significance, although most of the differences of which we shall be speaking are significant beyond the .01 level.

20. A scale of this sort provides a more accurate measure of perception of crime and distinguishes better between those who perceive little crime and those who perceive much crime. The values on this scale, and other scales we discuss in this chapter, have been converted from the values given in John E. Conklin, "Dimensions of Community Response to the Crime Problem," *Social Problems* XVIII (Winter 1971), pp. 373–385; and John E. Conklin, "Criminal Environment and Support for the Law," *Law and Society Review* VI (November 1971), pp. 247–265. The reason for this is that the scales are easier for the reader to interpret if they correspond with verbal descriptions of differences in attitudes. For example, by presenting "mirror image" values for the perception of crime scale, a perception of more crime corresponds to a higher score on the scale and a perception of less crime corresponds to a lower score on the scale.

21. Another possible influence on perception of crime was examined, the alienation of residents of the two communities. (See Appendix A, footnote 3, for a list of the items in this alienation scale.) Possibly, residents of Port City might perceive more crime because they are more alienated, with crime symbolizing a sense of helplessness and lack of power. There were in fact more alienated respondents in the urban community than in the suburb. Still, Port City residents of the same degree of alienation as Belleville residents perceived more crime in their community. *Within* each community, alienation was not strongly related to perception of crime. Thus the same conclusion that emerged when social traits were examined is also valid here: perception of crime is a function of the criminal environment rather than a function of the social or psychological characteristics of the individual.

22. Reiss, op. cit., pp. 30, 103–107.

23. Rosenthal, op. cit., p. 20.
24. Furstenberg, op. cit., p. 607.
25. Philip H. Ennis, Field Surveys II of the President's Commission on Law Enforcement and Administration of Justice, *Criminal Victimization in the United States: A Report of a National Survey.* Washington, D.C.: United States Government Printing Office, 1967, pp. 73–74.
26. Ibid., p. 74. The percentages for the national sample used here and for the following questions are only for whites. This makes the results from the national survey more comparable to our results, since there were almost no nonwhites in either the Port City or Belleville sample (see Appendix A).
27. Ibid., p. 75.
28. Ibid., p. 73.
29. Ibid., p. 75.
30. Ibid., p. 51.
31. "Fortress on 78th Street," *Life* magazine LXXI (November 19, 1971), pp. 26–35.
32. "Youth in California Carries Grenade to a Police Station," *The New York Times,* January 7, 1971.
33. Cited in "Shooting of a 'Prowler' Shocks Prosperous Suburb of Capital," *The New York Times,* October 18, 1970, p. 74.
34. James T. Wooten, "Murder Charge against Author in Negro's Death Stirs Passions in a Tennessee Town," *The New York Times,* November 23, 1970, p. 45.
35. Cited in Murray Schumach, "Connecticut Town Lives with Fear," *The New York Times,* October 1, 1970, p. 43.
36. Ibid.
37. Philip G. Zimbardo, "Vandalism: An Act in Search of a Cause," unpublished manuscript, p. 6.
38. David A. Andelman, "City Crime Wave Spreading to Suburbs," *The New York Times,* January 30, 1972, p. 49.
39. See Conklin, *Robbery and the Criminal Justice System,* passim.
40. This item was placed at some distance from the preceding one in the interview schedule.
41. Lee Rainwater, "Fear and the House-as-Haven in the Lower Class," in Robert Gutman, editor, *People and Buildings.* New York: Basic Books, Inc., 1972, pp. 309–311.
42. Reiss, op. cit., p. 25.
43. Albert D. Biderman, Louise A. Johnson, Jennie McIntyre, and Adrianne Weir, Field Surveys I of the President's Commission on Law Enforcement and Administration of Justice, *Report of a Pilot Study in the District of Columbia on Victimization and Attitudes toward Law Enforcement.* Washington, D.C.: United States Government Printing Office, 1967, p. 119.

44. Reiss, op. cit., p. 31.
45. Rosenthal, op. cit., pp. 19–20. At times, criminal actions by the government can have a similar effect. For example, victims of erroneous drug raids by government agents have been harassed and threatened as a result of making public the government's mistakes and suing for damages. Some have attempted to start a new life in a different community as a result of the government's actions. See Andrew H. Malcolm, "Harassed Victims of Drug Raids Are Moving," *The New York Times*, July 4, 1973, p. 40.
46. Migration can increase rates in both the cities and the suburbs. If those who move from the city to a suburb have higher crime rates as individuals than those living in the suburb, but lower rates than those who remain in the city, their migration will increase the crime rate in the suburb and will also increase the crime rate in the city, although the rate for the entire metropolitan area would not be changed by such migration.
47. Frank F. Furstenberg, Jr., "Fear of Crime and Its Effects on Citizen Behavior." Paper presented at the Symposium on Studies of Public Experience, Knowledge and Opinion of Crime and Justice Bureau of Social Science Research, Inc. Washington, D.C., March 1972, p. 7.
48. Ibid., p. 19.
49. Ibid., pp. 21–24.
50. Ibid., p. 14.
51. Ibid., pp. 20–21.
52. Ibid., p. 17.
53. Ibid.
54. Ibid.
55. Ibid., p. 20.
56. Conklin, *Robbery and the Criminal Justice System*, pp. 93–97.
57. Reports from around the country indicate that school principals have cancelled events at night to protect students from victimization. Such cancellations often follow a series of crimes against students, but such a response makes the streets even more deserted at night and increases the risk to anyone who is on the street after dark.
58. A similar view is expressed in Christopher Alexander, "The City as a Mechanism for Sustaining Human Contact," in Gutman, op. cit., pp. 409–412.
59. Rainwater, op. cit., p. 311.
60. "Boston Coeds Fearful after Slayings," *The New York Times*, December 10, 1972, p. 34.
61. For a discussion of the differences between "cosmopolitans" and "locals," see Robert K. Merton, *Social Theory and Social Structure*, revised edition. Glencoe, Ill.: The Free Press, 1957, pp. 387–420.

Defensive Responses to Crime

5

P E O P L E often react to their fear of crime by reducing contact with others and by avoiding situations that might lead to their victimization. They also take various security measures, such as purchasing firearms or installing burglar alarms. These changes harm the community at the same time that they may protect specific individuals. They erect barriers between neighbors and they generate distrust. The net effect of protective measures may be to shift crime to one's less protected neighbors rather than to prevent crime. Defensive measures also weaken public belief in the legitimacy of the government, since they draw attention to the inability of the government to protect the people.

Protective measures entail expense and inconvenience. Store-owners close their shops before dark, reducing their profits and inconveniencing their customers. Subway stations close early or shut down completely if the risk of crime is too great; people then have to confront the prospect of a mugging on their longer walk home rather than facing the risk in the station itself. Another instance of a negative effect of security measures involved a man who feared the depredations of neighborhood criminals to such an extent that he covered his apartment door with steel and a double-barred iron lock. When a fire began in his apartment, he could not unfasten the bars and locks and died before he was able to escape from behind his wall of security.[1]

Public response to a threat may involve *pathologies of defense.*[2] Craig Comstock says that "harm may come to us as much by the defenses we employ as by the dangers we seek to avert."[3] The defensive measures that people use to avoid criminal victimization —firearms, watchdogs, and bars on windows—often have such a pathological aspect.[4] A man becomes trapped in his own fortress.

A gun accidentally kills a child. A dog bites his owner's guest. By 1980, Americans will be spending one dollar on burglary-prevention equipment for every four dollars of property stolen.[5] Aside from the expense and direct harm involved in defensive measures, community solidarity is also undermined by the artificial barriers erected between neighbors, the same barriers intended as protection against criminals. An offender may stay away from a barking watchdog, but so will neighbors and their children.

Defensive measures are more common in communities where residents feel the threat of crime is great, although the real threat of crime in those areas is not necessarily very great. An appellate court recognized the significance of such an atmosphere of fear in the 1935 case of *Viliborghi v. State*.[6] In this case, a lower court was held to be in error for prohibiting the defendant in a murder case from using "the dangerous and lawless reputation of the vicinity" in which he lived as a defense for his actions.[7] The appellate court ruled that a man who lives in a community that is widely regarded as lawless, and who has been told that his premises are about to be burglarized, would have far more reason to fear for his property and his life than a man whose place of business was in an area where less threat existed. Fear of crime may thus produce violence in one's own defense, action that may even be legally justifiable.

However, the courts have not held that victims can use any degree of force to protect their property. For instance, after suffering a series of burglaries of an unoccupied house that he used for storage, an Iowa man installed a shotgun that would shoot anyone entering the building through a particular window. A burglar was later shot in the leg while climbing through the window. The burglar received a suspended sentence for his efforts, but he successfully sued the homeowner for $30,000. The law permitted the protection of property with "reasonable force," but not with enough force to "take human life or inflict great bodily injury" if no life were endangered.[8]

Defensive behavior may harm others, both criminals and innocent victims. Such behavior may protect people against certain types of threat, but it may be dysfunctional for the larger society if one considers injury to innocent people, the inconvenience and expense of such measures, and the reduction of social interaction and interpersonal trust that results from the use of such measures.

Defensive Behavior

Changes in behavior are made to avoid risks and to minimize the chance of victimization. In the previous chapter, we looked at the ways that people change their behavior to avoid potential criminals and dangerous situations. Such changes often reduce social interaction and informal social control of deviant behavior in the community. Defensive measures such as alarm systems and firearms can have similar effects on the community.

Defensive behavior and avoidance behavior are probably most common among people who most closely identify with the victims of highly threatening crimes. An example of such changes in behavior followed newspaper reports of seven murders of young Boston women in the fall and winter of 1972. At least two of the victims were regular hitchhikers, as were many young women in Boston, a compact city with a large number of universities and irregular patterns of public transportation. After reports of the murders, there was a noticeable decline in women seeking rides from strangers, an example of avoidance behavior. However, hitchhiking was shortly back to previous levels.[9] Other measures that were taken included going out at night only in groups of two or more, taking taxis rather than hitchhiking, and making inquiries about karate lessons, watchdogs, and stronger locks.[10]

In spite of the supposed vulnerability of hitchhikers to assault, rape, and murder, many continued to seek rides with strangers. It was an inexpensive and convenient means of travel, was quick because women did not have to wait long for a ride, and provided an opportunity to meet people. Some women said that if they did not hitchhike, they would have no way to get around the city. One even said that she did not spend much time thinking about the murders, because if she did, she might stop hitchhiking and that would cause her great inconvenience.[11] Some who continued to seek rides did so with greater care—they traveled with companions, carefully scrutinized drivers, refused some rides, and sat close to the door when in the car. A number of women adopted an "it can't happen to me" attitude; one said, "I don't know what all the fuss is all about. You only hear about the ones who get raped or murdered. You never hear about the great times you can have hitchhiking." [12] Where there is strong motivation to continue the practice, rationalizations develop to justify the failure to take defensive measures that would reduce risk but cause inconvenience.

One official reaction to the victimization of female hitchhikers was that they brought the crime upon themselves by their behavior. One Boston City Councillor stated that being raped or assaulted (probably not murdered) should teach a woman the lesson that hitchhiking is dangerous. A police captain in Maryland said that women who hitchhike "practically invite rape." [13] A somewhat more moderate statement with a similar implication was made by a Phoenix police sergeant who said, "If they are victims of any sex crimes, I wouldn't say they had it coming to them—but they placed themselves in the position where it could happen to them." [14] Many women respond bitterly to the suggestion that they should have to make drastic changes in their behavior to defend themselves from victimization or else be held partially responsible for their own victimization. The notion that the victimized women are partly to blame for their victimization stems not only from disapproval of their hitchhiking because of the risks it entails, but also from a more general condemnation of the life style of the young. [15] Few city councillors or police officers have told elderly ladies that they bring purse-snatches and assaults upon themselves by walking outside their apartments, yet such behavior certainly does enhance their vulnerability. Views of the victim's contribution to the crime thus vary not only with the actual behavior of the victim prior to the crime, but also with the observer's identification with the victim and with the victim's life style.

An interesting illustration of affixing blame was the reaction of 54 Los Angeles-area college students to the young women who committed a series of brutal murders with the Manson family. Female students were "much more apt to see the Manson situation in terms of a need for security and protection on the part of the girls in the group," whereas the male students emphasized the "stupidity and the gullibility" of the girls and called attention to their "weak characters." [16] The males stressed personality problems of the girls; the females felt more vulnerable and identified more closely with the girls, seeing them as victims of Manson's power over them. Women defined the female murderers as *victims;* men defined them as *offenders* who committed murder because of their own personality defects. Identification with the girls in the Manson family affected a person's assessment of their motivation and their guilt in the murders, just as identification with the girls who were victimized in Boston influenced assessment of their contribution to the crimes.

Identification with the victim not only influences attitudes toward the victims, but it also produces behavior changes among those who feel most threatened. For example, the rumor in Orléans, France, that women had been drugged and abducted into prostitution by dress shopkeepers was more commonly believed by women than by men. In fact, Morin suggests that the rumor originally developed among young schoolgirls because of their fantasy life and their lack of assimilation into an adult world in which sex could be openly discussed. Young women, who were most vulnerable to the rumored crimes, expressed the strongest belief in the myth and were most apt to alter their behavior. Morin says that a sense of vulnerability was also enhanced by the locale of the supposed abductions, the fitting room of a dress shop. He argues that because of the act of undressing there, an element of sexual fantasy was attached to that setting. As a result, those who felt most vulnerable—young women with active sexual fantasies but with little opportunity to fulfill their fantasies—were most affected by the rumors and were most likely to stay away from the shops to protect themselves from victimization.[17]

Another group that is especially likely to engage in defensive behavior and avoidance behavior is the elderly, a group that feels vulnerable because of age and weakness. A report from the Special Senate Committee on Aging found that the elderly often stay home night and day for fear of crime; they thus become prisoners in their own homes.[18] When they go out, they do so in groups or with escorts. In fact, attendance at the Committee's hearings by the elderly was poor because so few were willing to brave the streets to attend the meeting.[19] Not only do the elderly try to minimize risk, but their interpersonal contacts are often curtailed because of the high-risk environments (such as housing projects and low-rent areas) in which they live. According to one project resident, "Doctors won't make house calls, stores won't deliver goods, cabs won't make calls, movers are afraid to come in, sometimes the ambulance won't come and the undertaker is afraid to come to remove the deceased." [20] Taking advantage of project residents' need for services, criminals sometimes pose as maintenance men or agents of service organizations trying to help the elderly. If they gain entrance to an apartment, they assault and rob the victim. As a result, some tenants will not allow anyone into their apartments, thus creating additional barriers between people and further reducing access to outside services.[21]

Just as the elderly take defensive measures because they feel vulnerable, so parents may act to prevent crimes against their young children. Attacks on schoolchildren lead to demands for better security in the schools. A mayor of New York once said that "the single one greatest obstacle to progress in education is fear," and that security from violence and theft is the "first priority" in educational planning.[22] In some schools, lavatories are locked to prevent assaults in them; security guards are hired to protect school property and the safety of the students. In one school, only a single door exists for public use and it is made of metal and has a small peephole cut in it.[23] Even when security measures are taken in the schools, children still face threats on the streets between school and home. Thus, in some communities parents take their children to and from school, an inconvenience that is particularly bothersome if both parents work. Measures to defend children from attack and theft are especially common after reported crimes against the young. For example, after a series of crimes in Hamden, Connecticut, parents and teachers watched children en route to and from school and warned their children not to talk with strangers. Local libraries and playgrounds also fell into disuse because of the fear of crime.[24]

Defensive measures can reduce vulnerability, but they also have other effects. In the previous chapter, we saw that the avoidance of strangers and potentially dangerous settings can reduce social interaction in a community. Actions to minimize risk can also change the distribution of crime in a city. In a study of prostitution, it was found that white fears about entering black communities with high crime rates in order to find prostitutes can shift the working locales of the prostitutes to those areas of the city where white customers will go, such as the entertainment districts. Fears can thus move prostitutes from one area to another; this may also bring a shift in such crimes as assault, pick-pocketing, purse-snatching, and robbery.[25] Areas of the city that were once relatively safe may become high-risk areas, thus spreading crime throughout the city.

The feeling that public parks are dangerous places where predators lurk reduces public use of such places, thereby increasing the likelihood that potential criminals will indeed occupy those parks. One study found that crime in parks is uncommon in comparison to surrounding areas, but that fear leads people to avoid them anyway.[26] Possibly a robbery in a deserted park is more threatening than a robbery on a street where there are people and houses, even though no help may be forthcoming in either place. Protective measures to make parks more secure may stimulate fears of crime in those places. For example, a recent plan was proposed to enclose Washington Square Park in New York City with a fence having eight gates; this would reduce access and escape routes for criminals. At night, only two gates would be open and they would be guarded by policemen.[27] However, such security measures could easily intimidate citizens who would otherwise walk in the park; they might feel that any place that required such precautions could not be very safe. If people think that parks are unsafe, they will avoid them, abandoning them to potential criminals and making them even more dangerous.

An attitude of defensiveness has also produced changes in urban commerce, with storekeepers keeping their doors locked except for "safe" customers and closing before dark.[28] This reduces business for the shopkeepers and creates inconvenience for customers by limiting shopping hours to the times that they may be at work. It can also engender hostility among people who are denied admission because the storekeeper thinks that they look suspicious. Some proprietors have even shut down their businesses completely rather than face the threat of crime. A longitudinal study of urban areas that had experienced riots in the 1960's found that a number of local businessmen had closed their stores and businesses and moved elsewhere; in one Washington, D.C., precinct one of every four businessmen closed his business as a result of the riot.[29] More recently, a pharmacist in Boston closed his drugstore after being robbed four times in eleven days. In each holdup, the robbers had demanded narcotics and threatened to kill him. He liquidated his supply of narcotics after the third robbery, but in the fourth he was nearly murdered because he had no drugs to give the offenders. He decided to close his store, saying:

Nobody in America likes to run away from a problem, but I guess that this is what I have to do. . . . I wish I could give some advice as to how drug store robberies can be curbed, but I can't. I just don't see how they can be stopped. Maybe someday druggists will have to sell narcotics from a cage in back of some big department store.[30]

This man took the extreme measure of closing his store in order to protect himself, just as many people have moved from cities to suburbs to escape the crime problem. In both instances, the response may minimize the individual's risk but increase the threat of crime to the community as a whole. Just as the out-migration of residents destroys urban communities, so the closing of stores reduces the number of people on the street and thus weakens social solidarity. With fewer people on the street, there will be less business for those stores that are open, reducing their profits and increasing their risks. In New York City, the loss of business led a number of merchants to band together in a protest to the city government that the quality of the social environment and the lack of police protection had caused customers to stay off the streets and at home.[31] Fear of direct victimization by criminals leads storeowners to voice loud protest and demand better police protection; in some cities, storeowners have even been intimidated to pay protection money to juvenile gangs because of the ineffectiveness of the local police.[32]

The changes that people make in their behavior to defend themselves from depredations are many. They use cars and cabs rather than walk even short distances, as suggested by the following letter to a newspaper:

I live on a dark street off Utica Avenue in Brooklyn and therefore decided to take a cab home even though it was not late. The cab driver asked that I get off at the corner of Utica, saying he did not want to go down the dark street. If I had wanted to walk down the dark street, who needed him?[33]

This citizen relied on the cab driver for safety, but even he was unwilling to take any personal risk to provide security for his customer. Defensive measures such as this reduce human traffic on the streets and minimize social contacts. Such behavior may protect individuals, but only at great cost and inconvenience to them and their community.

Security Measures

One crime which elicits great fear from the public is burglary. This offense not only involves the theft of property, but also the invasion of private space in which the victim previously felt invulnerable. Victims ask themselves what would have happened if they had been there when the burglar entered their home. They feel frightened and outraged that someone broke into their home; some also react with resignation and despair. One victim of ten burglaries over a period of fifteen years did not even bother to replace her stolen property, saying, "Why buy jewelry and furs for a burglar?"[34] After a mistaken drug raid by government agents, the woman who had been victimized said, "I'm just a simple housewife. I want to clean up my home, but I can't. Our things seem dirtied somehow. They aren't ours anymore."[35] Not only did she and her husband feel that they had been terrorized and their privacy invaded, but they also saw their home and all their property as sullied by the violent intrusion.

Fearing burglaries and robberies in their homes, many people have installed devices to protect themselves and their property. Furstenberg refers to such measures as *mobilization* measures, security precautions such as extra locks, lights, bars, weapons, and watchdogs.[36] Protective measures involve expense and planning. As a result, fewer people take such measures than engage in avoidance behavior, which requires less effort and expenditure.[37] Only one person in four in a sample of Baltimore residents took *any* precautionary measure in the two years prior to the survey, and only one in three took any measure in the five years before the study.[38]

Furstenberg suggests that people may not take security measures because they feel that such steps would be ineffective in preventing victimization, especially victimization in a violent attack by a stranger on the street.[39] People may become resigned and fatalistic, much as did Myrt Clare after the Clutter murders; she suggested that if someone wanted to kill her, they would find a way no matter what she did.[40] Many residents of Baltimore felt that they should take some step to protect themselves, but most failed to do so or said that nothing they could think of would have any effect anyway. Mobilization measures involve expense and effort—the cost of a dog or a pistol, the installation of lights and locks. Wealthier people are more apt to take such measures because they are better able to afford them; they may also think that they have more to lose, or they may place greater value on material possessions. Aside from the lack of wealth, people also fail to take security measures because they do not know what to do, have not yet gotten around to doing anything, or refuse to believe that they will be victimized. Feeling immune prevents people from taking security measures, but it also makes it easier for them to live with crime in their community. Fear of victimization could cripple their mobility in the community and in the city; presumption of invulnerability prevents that from happening.[41]

Only one-fourth of the Baltimore sample took two or more of the five mobilization measures about which they were asked—locks, lights, bars, weapons, and watchdogs. People living in high crime-rate areas took such measures slightly *less* often than people who lived in low crime-rate communities, although the difference was small. Furstenberg concludes that the *objective* risk of victimization does not cause people to use security measures for self-protection. Also, perception of personal vulnerability to victimization was not related to mobilization behavior; those who felt that their neighborhood was unsafe or those who thought that the local crime rate was rising were no more likely to take mobilization measures than those who felt safer in their community.[42] However, Baltimore residents who had been victimized or had heard of a burglary in their neighborhood were more apt to take precautions than those who had not suffered a crime or heard of one. This relationship was especially strong among those who lived in high crime-rate areas. Specific precipitating events often provoke people to take mobilization measures because the threat of crime must be immediate before people will spend money and effort to protect themselves.[43] Once people see their neighbors take such mobilization measures, they too may employ protective devices.

Men and women did not differ in the frequency with which they took mobilization measures, although men bought firearms more often and women were more apt to install extra locks. Blacks were more apt than whites to take security precautions; the difference is attributable to the higher rate of victimization of blacks and the higher crime rates in the communities in which they live. Mobilization behavior was not related to attitudinal measures, although whites who were more resistant to social change and whites who saw crime as the most serious social problem were more likely to own firearms. Furstenberg concludes that social mistrust led to measures for self-protection, as it also led to avoidance behavior; however, avoidance behavior was more clearly tied to objective risks and fear of crime than was mobilization behavior.[44] A large-scale longitudinal study of a number of communities might provide more detailed information on stages of mobilization, resistance to taking security measures, the relationship of mobilization measures to actual victimization, and the effects of such measures on community crime rates.

The types of measures that people take to protect their homes are almost innumerable. They include the usual measures such as locks and alarms, but also more unorthodox measures such as decals on windows saying that the home is protected by a watchdog, cassettes of barking dogs that can be turned on if a prowler is heard, alarms for cars and boats to prevent theft and vandalism, pick-resistant locks, and engraving of property to prevent burglars from stealing it (since it could not then be fenced). Other measures include bright outdoor spotlights, impenetrable sliding glass doors on patios and "panic buttons" in bedrooms to be sounded if a burglar enters the home.[45]

The most common measure used by homeowners to protect themselves and their property from criminals is an alarm system. The sale of alarm systems is currently a boom industry. There are between 5,000 and 10,000 different companies now trying to garner part of the market; by 1980, it is expected that the alarm business will be a $400 million industry. Only about one American home in every 100 presently has an alarm system, although the ratio may be as high as one in ten for homes costing more than $40,000.[46] There are now three major types of alarm systems. Perimeter systems protect points of entry to the house. Space or area systems guard interior areas with photoelectric or ultrasonic devices. A third type involves listening devices that detect intruders in the home. All systems connect to an alarm, with a noise-producing signal in the home (which depends on action by neighbors who hear the alarm) or an alarm connected directly to a police station or central security office. Silent alarms which alert remote centers allow the police to surprise the offender and make an arrest; they also do not require action by neighbors, which is wise in light of widespread unwillingness to report crime and get involved in crime. Alarm systems do not offer perfect protection, since they often fail to function properly and may be circumvented by burglars.[47] They also create the problem that many false alarms are sounded. One study found that 94 per cent of the alarms that were sounded did not involve any illegal entry.[48] Another study discovered that only 2 per cent of sounded alarms in a two-week period were valid; many were set off because of poor installation, by mistake, or to see how quickly the police would respond.[49] Some alarms are too sensitive to the movement of occupants of the house. Others need to be turned on and off to prevent them from sounding when they should not; sometimes the alarm will have been left off when a burglary occurs. Because of the problem of false alarms, some communities now charge for excessive false alarms. In Tenafly, New Jersey, a homeowner is allowed three false alarms a year; he can then be fined $15 for the fourth one, $25 for the fifth one, and have his alarm system disconnected after that.[50]

Alarm systems are very expensive, both to install and to hook up to a central security office or to a police station. Police officers who monitor such alarms are not on the streets to prevent other crimes and to make arrests, so the net effect on crime of the alarms is unclear. Also, burglaries may be displaced onto unprotected targets rather than prevented. Less expensive ways to defend homes from burglary have been suggested. Etching a social security number or driver's license number on all valuable property and putting a sticker on a window saying that this has been done may prevent burglary. Burglars may also be deterred if a particular house appears to be occupied, if a light or a television is on. On the other hand, clear signs that no one is home, such as piles of mail or newspapers, no lights, no car in the driveway or garage, or unmowed lawns can be interpreted by potential burglars as indicators that a house is a safe target. In spite of people's fears, burglars try to avoid confrontation with their victims; this minimizes the risk of injury to the victim, which can result in a longer prison sentence for the burglar, and it reduces the chance of being arrested since no one will be able to identify the offender.

Many people keep firearms in their homes to protect themselves, their families, and their homes from intruders. These firearms sometimes harm children who accidentally fire them. They can also be turned on a spouse during a marital disagreement, leading to injury or death at times when less serious consequences would have followed had no firearm been present. Possession of a firearm may oversensitize a person to the behavior of others, as happened in Virginia when an eighteen-year-old shot and killed a newspaper boy he thought was trying to damage his car. Using a firearm for defense also means that the nature of the crime may change, from an assault if fists had been used or an aggravated assault if a knife had been used, to a murder if a firearm is available.

A survey conducted by *Life* magazine to which 43,000 readers replied found that 30 per cent of them kept a firearm in their home for self-defense.[51] This survey was carried out in 1971 on a

117

nonrepresentative sample, which may explain why the proportion owning firearms for self-protection was so much higher than the 7 per cent found in a 1966 survey of high crime areas in Boston, Chicago, and Washington, D.C., and the 8 per cent found in a 1966 survey of a group of Washington, D.C., residents.[52] Still, there is approximately one privately owned firearm for each person in the United States; many are used for protection from criminals. One politician says that in his city, "[s]ome people carry guns to take out the garbage."[53]

Other people carry bats, clubs, knives, tear gas sprays, or other devices. G. Gordon Liddy of the Watergate burglary once suggested to a woman that she carry a sharpened pencil for protection. He said, "Be sure the eraser is in good condition. It will protect the palm of your hand when you drive the pencil into an attacker's throat."[54] People who fear crime are sometimes desperate enough to try anything for self-defense. After the murder of a Columbia University law professor during a robbery, one man said:

"I've been thinking of what to do, and this is all I can think of." He displayed a roll of masking tape that he had just purchased.

"That's my response," he went on, "a roll of tape to put around the club I carry at night [on a tenant's patrol], so I can get a better grip. Pretty meaningful, huh?"[55]

Another man said, "What I rely on for security are my head and my sneakers and 30 good friends."[56]

Avoidance behavior is largely based on the notion that one is safer staying home than venturing onto the streets. As a result, people often go to great lengths to fortify their homes. Jesse Hill Ford, the author who shot and killed a black man he thought was menacing his family, had designed his home for protection, largely in response to reading about the Clutter murders in Truman Capote's *In Cold Blood*. Ford instructed the architect who was building his house to revise the original plans for the bedrooms to provide

"clear fields of fire around the house. Jay [his son] could cover almost the whole backyard out his window, Sarah [his daughter] could cover her side of the house from her window. . . ." When they moved into the house, they slept with firearms under their beds. "We weren't going to be slaughtered in our beds. If somebody did manage to get in the house, they sure as hell wouldn't get out again—we'd either hold them or kill them. We *all* decided this," Ford said.[57]

This extreme defensive posture was to prevent an extremely rare crime, a burglary in which the occupants of a home are murdered. Such a posture is probably related to Ford's willingness to shoot at the car which he thought held a man who was waiting to ambush his son.

Attempts to fortify the home sometimes reach extraordinary proportions. After "three burglaries, one robbery and an attempted rape" during two years of residence in an apartment, a New York City couple decided to secure their apartment, so they installed

a new door frame, two locks, double iron gates on the kitchen window, a city sewer grating bolted to the brick wall of the bathroom window, an air-conditioner and iron gate on the living room window, wooden shutters and a metal bar bolted across the bedroom window, and broken glass and flower pots on the fire escape. "In all," says Bill, "we've lost $3,000—and a lot of sleep."[58]

Looking at the security measures in one housing project, an observer said, "It's just a matter of time before everyone gets moats and crocodiles." [59] When fear of crime is this great, people become willing purchasers of any security device, even though no measure can insure total immunity from burglary. Alarm companies sometimes take advantage of the fear of crime to sell their wares. After a family of three was killed in a Connecticut town, neighbors soon began receiving mailed advertisements for burglar alarm systems that would protect them from harm. Under criticism, the company stated that it was only trying to help others avoid similar crimes, although the arrest of a suspect in the case showed that the crime was not a burglary and that the offender was in fact a member of the family.[60]

The attitude that one must defend one's family and property from criminals is widespread in American society. A survey carried out in 1968 asked respondents, "Do you think that people like yourself have to be prepared to defend their homes against crime and violence, or can the police take care of that?" More blacks (65 per cent) than whites (52 per cent) said that people had to defend their own homes; and more whites (41 per cent) than blacks (24 per cent) said that the police could defend their homes adequately.[61] Still, a majority of each racial group felt that some form of home defense was necessary.[62] Among whites, there was no difference between men and women in saying that such home defense was necessary, but more black men than black women felt that people had to defend their own homes. Within each racial group, older people were less apt than younger ones to feel that such defensive measures were necessary. Southern whites and northern blacks were the most defense oriented. Among whites, there was a decline in this attitude with increases in urban size, but home defense among blacks was most common in large urban centers. In rural areas and small towns, blacks were similar to whites in support of individual defense of the home, but in larger cities blacks were much more likely than whites to support individual home defense. In cities with a population of more than one million, 69 per cent of the blacks and only 33 per cent of the whites favored home defense measures over reliance on the police. For whites, there was a decrease in the home defense posture with increased education and higher occupational prestige; for blacks there was a decrease in this attitude with increased occupational standing.[63]

In examining the attitude of home defense, Joe R. Feagin looked at one behavioral index of this attitude, the ownership of firearms. He discovered that people who supported individual defense of the home were most apt to be armed. Sixty per cent of those whites favoring home defense also owned firearms; of those who did not favor home defense, only 35 per cent owned firearms. Of the blacks, 33 per cent of those favoring home defense and 27 per cent of those not favoring that view owned firearms. Thus in each racial group those who thought that individuals had to rely on themselves rather than on the police to protect their homes were more likely to own guns. Home defense oriented respondents were also more apt than others to know someone else who had recently bought a firearm. Whites were more apt to be armed than blacks, whether they were defense oriented or police oriented, an unexpected difference in light of the larger proportion of blacks who favored individual defense of the home.[64]

Fear of crime and violence was a major cause of the attitude of home defense. Criticism of the police was also common among those who favored home defense. Whites often criticized the police for their restraint in handling riots, but blacks did not make this criticism as much. The attitude toward how the police had handled riots influenced whether a white respondent would favor self-defense or reliance on the police, but it had no such effect on black respondents.[65] Whites who were home defense oriented were *more* likely than those who were not to attribute high crime rates to blacks; home defense oriented blacks were *less* apt than other blacks to feel that a high crime rate was characteristic of blacks. For each racial group, fear of crime and violence at the hands of the other group was related to a posture of home defense.[66]

A number of incapacitating devices other than firearms have become popular recently. Tear gas sprays, mace, and stun-guns[67] have all become commercially available to the general public. Such weapons are rarely controlled by federal or state law. Because such instruments are thought to be nonlethal, people buy and use them with little consideration of the real harm they may cause. The police think that many of these weapons may sometimes be lethal and at other times only provoke the offender to use violence against the victim. For example, robbery offenders are more apt to use violence against their victims if the victims resist their attempts to steal money, so weapons or protective devices held by victims may precipitate violence rather than prevent it.[68] After being robbed, victims make a number of changes to prevent recurrence of the crime. Twenty-two of a sample of ninety robbery victims installed bars on windows or locks on doors, sixteen made sure they always locked their house or car, eleven bought weapons or protective devices such as tear gas sprays, and nine installed alarms in their homes or their place of business. Robbery victims who had lost the largest sums of money were more apt to take such measures than those who lost less, suggesting that property loss as well as the threat of violence caused robbery victims to mobilize for self-defense.[69] Only one victim in nine had any protective device available to him at the time of the robbery, and only three actually used such a device. Two were used to summon the police by making noise after the robbery was completed, and one was used to scare the robber away. Providing individuals with protective devices will not necessarily reduce robberies, since many people will not have such a device available at the time of the crime or will hesitate to use it if it is available. Also, use of a protective device may lead to violence by the offender, harming the victim more than if he had been unprotected.

A national survey analyzed by Blumenthal et al. asked people when they thought it was appropriate to use violence; 32 per cent approved of the police shooting to kill someone who was a member of a hoodlum gang that was terrorizing a community, 30 per cent felt the police should shoot to kill people involved in a ghetto riot, and 19 per cent felt the police should shoot to kill students involved in a demonstration.[70] Even larger proportions felt that the police should shoot but not to kill; 64 per cent thought this was appropriate for the hoodlums, 61 per cent for the rioters, and 48 per cent for the student protesters. People were also quite willing to permit private citizens to shoot to kill in self-defense (89 per cent agreeing, and 60 per cent strongly agreeing), in defense of one's family (93 per cent agreeing, and 69 per cent strongly agreeing) and in defense of one's own home (58 per cent agreeing, and 23 per cent strongly agreeing). Thus widespread support existed for the use of lethal force against offenders who threaten life; there was also substantial but lesser support for the use of violence to protect property.[71] People who agreed most that one should be able to use violence in one's own defense were more apt to support the use of violence by the police. Feagin found that many Americans felt that self-defense was necessary to protect one's home because the police could not do the job, but this survey by Blumenthal et al. found that many Americans thought *both* that one had to defend oneself and one's home *and* also that the police should be permitted to use violence to defend life and property.[72]

Americans are somewhat more likely to support violence for purposes of social control if they have less education, are older, were raised in the South or in border states, are white, and are neither foreign-born nor have foreign-born parents. However, all these background traits explain little of the differences among respondents in their attitudes toward the use of violence for purposes of social control.[73] Support for police violence to control crime and rioting was strongest among those who lived in rural areas, those who lived in the South or in border states at the time of the interview, those who favored killing in self-defense, and those who favored retributive justice. The following is a portrait of an individual who is most likely to support the use of violence for purposes of social control:

He is a person who believes that his life will change for the worse if black protesters "get the things they want," and he believes with most Americans that few or no policemen dislike people like himself. He is a person who is likely to believe in retribution, and the right of a man to defend himself and his home with homicide. He probably thinks many forms of protest constitute "violence," and he is more likely than the average man to think that police activities such as shooting looters and beating students are not violence. He is more likely than most Americans to deny that violence has roots in such social problems as lack of jobs and poor education, and that poverty and discrimination cause violence. He is probably convinced that the courts treat everyone equally, that the Supreme Court has made it more difficult to punish criminals, and that the police need more power. Such an individual, compared to others who score lower on Violence for Social Control, is more likely to live in the South or in the border states, is more likely to be neither foreign-born nor of foreign parents, and is less likely to be well-educated.[74]

However, these factors still leave much variation in attitudes toward the use of violence unexplained. The inclusion of measures of crime perception, sense of safety, and interpersonal trust might help explain more of the difference among people in their willingness to use lethal force against those who are seen as a threat to life and property.

So far, we have focused on defensive measures used to protect home and family. Recently, threats to personal safety on college campuses have resulted in defensive measures to protect dormitory residents. Doors are locked so that all who enter the building must pass a security guard, have their identification cards checked, or sign in. Visitors and guests have their movements within the dormitories restricted. Student escort teams try to reduce vulnerability around the dormitory buildings. Additional locks are placed on doors and windows. Valuables are engraved to prevent theft. Closed circuit televisions are used to increase the range of surveillance within buildings. These defensive measures may make the formation of new friendships among students more difficult and may enhance feelings of vulnerability rather than decrease them. People may reason that if such drastic measures are necessary, the risk must be quite substantial. Also, such measures may merely shift crimes to areas near the campuses, much as measures to prevent burglary in a home may displace the crime to a neighbor's unprotected home.

Both in private residences and in college dormitories, people often use security guards or dogs to protect themselves. These measures present obstacles for offenders, but they also create barriers between people who would otherwise interact sociably. Private security guards have increased in number dramatically in recent years; some cities now have more private guards than public police officers. Private guards are not carefully regulated, and the licensing of such guards is only rudimentary. Often they are not well trained or well educated. Some guards have engaged in extortion by using their position to intimidate victims.[75] Lack of coordination among the guards makes it difficult for neighborhoods to be adequately protected. Instead, criminals simply seek unprotected targets. There has been an effort in New York City to integrate the activities of private security guards by using walkie-talkies to establish communication among the guards in a particular area. In that way, the guards could act as eyes and ears for the police, watching suspicious people in the neighborhood and alerting the police to behavior that might suggest a crime was about to be committed. This network of guards might bring people back to the streets because they would feel safer there. One person who has attempted to organize the guards says, "What we are trying to do is to create life in the area. We do not want the area to start going dead after sundown. We want people to come to the area to walk through it at night and enjoy it. We have fountains and a very pleasant setting. We will be scheduling special events in the evening." [76] The defensive measure of hiring guards could then create a public perception that an area is indeed safer, drawing people to the streets and increasing informal social control in the area; this might help reduce crime in the area.

A report from Argentina on the use of security measures by foreign businessmen suggests that the kidnapping of people by terrorists has had some effects on behavior, although reaction to the kidnappings seems to be one of uneasiness and anxiety rather than panic and hysteria. [77] A prerequisite for gardeners hired by these businessmen is that they know how to use a firearm and provide protection for their employer. Some businessmen even vary their daily activities and their routes to work, change the times they eat lunch, avoid late parties, move from hotel to hotel, rent a house in the suburbs, refuse to open their door at night, and hire bodyguards for themselves and their families. In spite of such measures, people feel resigned to the threat of kidnapping; one person said, "When it happens, it happens, and there's nothing to do but hope for the best." [78]

In desperation, people try almost anything to defend themselves from victimization. They spend thousands of dollars on alarm systems, drastically alter their habits, and place barriers between themselves and the rest of the world. Such defensive measures reduce social interaction, which may increase crime by diminishing informal social control. Protective steps also can cause direct harm, as when firearms are accidentally fired at innocent people. Security measures are expensive and create inconvenience for those who wish to approach the protected individual and for the individual himself. Attempts to prevent victimization can make people prisoners in their own homes.

Footnotes

1. Laurie Johnston, "Man Dies Here in Blaze, Trapped Behind Anti-violence Shield He Built," *The New York Times*, November 5, 1971, p. 38.

2. Craig Comstock, "Avoiding Pathologies of Defense," in Nevitt Sanford and Craig Comstock, editors, *Sanctions for Evil: Sources of Social Destructiveness*. Boston: Beacon Press, 1971, pp. 290–301.

3. Ibid., p. 290.

4. The President's Commission on Law Enforcement and Administration of Justice, *Task Force Report: Crime and Its Impact—An Assessment*. Washington, D.C.: United States Government Printing Office, 1967, p. 88.

5. Charles N. Barnard, "The Fortification of Suburbia against the Burglar in the Bushes," *Saturday Review of the Society* I (May 1973), p. 38.

6. *Viliborghi v. State*, Supreme Court of Arizona, 1935. 45 Ariz. 275, 43 P. (2d) 210. Cited in Jerome Michael and Herbert Wechsler, *Criminal Law and Its Administration: Cases, Statutes and Commentaries*. Chicago: The Foundation Press, Inc., 1940, pp. 70–75.

7. Ibid., p. 72.

8. Cited in Sid Ross, "The Thief Who Was Awarded $30,000," *Parade* magazine, December 13, 1970, p. 9.

9. Richard W. O'Donnell, "Girls Still Hitchhiking Despite Coed Slaying," *Boston Globe*, November 15, 1972, pp. 1, 10; George Vecsey, "More Women Defy Risks of Hitchhiking," *The New York Times*, December 26, 1972, pp. 1, 57.

10. Barbara Armstrong, "Girls in Back Bay Worried about Safety," *Boston Globe*, December 7, 1972, p. 3.

11. O'Donnell, op. cit.

12. Cited in ibid., p. 10.

13. Cited in Vecsey, op. cit., p. 57.

14. Cited in ibid., p. 1.

15. The life style of the young that is condemned by many adults in this country evokes a different response in other cultures. For example, a report from an Italian island finds that local residents accepted hippies from abroad, since the residents had long been accustomed to wanderers from foreign countries who provided additional labor for the island's economy. Since the people of the island were not concerned with hard and methodical work at regular hours, they were much more tolerant of the casual life style of the hippies than are many adult Americans. Other aspects or the hippies' life style, notably drug use, were condemned, but the rejection of regular work patterns was acceptable to residents of the island. On the other hand, these people were outraged when the Italian government exiled fifteen *mafiosi* to the island, not because the criminals were seen as direct threats to the life and property of the islanders, but because their presence would reduce the tourist trade that the islanders depended upon. Eric Pace, "Aeolian

Isles Get Influx of Hippies," *The New York Times*, June 13, 1971, p. 11; Eric Pace, "Italian Islanders Claim Victory," *The New York Times*, June 7, 1971, p. 2.

16. Gilbert Geis and Ted L. Houston, "Charles Manson and His Girls: Notes on a Durkheimian Theme," *Criminology* IX (August–November 1971), p. 350.

17. Edgar Morin, *Rumour in Orléans*, translated by Peter Green. New York: Pantheon Books, 1969, 1971, pp. 44–55.

18. "Fear of Crime Said to Immobilize Aged," *The New York Times*, January 10, 1971, p. 35; "Boston Elderly Tell of Terror," *The New York Times*, October 4, 1972, p. 29.

19. "Boston Elderly Tell of Terror," op. cit., p. 29.

20. Cited in ibid.

21. Ibid.

22. Cited in Paul L. Montgomery, "City Acts to Raise Safety in Schools," *The New York Times*, January 14, 1973, p. 1.

23. Martin Tolchin, "Rage Permeates All Facets of Life in the South Bronx," *The New York Times*, January 17, 1973, p. 22.

24. Murray Schumach, "Connecticut Town Lives with Fear," *The New York Times*, October 1, 1970, p. 43.

25. Charles Winick and Paul M. Kinsie, *The Lively Commerce: Prostitution in the United States*. Chicago: Quadrangle Books, 1971, p. 167.

26. Harold Lewis Malt Associates, *An Analysis of Public Safety as Related to the Incidence of Crime in Parks and Recreation Areas in Central Cities*. Phase I Report submitted to HUD, March 1971.

27. "Fencing of Washington Sq. Park Studied," *The New York Times*, April 6, 1973, pp. 1, 26.

28. Gary Kayakachoian, "Rash of Night Holdups Force Stores to Close Early," *Boston Globe*, February 1, 1973, pp. 1, 12; Lesley Oelsner, "Terrified East Flatbush Little Stirred by Slaying," *The New York Times*, August 26, 1971, p. 75.

29. Howard Aldrich and Albert J. Reiss, Jr., "The Effect of Civil Disorders on Small Business in the Inner City," *Journal of Social Issues* XXVI (Winter 1970), p. 191.

30. Cited in Warren H. Talbot, "Drug Addicts Win, Druggist Closes Store," *Boston Globe*, October 20, 1972, p. 3.

31. Isadore Barmash, "New York's Angry Retailers," *The New York Times*, November 29, 1970, Section 3, pp. 1, 8; also see Frank Ching, "Street Crime Casts a Pall of Fear over Chinatown," *The New York Times*, January 19, 1974, p. 16.

32. Wayne King, "In West Philadelphia, the Gang Wars Are a Way of Death," *The New York Times*, June 11, 1973, p. 30.

33. Cited in Jane Jacobs, *The Death and Life of Great American Cities*. New York: Vintage Books, 1961, p. 46.

127

34. Cited in Howard Whitman, *Terror in the Streets*. New York: The Dial Press, 1951, p. 268.
35. Cited in Andrew H. Malcolm, "Drug Raids Terrorize 2 Families —By Mistake," *The New York Times*, April 29, 1973, p. 43.
36. Frank F. Furstenberg, Jr., "Fear of Crime and Its Effects on Citizen Behavior." Paper presented at the Symposium on Studies of Public Experience, Knowledge and Opinion of Crime and Justice. Bureau of Social Science Research, Inc. Washington, D.C., March 1972, pp. 21–26.
37. Ibid., pp. 11–12.
38. Ibid., p. 13.
39. Ibid., p. 22.
40. Truman Capote, *In Cold Blood: A True Account of a Multiple Murder and Its Consequences*. New York: Random House, 1965, p. 69.
41. Furstenberg, "Fear of Crime and Its Effects on Citizen Behavior," op. cit., pp. 23–24.
42. Ibid., pp. 21–22.
43. Ibid., p. 24.
44. Ibid., p. 26.
45. "A Connoisseur's Catalogue of Modern Protective Aids," *Saturday Review of the Society* I (May 1973), pp. 41–44. One extreme measure is reported in Ronald Sullivan, "Barbed Wire to Ring Private Village after Residents Complain of Crimes," *The New York Times*, February 22, 1974, p. 33.
46. Barnard, op. cit., p. 38.
47. See John E. Conklin and Egon Bittner, "Burglary in a Suburb," *Criminology* XI (August 1973), pp. 223–224.
48. Barnard, op. cit., p. 40.
49. Richard Phalon, "Home Burglar Alarms Vex the Police," *The New York Times*, August 13, 1973, p. 33.
50. Ibid.
51. "Are You Personally Afraid of Crime? Readers Speak Out," *Life* magazine LXXII (January 14, 1972), p. 23A.
52. Albert J. Reiss, Jr., Field Surveys III, Part I, of the President's Commission on Law Enforcement and Administration of Justice. *Studies in Crime and Law Enforcement in Major Metropolitan Areas*. Washington, D.C.: United States Government Printing Office, 1967, p. 107; and Albert D. Biderman, Louise A. Johnson, Jennie McIntyre, and Adrianne Weir, Field Surveys I of the President's Commission on Law Enforcement and Administration of Justice, *Report on a Pilot Study in the District of Columbia on Victimization and Attitudes toward Law Enforcement*. Washington, D.C.: United States Government Printing Office, 1967, p. 129.

53. Cited in Barry Felcher, "Fear Stalks Gary, Ind., in Bloody Drugs War," *Boston Globe*, August 7, 1972, p. 31.
54. Cited in Jack Anderson, "Liddy's Odd Behavior," *Boston Globe*, July 24, 1973, p. 11.
55. Cited in Michael T. Kaufman, "After the Professor's Death, 'What Can You Say?' A Student Asks," *The New York Times*, September 22, 1972, p. 48.
56. Cited in ibid.
57. Marshall Frady, "The Continuing Trial of Jesse Hill Ford," *Life* magazine LXXI (October 29, 1971), p. 60.
58. "Fortress on 78th Street," *Life* magazine LXXI (November 19, 1971), p. 34.
59. Cited in "Living with Crime, U.S.A.," *Newsweek* LXXX (December 18, 1972), p. 32.
60. "Neighbors of Slain 3 Get Theft Alarm Ads," *Boston Globe*, August 19, 1972, p. 4.
61. Joe R. Feagin, "Home-Defense and the Police: Black and White Perspectives," *American Behavioral Scientist* XIII (May 1970), p. 799.
62. Ibid., p. 799.
63. Ibid., pp. 802–804.
64. Ibid., pp. 804–806.
65. Ibid., pp. 806–808.
66. Ibid., pp. 808–810.
67. A stun-gun is a weapon that fires a small bag filled with shot or some other projectile to stun or temporarily disable a burglar or assailant.
68. John E. Conklin, *Robbery and the Criminal Justice System*. Philadelphia: J. B. Lippincott Company, 1972, pp. 112–121.
69. Ibid., p. 96.
70. Monica D. Blumenthal, Robert L. Kahn, Frank M. Andrews, and Kendra B. Head, *Justifying Violence: Attitudes of American Men*. Ann Arbor: Institute for Social Research, 1972, pp. 28–31.
71. Ibid., pp. 108–109.
72. Fear of intrusion into one's home and a willingness to use violence in defense of one's home led one woman in Norfolk, Virginia, to shoot and kill a plainclothes policeman who burst through her bedroom door on a drug raid. Andrew H. Malcolm, "Violent Drug Raids against the Innocent Found Widespread," *The New York Times*, June 25, 1973, pp. 1, 22.
73. Only about 10 per cent of the variance in attitudes toward the use of violence for social control is explained by these background variables. Blumenthal et al., op. cit., p. 215.
74. Ibid., p. 225.
75. In response to such abuses, the Pennsylvania House of Repre-

sentatives has considered ways to more tightly regulate security guards and insure certain minimum qualifications for them. "Security Guards Stir Legislator," *The New York Times*, October 30, 1973, p. 11.

76. Cited in Murray Schumach, "Private Security Guards to Join Midtown Patrols," *The New York Times*, June 8, 1973, p. 43.

77. Jonathan Kandell, "Alien Executives in Argentina Take Steps to Foil Kidnappers," *The New York Times*, April 28, 1973, p. 7; "Most Foreigners Are Undaunted by Latin Violence," *The New York Times*, December 2, 1973, p. 24.

78. Cited in "Most Foreigners Are Undaunted by Latin Violence," op. cit., p. 24.

Informal Social Control of Crime 6

T H E imposition of punishment for a given crime is far from certain. Nonreporting, failure to arrest, and inability to convict all stand between the crime and the punishment of the criminal. As a result, the formal sanctions of the criminal justice system are probably less important in controlling behavior than informal sanctions such as group censure and bystander intervention. The loss of the esteem of significant others is probably a greater threat to an offender than a more objective judgment by a court that he has violated a particular law.

Crime generates fear, suspicion, and distrust and thus diminishes social interaction. As a community is atomized, solidarity weakens and informal social controls dissipate. The result is a higher crime rate, since restraints on criminal behavior are released. One author has suggested that a good indicator of how effective a community's standards are in controlling deviant behavior is the proportion of crimes in the area committed by local residents. From his study of Honolulu, Lind concludes: "An area capable of maintaining the strength of its prohibitions is likely also to discourage its wayward residents from attempting the violation of the taboos within the boundaries of the district, although it may not succeed in entirely repressing the behavior." [1] A similar conclusion emerged from a study of counter-riot activity in the 1960's: efforts to stop riot activity were most common in communities where residents had most contacts with each other. Riot activity itself was most widespread where there was no "extensive informal social interaction," and thus little informal social control.[2]

Both the Honolulu study and the riot study suggest that community standards and social interaction (through which residents learn shared norms and values) help control deviant behavior.

The restraining influence of informal controls was also found in a study of juvenile delinquency in Iraq: "Both the low rate of 'escapes' [from a juvenile institution] and the low rate of recidivism were explained by professionals dealing with these delinquents as resulting from the embarrassment caused to family or tribe during the initial conviction proceedings. The boys did not wish to cause additional embarrassment by running away or committing a second crime." [3] The restraining influence of group norms is particularly strong when it comes from a primary group, one in which people regularly interact on a face-to-face basis.

Social Control in Simple and Complex Societies

The argument is often made that as society and its division of labor become more complex and as interpersonal relations become less intimate, the force of informal social control is weakened. For example, Durkheim argues that in simple societies such as tribal villages and small towns, legal norms more closely accord with social norms than is true in larger and more complex societies. Moral disapproval of deviance is nearly unanimous in such communities; as Daniel Glaser says, "Tolerance of behavioral diversity varies directly with the division of labor in a society." [4] Because the law is often unwritten in tribal societies, the direct teaching of social norms to the children is necessary. Due to the lack of normative and structural complexity, socialization in such cultures does not present children with contradictory norms that create confusion and inner conflict. Intense face-to-face interaction in such simple societies produces a moral consensus that is well known to all members; it also brings deviant acts to everyone's attention quickly. [5] One observer has argued that in such homogeneous communities there is rarely any occasion to punish fellow tribesmen, because socialization is so thorough that nonconformity is rare. [6] This view leaves unanswered the question of how any deviance at all can exist in such a homogeneous community.

The view that tribal societies are very homogeneous is related to the notion that deviance is rare in such settings. As long ago as 1926, Bronislaw Malinowski provided evidence that this was not the case. He showed that acts that were supposedly in violation of strongly held norms were not always dealt with by great public horror and outrage, as the common view suggests. Citizens had to be mobilized by an accuser who made the deviant act public.[7] Patterned deviation from social norms was found by Malinowski, and such deviations often failed to evoke harsh censure and repressive measures. Only when the act became a direct challenge to the dominant norms was there a strong demand for punishment. This is consistent with Durkheim's argument that punishment follows a threat to the collective conscience; secret deviance does not present such a threat.

A recent summary of the literature on deviance in simple societies concludes that more deviance exists there than is commonly believed. Members of such societies often disagree about social norms; as a result, norms are often vague and inconsistently applied. Sometimes punishment does not follow deviant acts. The "rules are often very fuzzy around the edges, being relative to the situation, the actor, and the audience"; people in such simple societies are not "slaves to their customs."[8]

The argument that informal social control is stronger in small towns than in large cities is one that has a long history in this country.[9] For example, the child-saving movement of the late nineteenth century suggested that the problem of juvenile delinquency in the cities could be solved by making the urban social environment more like rural communities, or by actually moving the delinquent boys from their urban homes to institutions in idyllic rural settings.[10] In 1897 one penologist said that the "atmosphere of suspicion and distrust" in the city led to strangers being regarded with hostility and being excluded from social relations; "[t]hese conditions of existence are destructive of social cohesion in its highest forms, and have a tendency to develop selfish instincts till they overstep the borderland which separates selfishness from crime."[11] Early in this century, the murder of a gambler by a New York City policeman made headlines in small-town newspapers across the country; it was cited as a "sensational example of sin in the big eastern city."[12] This view of the city reinforced the attitude of rural and small-town residents that their way of life was superior to that in the cities.

Even today many urban dwellers express a preference for small towns and rural areas. One study found that many Boston residents said that they would most like to live in a homogeneous community with local self-government in which a proper sense of community could be instilled through informal social control of deviant behavior, a picture much like the ideal of a small town.[13] In 1972, a national survey asked 1,806 adults where they presently lived and where they would prefer to live, with the following results:

	Present residence	Preferred residence
City	36%	18%
Suburb	22%	22%
Town or village	15%	19%
Rural area	18%	38%
Unsure	9%	3%

Only half as many people who lived in cities said they preferred to live in cities, but nearly twice as many who lived rural areas or small towns preferred such communities.[14] A 1973 poll found that of people who actually lived in cities, 30 per cent preferred to live in a city, 24 per cent preferred a suburb, 20 per cent a small town, 9 per cent a rural area, 15 per cent a farm, and 2 per cent were uncertain.[15] Both polls suggest substantial dissatisfaction on the part of many city dwellers, a feeling that life would be better on a farm or in a small town. Desire to escape the crime problem is one cause of this preference,[16] but the image of a serene and healthy countryside reinforces the desire to leave the city.

Let us examine what evidence there is about informal social control in small towns and in large cities. In his study of deviance in the seventeenth-century Massachusetts Bay Colony, Kai T. Erikson concluded that the small size and the cultural homogeneity of the community helped control behavior, as all voices in the community pressured potential deviants to conform to dominant norms. The eyes of neighbors were everywhere, constantly watching for acts of deviance. Moral censure immediately followed any observed deviance.[17] Reaction to crime in such small, homogeneous, and closely-knit communities may be so intense and immediate that justice for a defendant in a criminal case may be difficult, since public pressure on the legal system to exact harsh and swift punishment may make the provision of due process rights doubtful. At times, a change of venue order may be issued to change the location of the trial so that such public pressure will no longer be present; such an order is probably more often necessary in small communities than in larger ones because of the greater impact of public opinion on the legal system.[18]

Informal controls operate more effectively in communities where people know each other and interact regularly. In general, small and homogeneous communities are probably better suited to this type of interaction than are large and heterogeneous ones. The police can probably expect better cooperation in smaller communities. In fact, the criminal justice system now in use throughout the country emerged when communities were much smaller. In today's large cities, law-enforcement agents are less able to depend upon the support of the citizenry which is necessary to make the criminal justice system operate efficiently. Residents of smaller communities are probably more likely to act as the eyes and ears of the police. One observer has said that in small towns "teachers, parents, and little old ladies keeping watch on flower gardens are apt to notice any strange or objectionable behavior and they will want to 'do something' about perceived threats to property." [19] A professional safecracker supports this view of the small town, as he assesses the opportunity for burglary:

But little towns are so hard to work in because you can't case the joint off, you know. The Hoosiers [small-town residents] know one another real well. And the bull [policeman] on the beat knows everybody in town—knows where he's supposed to be and what time he's supposed to be home and what he's doing in that neck of the woods and everything else. When he sees a stranger, a couple times in a evening, why right away he begins to think.[20]

Although this "box man" focuses on the police officer's surveillance of the community, he is also aware that a similar function is served by the people of the town, since anything out of the ordinary will attract their attention. They know normal patterns of social behavior, and a burglar looking over a target will be easily noticed. Of course, this public surveillance also limits the freedom of behavior for law-abiding citizens of the town, but in doing so it reduces the amount of crime in their community.

Surveillance is generally less thorough in large cities than in small towns. As the National Crime Commission noted in 1967:

A man who lives in the country or in a small town is likely to be conspicuous, under surveillance by his community so to speak, and therefore under its control. A city man is often almost invisible, socially isolated from his neighborhood and therefore incapable of being controlled by it. He has more opportunities for crime.[21]

In large cities, criminals are sometimes aware that they will not be molested by local residents; for example, the man who murdered Kitty Genovese (see Chapter 9) within the view of her neighbors later told the police "that he had known the people wouldn't come down because it was three o'clock on a cold morning and they wouldn't bother." [22] However, it is not clear that witnesses to such a violent crime in a small town would come to the victim's aid either. Law-enforcement officers in Perry, Iowa, note that the steady reduction of people living on farms in the United States "has left fewer people around to keep an eye on things." [23] Michael Lesy's compilation of newspaper clippings and photographs from a small Wisconsin town at the turn of the century suggests that life in small-town America even then was not as free of crime and deviance as is often thought.[24] Lesy cites one author from 1901 who casts doubt on the usual picture of social control in small towns and rural areas:

[O]ne of the greatest insufficiencies in country life is its lack of organization or cohesion, both in a social and an economic way. Country people are separated both because of the distances between their properties, and also because they own their own land. . . . There is a general absence of such common feelings as would cause them to act together unitedly. . . .[25]

Although small towns are probably more tightly-knit communities than large cities, small towns can be poorly integrated and large cities can incorporate a number of well-integrated communities, such as the North End of Boston. In highly cohesive communities there may also be a reluctance to report crimes by local residents to the police because the police are seen as outsiders and because people feel they will have to live with their neighbors in the future. Formal control of crime may thus be weakest in those communities where informal controls are strongest. High crime rates will be found where formal control agents lack public support and where informal controls are not strong enough to effectively restrain deviants in the community. Whether formal controls alone can reduce crime rates without the aid of informal controls is doubtful.[26]

A study of people's willingness to let strangers into their homes to use their phones found that residents of small towns were much more willing to permit entrance than were residents of middle-class housing developments in the city.[27] Willingness to admit strangers was more than twice as common in the small towns. Also, in the city many people talked to the strangers through the door without opening it, but in small towns doors were much more frequently opened so that the occupant could face the stranger. Unwillingness to admit strangers into the home was not just due to a fear of personal attack, since another study showed that urban dwellers were less likely than those who lived in small towns to help strangers who sought information over the telephone.[28] People were more willing to let females into their homes to use their telephones than they were to admit males, just as female hitchhikers wait shorter times for rides than their male counterparts. Women probably seem less of a threat than men, since their crime rate is much lower for the types of crimes most feared by the public. However, willingness to admit a stranger was *more* influenced by whether a person lived in a city or a small town than it was by the sex of the stranger who requested to use the phone.

Milgram suggests that because residents of cities encounter many more people in their daily lives, they have to ignore certain types of inputs and minimize the time they expend in processing other inputs in order to prevent informational overload. As a result, "moral and social involvement with individuals is necessarily restricted," creating a greater disparity between the treatment of friends and the treatment of strangers in cities than in small towns.[29] The frequency of interpersonal demands on urban residents generates *norms of noninvolvement*, which are related to distrust of strangers, desire for privacy, and withdrawal from social contacts.[30] Also, "the inhabitant of the city possesses a larger vulnerable space" in comparison to those who live in villages;[31] that is, urban residents feel threatened by crimes that occur throughout the city (with its large population), whereas those who live in small towns sometimes treat crimes in nearby towns as irrelevant to their lives. Of course, this is not always the case, as people throughout Kansas reacted strongly to the Clutter murders.

In looking at the social structure of cities, Alexander finds an *autonomy-withdrawal syndrome*, a tendency for people to sustain few if any intimate contacts with others.[32] The primary groups that support intimate contacts in simpler societies break down in the more complex and stressful urban setting. Instead, people in cities deal with each other in secondary or segmentalized role relationships that involve a minimum of personal involvement;[33] in a small town, the grocer will ask how your sick child is feeling, but in a large city the grocer will probably not even know if you have a family. Alexander does not feel that this lack of intimate contact in the city is a necessary part of urban life: "The ills of urban life which are commonly attributed to density and stress, are in fact not produced by the original stress itself, but by our own actions in turning away from that stress."[34]

In a study of formal and informal social controls, Sarah L. Boggs analyzed data collected from residents of central cities, suburbs, and small towns in Missouri.[35] She discovered that residents of large cities were more apt than suburban or small-town residents to feel that crime was likely to occur in their community. Those who lived in cities were also more likely to think that their neighbors would not report a burglary that they observed to the police, and more urban residents knew of a crime or a suspicious incident in their community within the previous year. Most people in all areas felt that their own neighborhood was safe, but fewer felt that way in the cities. When they were asked *what* it was that made their neighborhood safe, 83 per cent of those in rural areas and small towns said that it was informal controls; 70 per cent of those in the suburbs and 68 per cent of those in the cities attributed safety to informal controls. When they said that their neighborhood was kept safe by informal social controls, the people meant that they felt secure because of the character of the community and its residents ("good, decent, law-abiding, middle-class citizens"[36]) and because of the social network in the community which might lead to bystander intervention in a crime. People who lived in suburbs and in large cities were more apt than those who lived in rural areas and small towns to attribute safety to such formal control agents as the police.[37] Overall, people thought that formal controls were less important than informal controls in producing a sense of security, but this difference was more pronounced in rural areas and small towns.[38] In summary, people in cities were most apt to expect crime, but least likely to feel that they could rely on their neighbors rather than the police to protect their community. As a result, they were more apt to take precautions (such as buying a watchdog or a weapon) than were people who lived in suburbs, small towns, and rural areas.

Richard D. Schwartz has examined the use of formal controls and informal controls in a study of two Israeli agricultural settlements.[39] The communities were similar to each other when they began, to the extent that there was no significant difference between them in ideas of legal control. One settlement was a collective or *kvutza* with no formal mechanism to resolve disputes of a legal nature, and the other was a semi-private settlement or *moshav* which had a judicial committee to handle legal disputes. The collective had no legal committee because the intense and frequent face-to-face interaction provided an effective means of social control by group pressure. On the other hand, in the semi-private settlement there was less interaction and less consensus; behavior was less visible to members of the community than it was in the collective. Informal social control was less effective in the semi-private settlement than in the collective, where the flow of information soon made any deviant act known to all members of the community. The type of informal social control that is commonly attributed to small communities (such as tribal societies and small towns) was found in the *kvutza* but not in the *moshav*, although the two settlements were not much different in size. This raises an important point: *It is the structure of social interaction and social relationships rather than size alone which determines the degree of informal social control in a community.* If there is intense social interaction on an intimate face-to-face basis, if there is normative consensus, and if there is surveillance of the behavior of members of the community, social control will be strong, to the extent that legal or formal controls may be unnecessary. These social conditions are probably more common in small communities; however, the correlation of these conditions with size of a community is far from perfect. For example, the Ik of Africa live in buildings which isolate people from each other, and they have minimal social interaction and shared values. As a result, there is comparatively little informal control over aggressive and destructive behavior, even though the tribe is a small and simple society.[40] As we shall see, communities with the structural characteristics that strengthen informal social control also exist or can be created in large cities.

Informal Social Control in Urban Communities

The difference between social control in small tribal societies and social control in large urban communities has been examined in the context of developing nations. As people migrate from tribal villages where social ties are strong and where deviance is followed by group censure to large cities where solidarity is weak and people do not even know their neighbors, social control over deviant behavior diminishes. One writer has observed about Liberia:

The effectiveness of tribe and family as agents of social control has always depended upon the cohesiveness of the particular unit. In the urban areas the cohesiveness increasingly gives way to individualism and the vacuum created by the decline in family and tribal authority has only been filled by the impersonal sanctions of the law.[41]

In comparing a low crime-rate community and a high crime-rate community in Kampala, Uganda, Clinard and Abbott found that the areas with less crime showed greater social solidarity, more social interaction among neighbors, more participation in local organizations, less geographical mobility, and more stability in family relationships. There was also greater cultural homogeneity and more emphasis on tribal and kinship ties in the low crime community, helping to counteract the anonymity of recent migrants to the city. The stronger primary group ties among residents of the low crime area made it more difficult for strangers in the community to escape public notice and thus helped to prevent theft from neighbors. To prevent theft, residents of an area must feel that theft is wrong, share some responsibility for protecting their neighbors' property, be able to identify strangers in the area, and be willing to take action if they observe a theft.[42]

Comparing offenders and nonoffenders in Uganda, Clinard and Abbott discovered that offenders were less apt to have received aid from a member of their tribe, a relative, or a friend when they arrived in the city. They were thus cut loose from traditional social ties and their behavior was less subject to informal social controls. As a result, they sought out others for companionship and assistance in adjusting to city life; this exposed them to possible criminal influences.[43] Thus, evidence both about offenders and about communities as units shows that informal controls *in the city*, as well as in the small tribal villages from which the migrants came, are important in determining the extent of criminal behavior.

Support for this conclusion comes from a study of two neighborhoods in Cambridge, Massachusetts, one with a high rate of juvenile delinquency and one with a low rate.[44] Residents of the two communities were quite similar in terms of social background characteristics. However, the high delinquency area was less *integrated:* residents were more heterogeneous in terms of religion and ethnicity, they knew fewer neighbors by name and fewer neighbors from whom they could borrow, they felt they had fewer interests in common with their neighbors, and they disliked their community more. Maccoby, Johnson, and Church reasoned that many juveniles in each community would engage in occasional delinquent acts. If the community in which they lived were disorganized, there would be little chance that they would be seen, interfered with, or reported to their parents by a neighbor. If they got away with their delinquent act, they would probably commit additional offenses, producing a higher rate of delinquency in the disorganized community.

Maccoby et al. did find that adults in the high delinquency area were no more *tolerant* of deviance than the adults in the low delinquency area, but that those in the high rate area were less likely to *do something* about delinquent acts if they observed them. In each community, *victims* of a delinquent act were equally likely to take action, but people who were not *directly* victimized by an act were more likely to do something in the low rate area than in the high rate area. Overall, people were less likely to take actions against delinquents in the high rate area. Many people in both communities were reluctant to act when their neighbors' children were involved, but more of those in the high rate area said that neighbors ought to mind their own business and not interfere. In sum, the low rate area was better integrated than the high rate area, and residents of the low rate area were more likely to take action if they saw a delinquent act in progress. When people ignore such acts, there develops "an atmosphere in which delinquency can grow more easily. . . . [T]he lack of social integration appears to have certain direct effects in a lowered level of social control of delinquent and pre-delinquent activities." [45] Here again we see that informal social controls do indeed exist in urban communities and that the strength of such controls is related to the nature of social relations in the community rather than simply to the size of the community.

The problem of informal control of deviant behavior in the city has been dealt with by Jane Jacobs. [46] She suggests that when people say a city is not safe, they mean that they feel insecure on its streets and sidewalks. If people are afraid to venture onto the streets at night, the streets become dark and deserted and thus more dangerous, as informal controls that would otherwise check criminal behavior are absent. Jacobs suggests that order in public places is kept not by the police, but by an intricate and nearly unconscious network of involuntary controls by private citizens. A well-used street is a safe street, because the presence of people restrains deviant behavior and attracts the attention of neighbors. Surveillance of the streets by the eyes of the community reduces opportunities for crime. Jacobs calls these eyes the natural proprietors of the street, claiming that if they are continuously trained on public areas, the community will be safe.[47] Surveillance is more common if there are things of interest to watch on the streets, such as the customers of local stores and restaurants. By extension, anything that brings people onto the streets will enhance the safety of the community.[48] Better lighting may inspire confidence in citizens that the streets are actually safer, even if the lights themselves do nothing to prevent crime. Year-round use of daylight savings time might have a similar effect. More people will be drawn to the streets, and their perception of greater safety will become a self-fulfilling prophecy. Effective crime control by the local police may also draw more people into public places, thereby augmenting informal social controls as well. In fact, one observer has suggested that the following quality-of-life measures might be used as indices of how well the *formal* social control system is operating:

a. The number of individuals at various hours using public transportation, walking on streets, and using public libraries, museums and recreational facilities;
b. Hours and days of operation of public facilities, private service units (gas stations), and retail stores.[49]

In a study of a Chicago slum neighborhood, Gerald D. Suttles noted certain *impersonal domains*, nonresidential areas where the safety of passersby was in the hands of such local "authorities" as store proprietors. Businessmen, bureaucrats, and customers established informal social control of deviance in those areas during the day, but at night the streets were dark and deserted except for the police. Residents of the rest of the city saw these areas as dangerous and doubted that the police could keep them safe. As a result, human traffic in the areas was scarce and the dangerousness of the areas high.[50]

For a street to be a safety asset for a community, people's eyes must be trained on the streets and buildings must be oriented so that windows look onto public areas.[51] The sidewalk must be in use fairly continuously to attract attention. Because of the large number of people who have no intimate contacts with or knowledge of their neighbors in large cities, it may be necessary to create safety zones in public areas to draw people to small parks and shopping districts. Human traffic will then increase surveillance of those areas, and also increase surveillance of the streets by people inside their homes. One prerequisite of informal social control in the community is that a significant number of people have roots in the community and know what constitutes unusual activity and who is a stranger in the neighborhood.

The high-rent tenants, most of whom are so transient we cannot even keep track of their faces, have not the remotest idea of who takes care of their street, or how. A city neighborhood can absorb and protect a substantial number of these birds of passage, as our neighborhood does. But if and when the neighborhood finally *becomes* them, they will gradually find the streets less secure, they will be vaguely mystified about it, and if things get bad enough they will drift away to another neighborhood which is mysteriously safer.[52]

Informal social control in a community operates though a web of social relationships that develops over time. Relatively trivial interpersonal contacts gradually generate a network of trust and interdependence. This process is strengthened by the influence of public characters such as shopkeepers and newspaper salesmen who are in frequent though limited contact with many residents of the community.[53] They spread news among the people and help bind the community together. Most of their interactions with local residents are not intimate or involved, but they do help maintain a sense of community that informally controls deviant behavior in the area. However, if neighbors do not know each other and if no web of social relationships exists, people will not be able to guard each other from harm. Without minimal contacts among residents, people will not even know who is a neighbor and who is a stranger to the area. An indicator of how social control might be absent from a community because of lack of contact among residents is suggested in the following letter and answer from a Boston newspaper column:

Q. I have complained for two months about an abandoned car on Mt. Vernon St. Why don't the police take action?

—B. F., Charlestown

A. The car is not abandoned. It is properly registered, according to police, and belongs to your neighbor, who has been too ill to drive it.[54]

Not only would this letter-writer fail to call the police if the car were stolen by a stranger, but he would also not be able to help his sick neighbor if it were necessary.

If people react to crime with fear and distrust, they may withdraw from social contacts in public places. As a result, there will be fewer people on the streets and residents of the area will be less likely to watch the streets. This weakens social control and leaves public areas to criminals. They will not be seen committing crimes or will not be reported if they are seen. Fear of crime can thus become a self-fulfilling prophecy, one which can be reversed by creating attractions that increase human traffic in public places and thus strengthen informal social controls in the community.

Informal Social Control and Architectural Design

Oscar Newman has shown how architectural design can reduce the autonomy-withdrawal syndrome that contributes to the crime problem in large cities.[55] He argues that because community solidarity has broken down in large cities, especially in housing projects, citizen involvement is needed to prevent crime. He suggests that it is possible to construct residential complexes to deter crime by creating *defensible space*. Defensible space involves the subdivision and design of housing to allow residents to distinguish stranger from neighbor. Housing design itself can reinforce or create opportunities for surveillance of buildings and surrounding grounds by eliciting from residents a feeling of territoriality and a sense of proprietary interest in the protection of their community.[56]

A survey in New York City found that over half of the residents of housing projects felt unsafe. "Fear, in itself, can increase the risk of victimization through isolating neighbor from neighbor, witness from victim, making remote the possibility of mutual help and assuring the criminal a ready opportunity to operate unhampered and unimpeded." [57] However, project residents who knew a number of their neighbors at least moderately well felt less threatened by crime, and people were more apt to know their neighbors if the design of their housing project facilitated social interaction. Newman suggests ways that housing can be designed to enhance social interaction and proprietary interest over nearby territory, thereby generating informal social control over behavior.

Crime in housing projects is most common in interior spaces, particularly in tall buildings and in those with long corridors. Newman suggests that crime can be reduced by making these interior spaces more visible to people outside the building and by defining more clearly the entry to the building.[58] Design can also help define building groups and interior spaces as zones of influence for the residents; for example, a housing project with L-shaped buildings can create a sense of semi-privacy within the areas partly enclosed by the L's. Building design can also create a hierarchy of increasingly private zones as one moves from public space to private apartments. Either physical barriers or symbolic design can be used to suggest to potential intruders that certain areas belong to the residents. The strangers must read the symbols accurately and the residents must be willing to challenge intruders if crime in the housing project is to be reduced.

Multiple entries create shared concern for the safety of common areas and allow residents to get to know each other and thus recognize who is a stranger to the building. In high-rise proj-

ects, strangers often cannot be distinguished from residents because of the large number of people living in the unit. If the
social community is relatively small, informal controls will be
stronger. Newman shows that housing units can be constructed
so that tightly-knit communities of the sort usually associated
with tribal societies or small towns can be created in urban settings. Lee Rainwater reached a similar conclusion in his study
of low-income housing in St. Louis:

A measured degree of publicness within buildings can also contribute
to a greater sense of security. In buildings where there are several
families whose doors open onto a common hallway there is a greater
sense of the availability of help should trouble come than there is in
buildings where only two or three apartments open onto a small hallway in a stairwell. While tenants do not necessarily develop close
neighborly relations when more neighbors are available, they can
develop a sense of making common cause in dealing with common
problems. And they feel less at the mercy of gangs or individuals intent
on doing them harm.[59]

Clusters of apartments also create zones of influence or social
control if shared areas are defined as private and are watched by
residents. If children play in hallways or on playgrounds, parents
will watch those areas to guard their children from strangers.
Filling private or semi-private areas near housing projects with
amenities such as play equipment or benches will attract people
and attention to the area. Placing basketball courts and baseball
fields near the project will allow residents to watch their children;
lack of such facilities will draw juveniles to parks and streets
outside the view of their parents, reducing social control and increasing the likelihood of delinquent acts.[60]

Surveillance of exterior nonprivate areas (such as play areas)
can be increased by juxtaposing such areas with interior areas of
activity (such as kitchens). The provision of windows and exterior lighting augments the capability of residents to observe
activity outside the building. Also, the juxtaposition of housing
projects with safe areas of the city will minimize risks within the
project grounds, since human traffic in those safe areas will pro-

vide surveillance over the project grounds. On the other hand, placing projects near schools will increase the possibility of crime, since schools contain large numbers of high-risk individuals, young males who engage in delinquent acts.

Newman claims that residents of housing projects will be safer if they can "see and be seen, hear and be heard, by day and night."[61] Surveillance not only deters crime, but it also reduces anxiety and creates an image of a safe environment. People who feel less anxious will be more likely to walk outside and visit their friends, further enhancing surveillance and increasing the safety of the area. Physical design of housing projects should thus allow residents to pre-scan pathways and objectives within the project grounds, since corners and alleys can hide criminal predators or at least create that impression among residents of the project.

Buildings can be designed to provide areas for which residents will adopt a territorial concern.[62] In the past, ethnic communities often took responsibility for controlling deviant behavior in an area, but the influence of ethnic groups has diminished with their assimilation into the larger society. Newman suggests that by thoughtful architectural design, it is possible to evoke public willingness to take responsibility for crime prevention and thus counteract the "deterritorialized existence in contemporary cities." [63] He states:

Where building design provides opportunity for tenants to observe and maintain surveillance over their living areas, security will be enhanced; where design allows tenants to feel the presence and shared concerns of their neighbors, security will be preserved; and where buildings relate adequately to streets and other surrounding zones, large public areas of the city can profit as a byproduct of local community concern.[64]

One difficulty with the ideas of Newman, Rainwater, and Jacobs about informal social control is that surveillance of public areas presupposes some degree of solidarity and some active support for the law. If a potential offender feels that he will be observed committing a crime but will not be interfered with or reported to the police by the observer, he will not be controlled by mere surveillance. The offender must not only feel that he will be watched; he must think that local residents will take some effective action against him if they see him committing a crime.

An experiment by Zimbardo shows that public surveillance alone is not enough to inhibit deviant behavior. He left a car with a raised hood and no license plates (releaser stimuli) on a street in a middle-class community near a college campus in California, and another car on a street near a campus in the Bronx. The car in California was left untouched for more than a week, but the one in New York was soon destroyed. In daylight, within a few hours, adult and young men stripped the car of usable or salable parts. Bystanders watched with no sign of disapproval. Then younger children began smashing windows, and adults began breaking or ripping parts of the car and smashing it with rocks and tools. Within three weeks, there were twenty-three separate incidents of destructive contact. Norms in the California community helped control vandalism, but in the New York City community even the observation of vandalism by passersby did not inhibit destructive behavior.[65] Surveillance of public behavior must be reinforced by a willingness to exercise direct control over deviant behavior, whether by subtle cues of disapproval, direct interference with the act, or reporting of the behavior to the police. If no action is taken, surveillance by itself will have no effect on crime in the community.

Footnotes

1. Andrew W. Lind, "Some Ecological Patterns of Community Disorganization in Honolulu," *American Journal of Sociology* XXXVI (September 1930), p. 218.
2. Donald I. Warren, "Neighborhood Structure and Riot Behavior in Detroit: Some Exploratory Findings," *Social Problems* XVI (Spring 1969), pp. 464–484.
3. Carl D. Chambers and James A. Inciardi, "Deviant Behavior in the Middle East: A Study of Delinquency in Iraq," *Criminology* IX (August–November 1971), p. 300.
4. Daniel Glaser, "Criminology and Public Policy," *The American Sociologist* VI (June 1971), p. 32.

5. The strength of informal means of inducing conformity is shown in Leonard Berkowitz and Nigel Walker, "Laws and Moral Judgments," in Lawrence M. Friedman and Stewart Macaulay, editors, *Law and the Behavioral Sciences*. Indianapolis: The Bobbs-Merrill Company, Inc., 1969, pp. 198–211.

6. Ellsworth Faris, "The Origin of Punishment," *International Journal of Ethics* XXV (October 1914), pp. 54–67.

7. Bronislaw Malinowski, *Crime and Custom in Savage Society*. Paterson, N.J.: Littlefield, Adams & Company, 1926, 1964.

8. Robert B. Edgerton, *Deviant Behavior and Cultural Theory*. Reading, Mass.: Addison-Wesley Publishing Company, Inc., 1973, p. 23.

9. C. Wright Mills has attributed this view in part to the small-town background of many social scientists who wrote about social problems and social disorganization in the early twentieth century. See C. Wright Mills, "The Professional Ideology of Social Pathologists," in Irving Louis Horowitz, editor, *Power, Politics and People: The Collected Essays of C. Wright Mills*. New York: Ballantine Books, 1963, pp. 525–552.

10. Anthony M. Platt, *The Child Savers: The Invention of Delinquency*. Chicago: The University of Chicago Press, 1969, passim.

11. Cited in ibid., p. 39.

12. Andy Logan, *Against the Evidence: The Becker-Rosenthal Affair*. New York: The McCall Publishing Company, 1970, p. 33.

13. James Q. Wilson, "The Urban Unease: Community vs. City," *The Public Interest*, No. 12 (Summer 1968), pp. 28–29.

14. Jack Rosenthal, "Nonurban Living Is Gaining Favor," *The New York Times*, December 17, 1972, p. 31.

15. "Americans Return to Gardening," *Boston Globe*, June 29, 1973, p. 12.

16. This desire is reflected in the popularity of David and Holly Franke's *Safe Places*. New Rochelle, N.Y.: Arlington House, 1972. This book provides information about cities and towns in the United States which are relatively safe places to live.

17. Kai T. Erikson, *Wayward Puritans: A Study in the Sociology of Deviance*. New York: John Wiley & Sons, Inc., 1966, pp. 169–170.

18. Alfred Friendly and Ronald L. Goldfarb, *Crime and Publicity: The Impact of News on the Administration of Justice*. New York: The Twentieth Century Fund, 1967, pp. 96–101.

19. James Q. Wilson, *Varieties of Police Behavior: The Management of Law and Order in Eight Communities*. Cambridge: Harvard University Press, 1968, p. 115.

20. Bill Chambliss, editor, *Box Man: A Professional Thief's Journey*. New York: Harper and Row, Publishers, 1972, pp. 102–103.

21. The President's Commission on Law Enforcement and Administration of Justice, *The Challenge of Crime in a Free Society*. Wash-

ington, D.C.: United States Government Printing Office, 1967, p. 6.

22. Jonathan Craig and Richard Posner, *The New York Crime Book.* New York: Pyramid Books, 1972, p. 181.

23. B. Drummond Ayres, Jr., "Rural Crime Spreads Fear and Distrust," *The New York Times,* January 16, 1972, p. 46.

24. Michael Lesy, *Wisconsin Death Trip.* New York: Pantheon Books, 1973.

25. L. H. Bailey, cited in ibid., no page number.

26. For example, see David Burnham, "A Police Study Challenges Value of Anticrime Patrol," *The New York Times,* November 11, 1973, pp. 1, 67.

27. Cited in Stanley Milgram, "The Experience of Living in Cities," *Science* CLXVII (March 13, 1970), p. 1463.

28. Ibid., p. 1465.

29. Ibid., p. 1462.

30. Ibid., p. 1463.

31. Cited in ibid., p. 1463, from a study by J. Villena.

32. Christopher Alexander, "The City as a Mechanism for Sustaining Human Contact," in Robert Gutman, editor, *People and Buildings.* New York: Basic Books, Inc., 1972, pp. 415–421.

33. Hartmann et al. found in a study of bystander response to acts of shoplifting that witnesses who had grown up in larger cities were less apt to report the behavior to the storekeeper than were people who had grown up in smaller communities. See Donald P. Hartmann, Donna M. Gelfand, Brent Page, and Patrice Walder, "Rates of Bystander Observation and Reporting of Contrived Shoplifting Incidents," *Criminology* X (November 1972), p. 258.

34. Alexander, op. cit., p. 431.

35. Sarah L. Boggs, "Formal and Informal Crime Control: An Exploratory Study of Urban, Suburban, and Rural Orientations," *The Sociological Quarterly* XII (Summer 1971), pp. 319–327.

36. Ibid., p. 323.

37. Ibid., p. 324. Also, fewer blacks than whites felt that they could rely on their neighbors *or* on the police to prevent crime, but the two racial groups were equally likely to take special precautions against crime. Whites placed relatively greater emphasis on informal controls; blacks stressed formal controls relatively more. The blacks felt more dependent upon, but less satisfied with, the local police in their crime prevention efforts. Ibid., pp. 325–326.

38. Ibid., p. 324.

39. Richard D. Schwartz, "Social Factors in the Development of Legal Controls: A Case Study of Two Israeli Settlements," in Friedman and Macaulay, op. cit., pp. 509–522.

40. Colin M. Turnbull, *The Mountain People.* New York: Simon and Schuster, 1972, p. 83.

41. Cited in Marshall B. Clinard and Daniel J. Abbott, *Crime in Developing Countries: A Comparative Perspective.* New York: John Wiley & Sons, 1973, p. 89.

42. Ibid., p. 149.

43. These influences could provide new migrants to the city with "definitions favorable to violation of the law," which according to Sutherland and Cressey's "theory of differential association" would increase the likelihood of their becoming criminals. Edwin H. Sutherland and Donald R. Cressey, *Criminology*, eighth edition. Philadelphia: J. B. Lippincott Company, 1970, pp. 71–93.

44. Eleanor E. Maccoby, Joseph P. Johnson, and Russell M. Church, "Community Integration and the Social Control of Juvenile Delinquency," *Journal of Social Issues* XIV (June 1958), pp. 38–51.

45. Ibid., pp. 49, 51.

46. Jane Jacobs, *The Death and Life of Great American Cities.* New York: Vintage Books, 1961.

47. For a discussion of surveillance of public places in East European nations, see James Feron, "Everybody Watches Everybody in East Europe, But Nobody Really Notices," *The New York Times*, March 20, 1973, p. 14.

48. For example, a number of record stores in Boston and Cambridge have "midnight sales" from 11:00 P.M. to 3:00 A.M. on Friday and Saturday nights. These sales draw a number of young people to the streets at hours when the streets would otherwise be relatively deserted. This increases surveillance of certain public areas and may reduce the number of street crimes committed in well-traveled places.

49. Richard B. Hoffman, "Performance Measurements in Crime Control," *Journal of Research in Crime and Delinquency* VIII (July 1971), p. 174.

50. Gerald D. Suttles, *The Social Order of the Slum: Ethnicity and Territory in the Inner City.* Chicago: The University of Chicago Press, 1968, pp. 36–37.

51. One California school district has effectively eliminated vandalism to the school by providing surveillance of the grounds; families with mobile homes have been given rent-free space on the school grounds. Jeane Westin, "A Novel Way to Stop School Vandals," *Parade* magazine, January 20, 1974, pp. 12–14.

52. Jacobs, op. cit., p. 39.

53. Ibid., pp. 68–71.

54. "Ask the Globe," *Boston Globe*, May 17, 1973, p. 2.

55. Oscar Newman, *Architectural Design for Crime Prevention.* Washington, D.C.: United States Government Printing Office, 1973; Oscar Newman, *Defensible Space: Crime Prevention through Urban Design.* New York: Macmillan Publishing Co., Inc., 1972.

For a more general treatment of the impact of social environment on crime, see C. Ray Jeffery, *Crime Prevention through Environmental Design*. Beverly Hills: Sage Publications, 1971, especially pp. 214–225.

56. Newman, *Architectural Design for Crime Prevention*, p. ix, in foreword by Martin Danziger.
57. Ibid., p. 92.
58. Ibid., pp. 117–118.
59. Lee Rainwater, "Fear and the House-as-Haven in the Lower Class," in Gutman, op. cit., p. 312.
60. This point is also made by Jacobs, op. cit., p. 77.
61. Newman, *Architectural Design for Crime Prevention*, p. 59.
62. Ibid., p. xv.
63. Ibid., p. 14.
64. Ibid., p. 19.
65. Philip G. Zimbardo, "The Human Choice: Individuation, Reason, and Order versus Deindividuation, Impulse, and Chaos," in William J. Arnold and David Levine, editors, *1969 Nebraska Symposium on Motivation*. Lincoln: University of Nebraska Press, 1969, pp. 285–290.

7 Crime and Support for the Law*

S O C I A L scientists have often approached the question of support for the law as a problem in social stratification analysis. Pressure to pass certain laws and willingness to assist law-enforcement agents are often related to social status and political power. For example, Marx and Engels saw the law and support for the law in terms of class interests, arguing that the law is used by capitalists to oppress and exploit the proletariat.[1] They regarded the law as reflecting the dominant economic mode of production in a society. In his *Moral Indignation and Middle Class Psychology*, Svend Ranulf concluded from an examination of different cultures that the "disinterested tendency to inflict punishment" is concentrated in the lower middle class.[2] Not too different from the conclusions reached by Marx and Engels and by Ranulf is James Marshall's argument that middle-class values have long been instrumental in determining what sorts of social behavior will be called criminal.[3]

Aside from historical analysis, similar conclusions about the class basis of support for the law emerge from studies in which people have been asked to assign hypothetical punishments to various criminal acts. These studies have found that people from backgrounds of higher socioeconomic status assign *harsher* penalties for crimes than do people from lower status backgrounds.[4] They have also discovered that lower status subjects are more *flexible* in assigning penalties for specific acts than are higher status subjects; that is, they are more apt to vary the punishment with the type of victim and the background of the offender.[5]

* Portions of this chapter originally appeared in John E. Conklin, "Criminal Environment and Support for the Law," *Law and Society Review* VI (November 1971), pp. 247–265. Used with the permission of the Law and Society Association.

These studies reinforce the finding of Marx and Engels, Ranulf, and Marshall that the middle class supports the law with the greatest strength.

Support for the law can fruitfully be seen in a context different from the stratification system of a society. Support may be examined in the context of the criminal environment of a society, a city, or a neighborhood. How *support for the law* is related to *amount of crime that is perceived* in a community is not clear without empirical testing. We might guess that if crime is more noticeable to residents of a community, they will be more willing to support the law by reporting crime to the police, testifying in court, and generally assisting the agents of the criminal justice system. This argument is a specific instance of the more general idea that when people face a social problem that bothers them greatly, they will try to solve that problem. On the other hand, we might guess that if crime is salient in the social environment, it will be threatening. The threat may reduce support for the law because people fear reprisals from criminals they report to the police and testify against in court, or because people feel they cannot do anything about the frightening problem of crime. In such a situation, people may find the easiest solution is to turn over all responsibility for crime reduction to the police and minimize their own role in fighting crime. This will reduce public support for the law. In this chapter, we explore the actual relationship of perception of crime to support for the law.

Measuring Support for the Law

There are a number of ways to measure public support for the law. One way is to ask people directly about their agreement with existing laws. However, people may agree with existing laws simply because they already exist, thinking that there must be a good reason for laws to be as they are. Another way to measure support for the law is to ask people how they would decide certain problem cases and then compare their responses with the actual legal solutions for the same problems.[6]

We might also examine support for the law by observing people in situations in which their *active* support of the law might be appropriate. Personal intervention to prevent law-violating behavior might be an indicator of support for the law. However, active involvement in support of the law is difficult to measure because of problems in observing such behavior. One study of this sort involved staging crimes of shoplifting in stores and having observers note the reactions of witnesses, whether the witnesses even saw the "crime" and what actions they took if they did.[7] Witnesses were interviewed later. Only one-fourth of the witnesses even noticed the shoplifting, in spite of attempts by the "shoplifter" to draw attention to the act. One reason for lack of reporting crime is thus that crime often passes unobserved. On the other hand, people may intentionally fail to notice such acts in order to avoid involvement; they may keep their eyes to themselves or quickly turn away if they see something suspicious. Of those witnesses who did observe the shoplifting, only one-fourth reported the crime to a store employee. Those who reported the act said they did so because it was immoral or wrong. Those who failed to report the crime said that the offender left the store too quickly, that no employee was available to take a report, or that the store was too crowded. Nonreporters also felt that if they reported the offense they might face a countersuit, and they saw no personal advantage in reporting the crime.[8] Studies of this sort are relatively uncommon, although staged incidents can be used to test actual response to crime and willingness to support the law.[9]

Another way to test support for the law is the victimization survey, which we discussed in an earlier chapter. Such a survey asks people about actual crimes they have suffered. They can also be asked if they reported the crime to the police and their reasons for reporting or failing to report the crime. Crime reporting by the public is critical to the functioning of the criminal justice system, for most of the crimes of which the police learn are reported by private citizens.

People give a number of reasons for not reporting crime to the police.[10] Sometimes a victim knows the offender personally and does not want to get him into trouble with the law. Others fear reprisals by the offender, although a study of robbery victims and robbery offenders suggests that this fear is exaggerated.[11] Few offenders seek revenge against their victims, since they feel that reporting a crime is part of the game. However, the fear itself may reduce the number of crimes that are reported. People often fail to report crimes because they feel the police are ineffective and will be unable to do anything such as arrest an offender or recover the lost property. Also, some people are confused as to exactly how to report a crime, and others feel it will take too much time or cause too great an inconvenience. Studies in both India and Uganda have also discovered that inconvenience was a major reason for failure to report crime: in rural areas the distance between the victim's home and the nearest police station was too great to traverse just to report a crime, and there were no telephones with which to call the police.[12] The feeling that reporting a crime is too much trouble may be produced by actual experience with the criminal justice system. People who have to testify in court often find that their experience is wasteful of time, wearying, and pointless. Not only do delays in court deprive criminal defendants of a speedy trial, but they also make victims and witnesses less willing to report future crimes, meaning that offenders may have no trial instead of a speedy or even a slow one. One survey of public attitudes toward the police found that people do not call the police unless they are seriously wronged or have something to gain—for example, being able to collect on an insurance policy if a crime is reported to the police. The gain must outweigh the effort of calling the police and the psychological cost of getting involved with the legal system; otherwise, the call will not be made.[13]

Another common reason for failure to report crime is the opinion that "it's none of my business." Some people even adopt the attitude that "the process of apprehending and identifying a criminal [is] a sort of game in which both sides—the police and the offender—are given equal odds and from which they, as bystanders, must remain detached so as not to introduce a degree of unfairness by tipping the scales in one direction or another."[14] This attitude of noninvolvement acts as justification for failure to report crime, as well as for failure to assist a victim or a police officer in need of aid.

Unwillingness to support the law even to the extent of reporting an offense was found in a Gallup poll in which nearly half of a sample of college students said that they would not report such behavior as illegal hunting, underage drinking, and carrying a concealed weapon.[15] A more recent report concluded: "Students say they do not go to the police for many reasons—they have had unpleasant personal experiences with police harassment; have seen too many films and descriptions of police brutality; fear becoming enmeshed in the complex and time-consuming judicial system; and, in some cases, fear retaliation by the student criminals themselves."[16] The reasons the general public fails to report crime may thus be reinforced by a student subculture with an even greater distrust of the police, just as blacks are less trusting of the police than whites. Subcultural norms may inhibit victims and witnesses from calling the police. Norms may support personal revenge against the wrongdoer rather than bringing in an outside party to settle the dispute. Norms may define those who report crimes as "stool pigeons" or "rats." Such normative expectations make it difficult to formulate and carry out a consistent law-enforcement policy in a community. If the police follow popular demands, they may underenforce the law and fail to protect the residents of a community, but if they enforce the written law they may face bitter opposition and lack of cooperation from the residents of a community.[17]

Sometimes there will be an element of self-interest in the failure to report a crime. There is usually no complainant in crimes without victims such as homosexuality and drug addiction because all parties to the crime gain from the activity and none would gain from police intervention.[18] The desire to avoid public embarrassment often prevents a rape victim from reporting the crime to the police. Large corporations rarely report embezzlement and employee theft to the police, since executives believe that if such offenses were known to the public, corporate good will would decline and the public would lose faith in the honesty of the company and its employees. Instead, corporations usually absorb such losses as part of overhead or inventory shrinkage.

People may not report a crime to the police because they feel that the law metes out too severe a penalty or because they think that a particular type of behavior should not be illegal. A belief that the criminal justice system is unjust and discriminatory may also cause a reluctance to report a crime; for example, the experience of blacks with the police, the courts, and the prisons creates an unwillingness to report crime and testify in court among blacks. If specific laws are regarded as unfair or if the penalty for violation of a particular law is thought too harsh, support for the law may be weak. For example, in early nineteenth-century Great Britain, more than two hundred criminal offenses could be punished by the death penalty. Severe penalties for seemingly trivial acts meant that juries often acquitted defendants who were clearly guilty rather than send them to the gallows.[19] Not only were fewer penalties meted out because of the stringency of the laws, but many crimes for which the death penalty might have been used were probably not even reported. Another example of this process occurred in Connecticut in the 1950's. After a more severe penalty (suspension of driver's license) was imposed for speeding violations, there was a rise in the proportion of defendants charged with such violations who were acquitted.[20] Again this suggests that harsh penalties may reduce willingness to apply the full measure of the law.

All these reasons for not reporting crime to the police suggest that a substantial amount of *social disorganization* exists regarding the enforcement of the law. People feel that theft is a crime against the person who loses property, not an offense against the state. However, the criminal law sees crime as an offense against the state, involving a victim who suffers a wrong and makes a complaint, but with primary harm being done to the society as a whole. Because victims want their property back, they are sometimes willing to drop charges in return for having their property restored. This weakens the criminal justice system, since individuals place their personal welfare over the welfare of the society and thus undermine the law that is supposed to protect the entire society.[21]

There are, then, a variety of ways to measure support for the law. Because of difficulties of observation studies, we did not try to measure reporting behavior or intervention in crimes in such a direct way in Port City and Belleville. Victimization surveys are time-consuming to administer and require large samples in order to produce a significant number of victims who have even had the opportunity to report a crime. We did ask about actual victimization and crime reporting in the two Boston-area communities, but too few residents had been victimized in recent years to form any solid conclusions.

We first asked people about their attitudes toward violation of the criminal law in general. They were then asked whether they thought there should be a law against thirteen specific types of behavior (all of which were in fact illegal) and whether they would report each type of behavior to the police if they became aware of it. Our measures of support for the law thus rely on verbalized attitudes about the law and how people think they would react to violations of the law. These measures probably overestimate the extent to which people would report a crime to the police if they were faced with a real chance to do so. However, this method makes it possible to gather data for all respondents, whereas collecting data only on actual reporting experiences would have limited us to those who had been victimized. Also, as we shall see later, *expressed* willingness to report crime has an important effect on the way that other people in the community form their attitudes toward crime.

Willingness to Report Crime in Port City and Belleville

The residents of the two communities were asked whether they thought it would be all right for a person to break the law under some conditions. People in Port City were considerably more opposed to ever violating the law than were the Belleville residents. However, this difference was due to a difference in authoritarianism of the residents of the two communities.[22] In both Port City and Belleville, those who were more authoritarian were more apt to say that one should *never* break the law; this is consistent with the fact that *authoritarian submission* to power is one dimension of the authoritarianism scale. If we compare residents of each community who were high on the authoritarian scale, there is no difference in response to the question of whether violation of the law is ever justified. Similarly, if those of medium authoritarianism are compared, and if those of low authoritarianism are compared, there are no differences between communities in response to this question. In other words, whether or not a respondent thought that the law could ever be broken with impunity was a function of his authoritarianism rather than a function of his attitude toward the law per se.

Residents of each community were asked about thirteen offenses: rape, manslaughter, robbery, auto theft, murder (two different cases), aggravated assault, larceny, burglary, embezzlement, marijuana use, trespass during a student protest, and gambling. Statements were read to respondents describing each type of behavior (see Appendix B, Table B-5). Subjects were then asked for each crime: "In your opinion, should there be a law to punish this person [the perpetrator of the act]?" People were quite unanimous in their opinions that laws should exist to punish offenses now included in the FBI crime index, as well as the crime of manslaughter (see the first two columns of Table B-5, Appendix B). This consensus probably reflects the obvious harm to person and property that results from such offenses. In fact, this was a major reason for the inclusion of these crimes in the FBI crime index.[23] Another reason for consensus is the *fait accompli* effect, the fact that the mere existence of laws influences the formation of social norms; the law serves a didactic function in teaching people to condemn what the law condemns.[24] Making an activity illegal may over time generate informal norms prohibiting such behavior, although the law will be more easily enforced and more often adhered to if it is consistent with informal social norms when it is passed.

Although nearly all residents of Port City and Belleville condemned the FBI index crimes, they differed on other offenses. There was near unanimity on the point that embezzlement should be a crime, but more Belleville residents than Port City residents felt that way. Although the difference is small, the direction is opposite to what would be suggested by class interests, if one assumes that Belleville residents would be more likely to work at a job at which they could embezzle money than would the working-class residents of Port City. However, the finding is consistent with the conclusion we discussed earlier in this chapter that the demand for punishment is more widespread among the middle class than among the working class.

About one-quarter of each sample felt that there should be no law to prohibit the use of marijuana, but more residents of Belleville felt this way. About a third of each sample—more in Port City than in Belleville—thought that there should be no law to punish a college student who takes over a building during a protest. Considerably less than half of each sample felt that the law should punish those who took gambling bets; significantly more Port City residents disapproved of the laws against gambling. There are thus differences between residents of the two areas in their support for existing laws, laws which do not involve behavior classified as serious by the FBI. On a number of these offenses there is less than full agreement that the law should prohibit behavior that is currently illegal.

Asking people whether the law should punish behavior which most people know is already illegal may not go far enough in measuring public support for the law. Respondents were therefore asked another question about each of the thirteen crimes: "If you knew someone had done this thing, would you report it to the police?" (Answers to this question appear in the third and fifth columns of Table B-5, Appendix B.) Probably *fewer* subjects would actually report a crime to the police if faced with the real choice of doing so than *said* that they would report the crime. On the other hand, few who stated that they would *not* report the offense would *actually* report it if they knew about it. In other words, the percentage expressing willingness to report crimes to the police probably represents the *maximum* number who would *actually* report the crime if faced with the real situation.

While there was agreement between samples on the desirability of laws to prohibit and punish many of the crimes, there was less agreement about whether or not one should *report* such behavior to the police. Although residents of both communities thought that the law should punish people for committing FBI index crimes, for *all* such crimes the residents of the high crime-rate community were *less* willing to call the police. For the eight index offenses, the mean percentage of Port City residents expressing a willingness to report the crime was 75 per cent, compared to 86 per cent for the Belleville residents. In other words, substantially more residents of the low crime-rate area said that they would report index crimes to the police. The residents of Belleville were also more willing to call the police on three crimes (manslaughter, embezzlement, and gambling), about as willing to call on one offense (trespass—protest), and less willing to report one other (marijuana use).[25]

The number of crimes a person said he would report was used as an index of his willingness to support the law. The difference between communities was statistically significant, with Port City residents willing to report fewer crimes than Belleville residents. On the average, the urban residents said they would report one less crime than the suburban residents. In neither community was the number of crimes a person was willing to report related to authoritarianism, indicating that using this index of support for the law avoids the problem faced earlier in using a global measure of approving or disapproving of violation of the law under any circumstances.

Not only does the difference between residents of each community on willingness to report crime to the police hold up when authoritarianism is controlled, but it also obtains when various social background characteristics are used as controls. One variable that we might expect to be related to willingness to report crime is a person's education; that is, a more educated person might be more apt to tell an interviewer that he would report crime. The mean numbers of crimes that respondents said they would report to the police, by level of education, are:

	Belleville	Port City
Less than high school	8.88 (16)	8.23 (66)
Completed high school	9.62 (39)	8.11 (35)
Some college	9.46 (82)	9.22 (27)

Comparing residents of each community with the same amount of education we find that at all levels those who live in Port City are less willing to report crime than those who live in Belleville, although the difference is smaller at the higher and the lower educational levels than at the "completed high school" level. *Within* each sample, there is no clear tendency for the more educated to say that they would report more crime. The college-educated were more willing to report crime than those with less than a high school education in each community, but there was no linear increase in willingness to report crime with amounts of education in either sample. Willingness to report crime to the police does not seem to be a function of a respondent's education. Similarly, the data in Table B-6 of Appendix B suggest that the difference between Port City and Belleville in willingness to report crime still exists after people of similar background characteristics in the two communities are compared, although in some instances the difference between communities is diminished. As with the amount of crime perceived in the community, willingness to report crime is largely unaffected by such characteristics as sex, age, ethnic group, religion, education, income, prestige of occupation, self-designated class, and father's occupation.

While there is a substantial difference between the residents of the two communities in support for the law (as measured by number of crimes they are willing to report to the police), there is no difference in the *relative seriousness* with which residents of the two communities view the different offenses. When crimes are ranked by the percentage of each sample willing to report the crime to the police (see the fourth and sixth columns of Table B-5, Appendix B), there is near-perfect agreement between the two samples on the relative ranking of the various crimes.[26] This is consistent with other research on the relative seriousness of different offenses.[27] However, to judge the comparative seriousness of crimes, these other studies used people from middle-class backgrounds; we have shown that even for respondents from quite different social backgrounds and from communities with quite different criminal environments, the ranking of offenses by seriousness is much the same.

The thirteen crimes were also ranked by seriousness using the maximum legally allowable penalty under Massachusetts law (see the last column of Table B-5, Appendix B). Agreement on the relative seriousness of the crimes between the two communities is greater than agreement between the relative ranking of crimes in either community and the ranking by maximum allowable penalty under the law.[28] However, there is nevertheless substantial agreement between the respondents in each community and the law in the ranking of crimes by seriousness.[29]

Another question we asked people was what they thought their response would be to observing a woman being attacked by a man with a knife outside their home, a situation meant to resemble the Kitty Genovese murder in New York City in 1964 (see Chapter 9). In that case, thirty-eight witnesses watched a woman stabbed to death outside their apartments. In our study, we did not think that verbalized responses of what action people would take in such an emergency would closely reflect how they would actually behave, but their responses do provide additional information on the extent to which they are willing to report such a crime to the police. In Port City, 62 per cent of the residents said that they would call the police if they witnessed such an attack, and in Belleville 75 per cent said that they would call the police. This difference is consistent with our finding that willingness to support the law by reporting crime to the police is less widespread in Port City than in Belleville. A few years before our survey, a young man was beaten to death in Port City by a gang while an estimated three hundred people watched. No one called the police or took any direct action to protect the victim. Although the bystanders might have offered aid if the victim had been a woman—because of different expectations about how men and women should be able to defend themselves—this event does suggest that the Port City respondents overstated their willingness to report an observed crime to the police. Still, it is important that they were less likely to verbalize a willingness to call the police than were the Belleville residents; whether similar differences would exist between the two samples in actual responses to observed crimes is unclear.

In summary, the community in which people perceived more crime (Port City) was also the community in which there was less support for the law, as measured by willingness to report a crime to the police. For the two communities we studied, there was thus an inverse relationship between perception of crime and support for the law: *the more salient crime was, the less support there was for the law.*

Perception of Crime and Support for the Law

The inverse relationship that exists between criminal environment and support for the law at the community level must also be examined for residents who live in each community. To do this, a score ranging from 0 to 4 was calculated for each person, this score being a measure of the number of items on which he perceived a high rate of crime. A score of 4 was given if a respondent ranked high on the overall perception of crime scale, felt that crime was either the first or second most important social problem of the seven problems mentioned, thought that the local crime of greatest importance was a "serious" crime, and believed that people who committed crimes in the community also lived there. A score of 0 was assigned if a respondent perceived little crime or little threat on all these items.

The following shows the average number of crimes a person was willing to report to the police, for those who perceived varying amounts of crime: [30]

Number of items indicating a high perception of crime	Belleville	Port City
Low perception of crime (0 or 1 item)	9.98 (41)	9.34 (32)
Medium perception of crime (2 items)	9.62 (47)	9.30 (43)
High perception of crime (3 or 4 items)	9.50 (12)	8.86 (22)
Total	9.75 (100)	9.22 (97)

These data point to slight inverse relationships between perception of crime and support for the law in each community. Although the relationships were not statistically significant in either sample, they were in the expected direction: in both Belleville and Port City, *those who perceived more crime were somewhat less inclined to report crimes to the police*.[31] As was true at the community level, so at the individual level was support for the law inversely related to perception of crime.

This inverse relationship between perception of crime and willingness to report crime to the police can be explained in various ways. First of all, *the threat of crime may cause unwillingness to report crime*. Fear of crime may lead people to retreat from responsibility to help prevent crime, even to the point of being unwilling to report crime to the police. The presence of the threat of crime, in conjunction with the existence of an established institution to deal with crime (the police), makes it possible for people who live in a high crime-rate area to say that the police rather than the public should prevent crime, that such actions are too risky for private citizens to undertake.

Residents of Port City and Belleville responded to the following statement: "Preventing crime is the job of police, not the job of the average citizen." Two of five (40 per cent) of the Port City residents and fewer than one in five (18 per cent) of the Belleville residents agreed with this statement, a statistically significant difference. The greater tendency to assign crime-prevention duties to the police in the high crime area probably arises in part from the threat that crime presents to residents of that community. This tendency to hold the police responsible for crime prevention, even when people refuse to report crimes to the police, was also found in a study of police and the public in Uganda: "Although the people are dubious about the crime-detecting skills of law enforcement officers, they recognize their role as the formal barrier between themselves and the numerous forms of personal violence that threaten their lives."[32] Another example of the people turning to the police when crime presents a great threat occurred after a series of forty or fifty burglaries in a working-class community of Chicago in 1888. Although residents spoke of vigilance committees and better security measures, they also demanded that

167

the police spend less time on morality offenses and more time on serious crimes that threatened community stability; they demanded that the police "make the community riotproof and crimeproof."[33] More recent surveys have found that pro-police sentiments decline with increased anxiety about crime, suggesting that there may be unwillingness to assist the police at the same time that there is a great reliance on the police to solve the crime problem.[34] Those who most fear crime dislike the police most and also rely most on the police to fight crime.

Because fear of victimization is greatest in high crime areas, those places where surveillance of the streets most needs to be reinforced by willingness to report crime to the police are just the areas where such support is least likely to occur. In fact, surveillance in such high crime areas may even work against the efforts of law-enforcement agents. For example, in a Brooklyn neighborhood which is controlled by organized crime: "A raid on organization activities or even surveillance of its members is virtually impossible because the neighborhood residents quickly identify any 'stranger,' make his presence known, and often hasten his exit from the area."[35]

The collapse of informal social controls in a community sometimes increases the demand for action by institutional and formal control agents such as the police.[36] For example, parents who learn of the delinquent acts of their own or others' children often react by blaming the police for their inability to prevent such behavior, rather than looking to themselves as a possible cause of the youths' actions. In his study of community reaction to adolescent drug use in a small town, Poveda found that a get-tough stance was adopted at a City Council meeting; the police were blamed for their ineffectiveness in combating drug use, although it seems there was little they could have done.[37] Also, the parents of some of the twenty-seven young men killed in Houston by a homosexual sadist blamed the police, saying they should have found their runaway sons. The police responded that they lacked the resources to find all runaways, but the parents found it easier to blame the breakdown of formal controls than the breakdown of informal controls often exercised by parents over their children.[38]

Failure to report crime to the police or help the police apprehend suspects is not inconsistent with reliance on the police to fight the crime problem, since people often are able to justify their lack of active support for the police when faced with the need to act.[39] An example of public demand for police action but unwillingness to help the police in their fight against crime occurred following the Jack the Ripper murders in London. An indignant public blamed the police and the government for their failure to protect their security. Some merchants complained that police ineffectiveness in arresting the murderer kept people off the streets and thus decreased their volume of business. However, the indignant public was not always willing to assist the police in their efforts to arrest Jack the Ripper. For instance, a crowd of hundreds gathered around a constable who was trying to arrest a man thought by the crowd to be the murderer. A newspaper later reported, "Men hooted the prisoner and women shrieked at him, but none offered to help the unfortunate constable who was being liberally kicked, beyond the advice to 'Catch hold of his legs.' "[40]

Furstenberg and Wellford argue that the police themselves contribute to this excessive reliance on them for reducing crime, by their emphasis on crime statistics—especially the clearance rate —as the major indices of police effectiveness:

Focusing on crime rates to measure effectiveness—and thereby persuading the public that the police hold the key to solving the crime problem—may have the short-term advantages of obtaining larger budgets and gaining greater public support for strict enforcement. Eventually, however, public confidence in the police is likely to be eroded. People may come to hold the police partly responsible for the level of crime in the community, and the police may, in turn, feel unappreciated and resent the public's loss of faith in them.[41]

If crime is salient, people will put pressure on the police. Community groups may demand from the mayor more police protection in their area. The political power and organization of a community will thus affect the level of police protection it receives. Although those who feel that crime is a great threat will probably favor strongest police actions to prevent crime, it is not certain that they will also have the power to implement their demands. In fact, they may be the people with the poorest communications with local police, since their denial of civilian responsibility for crime prevention and their unwillingness to report crime to the police suggest that police-community relations in their high crime-rate areas will not be very good.

Because they are public servants, the police are not in a position to make their services contingent on public cooperation and support. In New York City, a newly appointed park administrator publicly stated that he refused to take all responsibility for the upkeep of the city's parks. He insisted that people become involved in the prevention of vandalism in parks, stating, "We will insist—no, we will demand—that the public stop complaining and start helping."[42] He threatened to withdraw maintenance men and services from the parks unless local residents took a more active role in maintaining recreational facilities. His approach was somewhat unique, in that the public is accustomed to paying taxes and then expecting that appropriate agencies will take measures to stop crime. The park administrator's suggestions met with anger and criticism from the public.[43] He had demanded that people provide the input necessary for his agency to carry out its assigned function. A police department may ask for better cooperation from the public, but none has yet dared withdraw its men and services until it receives what it feels is adequate public support. The morale of the police undoubtedly suffers when they know that people will not even report a crime to them, but will criticize them vehemently for failing to prevent crime.

So far we have examined the possibility that perception of crime may lead to lack of citizen support for the law, as well as to reliance on law-enforcement agents for reduction of crime rates. A second possible explanation for the inverse relationship between criminal environment and support for the law is that *lack of support for the law may indirectly cause changes in the perception of crime.* Lack of support for the law may increase the actual amount of crime in a community by reducing informal social controls over potential criminals and by weakening formal controls over them; public perception of crime may then rise as a result of actual increases in crime rates.

This explanation is implicit in Sutherland and Cressey's "theory of differential association," with failure to punish, report, or otherwise sanction criminal behavior constituting a "definition favorable to violation of the law."[44] An increase in definitions favorable to violation of the law over definitions unfavorable to violation of the law will lead to higher rates of crime and delinquency. To the extent that people are aware of this rise in crime rates, their perceptions of crime will also change. Durkheim formulates a special case of Sutherland and Cressey's idea, stating that by punishing certain types of behavior, community sentiments about acceptable social behavior are transmitted to members of the community, thereby affecting the chance that they will engage in such deviant behavior.[45] The theories of Durkheim and of Sutherland and Cressey suggest that lack of support for the law will produce a rise in criminal behavior, since the absence of negative sanctions will be interpreted as a definition favorable to violation of the law.

Another way to state this point is to distinguish *proscriptive* norms from *prescriptive* norms.[46] A proscriptive norm is an expectation that those who occupy certain roles will avoid, abstain from, or reject a certain type of behavior; it is a *thou shalt not* norm that states a negative goal. A prescriptive norm is an expectation that a person will act in a particular manner in a given situation; it is a *thou shalt* norm which posits an affirmative goal. Although communities may hold norms which prescribe or support criminal behavior, probably community *tolerance* for crime is more common than outright support for such behavior. People tolerate crime if they fail to report crime to the police. This tolerance may be transmitted from generation to generation in a community, even if the characteristics of community residents change over time.[47] Although norms that prescribe criminal behavior are probably less common than norms which tolerate such offenses, even the acceptance of such behavior has a significant impact. As Ramsey Clark has said, "By accepting the unacceptable—minor crimes—we invite worse. Young people sense this and they are not motivated toward decency. To succeed with one crime may well encourage another. Indifference to crime causes its repetition." [48]

Even without norms that prescribe criminal behavior, crime still may be stimulated by the absence of norms that proscribe

171

illegal actions. If there are no norms that say that certain acts are wrong or if there are no norms that say that such offenses should be reported to the police, social toleration of crime may generate more crime. There may be no *pre*scriptive norm to call the police, but there may also be no *pro*scriptive norm that failure to call the police is wrong. Crime may not be actively supported, but if it is not actively opposed the result may be the same. A number of offenders do not rationally plan their crimes, but many do consider the risk they run of being caught.[49] If they know that a particular community is an easy mark because no one there will report crime to the police, they will be more apt to commit a crime there than in a community where residents are more active in their support of the law.

Direct evidence that criminals are deterred by the willingness of residents to report crime is lacking. Indirect suggestion that awareness of the risk of getting caught may influence behavior comes from a study that found that offenders were less inclined than nonoffenders to feel that lawbreakers are almost always caught. If this feeling that there was a low risk of being apprehended preceded the criminal behavior, it might be the case that such behavior is more common where the risk is low, or is perceived to be low.[50] The possibility that offenders have some idea of the relative risks they face in different communities was suggested as long ago as 1892, when the Chief of Police of Omaha, Nebraska, said, "[T]he resident districts of Omaha usually have no police protection, and are left to the mercy of tramps, sneak thieves, burglars, house-breakers, veranda climbers, and other criminals, who, besides our local law breakers, are *always well informed as to the localities that have no police protection.*"[51] In this author's study of robbery in Boston, one heroin addict said that he committed burglaries to support his habit, but never committed such crimes in the neighborhood in which he lived because the local citizens are highly intolerant of crime and would personally intervene to prevent a burglary.

Another example of public support for the law affecting the crime problem comes from a study of prostitution. Brothels are often started in rundown areas of the city because the poor residents of those communities are less apt to call the police or have political influence than the residents of wealthier areas.[52] Business districts were preferred for the establishment of brothels because they had few residents during the night, when the houses were busiest. This suggests that if there is little surveillance of public places, or if those who would watch the streets are unwilling to call the police or unable to exert political power, people who run houses of prostitution will see those areas as good locations to set up business. The presence of brothels may then bring other crimes such as robberies and assaults to the neighborhood. The higher crime rates and the presence of houses of prostitution could be avoided if residents of the area were more actively involved in supporting the law and more willing to exercise informal social controls themselves.

No criminals were interviewed to determine how aware they were of the chance of being reported to the police in Port City or Belleville. It is not even clear how we would find a representative sample of offenders to question about this, since those who committed offenses where they correctly thought the crime would not be reported would not be available for questioning. We did ask our respondents in each community if they thought that their neighbors would report most crimes to the police if they knew about them. In Belleville, 78 per cent said yes to this question, but in Port City only 47 per cent responded affirmatively. Not only did the residents of the high crime area say that they would be less willing to report crimes to the police, but they also thought that their neighbors would not be too willing to do so either. If a sample of the residents of Port City is aware of community unwillingness to support the law by calling the police, probably potential criminals in the area—and probably some potential criminals who live elsewhere—will also be aware of the state of social disorganization regarding support for the law in that area. To the extent that such a consideration affects the selection of a criminal's target, residents of Port City contribute to even higher crime rates by failing to report crimes to the police.

So far we have looked at the link between support for the law and perception of crime in terms of each as cause and the other as effect. Another way to explain the inverse relationship between the two is to look at *variables which are related to each in a way that would produce such a negative relationship.*[53] One such variable might be the concept of *trouble* discussed by Walter B. Miller. Trouble as a focal concern of lower-class culture implies a shallow commitment to legal norms and compliance with the law primarily to avoid "the complicating consequences of the action."[54] Where such a focal concern exists, restraints to avoid law-violating behavior will be weak and the probability of criminal behavior great. Such increased criminal activity will in turn affect public perception of crime. Not only will concern with trouble affect the criminal environment in this way, but it can also affect support for the law. In a subculture where trouble is a focal concern, individuals are apt to feel that *any* involvement with the law should be avoided as complicating and troublesome. People will feel that reporting crime may cause trouble in the form of reprisals, that assisting the police may cause trouble in the sense of hostile reactions from friends and neighbors, and that testifying in court may cause trouble in the shape of difficult questions posed by lawyers and judges. This concern can therefore reduce support for the law at the same time that it increases the actual and perceived amounts of crime in the community. The diagram shows that a variable such as trouble which decreases (−) support for the law and increases (+) perception of crime will create or contribute to an inverse relationship between support for the law and perception of crime.

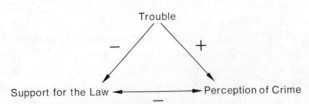

Probably all three of the explanations of the inverse relationship between support for the law and perception of crime have some merit. It is plausible that if crime is perceived as a threat, people may assign full responsibility for preventing crime to the police but deny their own role in crime prevention. It is equally likely, and not inconsistent with this explanation, that unwillingness to support the law may lead to more crime in the community and thus increase residents' perceptions of crime in the area. A number of underlying variables might also explain the inverse relationship because they are related in opposite ways to support for the law and perception of crime.

Support for the Police

So far we have examined support for the law in terms of expressions of willingness to report crime to the police. We now look at attitudes toward the local police held by residents of Port City and Belleville. In general, the residents of Port City are less satisfied with the local police than those who live in Belleville. Only 3 per cent of the suburban residents expressed dissatisfaction with the police, but 32 per cent of the Port City residents expressed dissatisfaction. Also, 82 per cent of the Port City residents felt that more policemen were needed in their community, but only 40 per cent of the Belleville residents felt that way.

Dissatisfaction with the local police was thus higher in the community with the higher crime rate. Findings in other studies show that blacks are more dissatisfied than whites with the police. This may be partially accounted for by differences in crime rates in the communities in which blacks and whites live, with blacks more likely to live in high crime areas and thus more apt to blame the police for their failure to control crime.[55] On the other hand, both in the Port City-Belleville comparison and in the black-white comparison, we must recognize that complaints about the police may be valid, based on personal experiences with the police. However, the police may feel that people in high crime areas tolerate crime by their failure to report crime and do not really want effective law enforcement in their community. Such a view could lead to lack of police attention to the high crime communities, thereby causing legitimate complaints about police inadequacy.

One study found that business managers and store owners in high crime areas were generally less favorably disposed toward the police than those who worked in low crime areas.[56] Similarly, in communities near the welfare hotels in New York City, the police

175

were called upon to reduce crime. When they did not do so immediately, there were loud complaints that the police were ineffective and corrupt. There were reports that the police were allowing or even participating in drug sales. The police denied these charges, but it seems clear that public dissatisfaction with the police grew as a result of their ineffectiveness in controlling the crimes committed by welfare hotel residents.[57]

There was no relationship in either Port City or Belleville between the number of crimes a subject said he would report to the police and his satisfaction with the police. This suggests that our index of willingness to report crime measures support for the laws themselves rather than satisfaction with the police to whom the crime would be reported; this is substantiated by other research as well.[58] In Port City, people who were satisfied with local police perceived significantly less crime in the community than those who were dissatisfied with the police; this relationship did not emerge in Belleville. Dissatisfaction with the police and perception of crime are thus only related to each other in the high crime-rate community, again showing the threshold effect that *relationships* between variables exist in the high crime area but not in the low crime area.

Two surveys have found that victims and nonvictims do not differ in their sentiments toward the police.[59] However, another study concluded that victims were less likely than nonvictims to support the police, in terms of being willing to give them the right to stop and frisk citizens.[60] Fear of crime was related to support for increased police power only among those who felt an attack on the street was highly likely. Victims were more apt than nonvictims to favor greater protection of civil liberties by providing a civilian review board to check police behavior and by furnishing suspects who were being interrogated by the police with a lawyer. Those who favored greater police power were more opposed to increased protection of civil liberties.

Residents of Port City and Belleville were asked if they thought that people helped the police as much as they should. The difference between samples is negligible, but it is interesting that three-fourths of each sample—76 per cent in Belleville and 74 per cent in Port City—felt that the public did *not* help the police as much as they should.[61] What is puzzling is that as many residents of the high crime-rate area as in the low crime-rate area thought that people did not help enough, even though our data show that the Port City residents were less willing to help the police by reporting crime than were the Belleville residents.

Respondents were asked whether they would favor institutionalizing an obligation to assist the police: "A policeman who is arresting a criminal asks a bystander for help. Should there be a law to punish this bystander if he refuses to help?" About the same proportion of each sample—60 per cent in Belleville and 59 per cent in Port City—said that there should *not* be a law to compel citizens to help the police in such a situation. Thus, three-quarters of each sample said that the public did not help the police enough, but three-fifths would not favor a law to require such assistance. Interestingly, there was no relationship between these two questions in either sample. In other words, a person's view of whether or not the public neglects to help the police is unrelated to his view of whether the law should require people to help the police. Those who feel the public is negligent are no more likely to call for a law to require citizen aid to the police than are those who feel the public helps the police enough.

Although equal proportions of each sample thought that others did not aid the police enough and that people should not be compelled by law to do so, the residents of Port City were more apt to rely on the police to prevent crime in their community. We have already seen that they were more likely than Belleville residents to say that crime prevention is a job for the police, not the average citizen. They were also more likely to agree that "policemen are the most important protectors of law and order in the community"; 86 per cent of the Port City sample and 73 per cent of the Belleville sample agreed with this item. Responses to this statement are highly correlated with responses to the statement that crime prevention is a job for the police rather than the public.

James Q. Wilson has argued that in large cities the officer patrols a neighborhood and is in a position to initiate complaints, engaging in a *proactive* stance with regard to crime.[62] The officer may interfere with and regulate the conduct of residents of the community, leading to a belief that the police are invaders of

177

privacy or even an army of occupation. In suburbs and small towns, the police are more often engaged in a *reactive* response to crime, being called to the scene of a crime by people who see them as protectors of their privacy. Wilson suggests that the police in large cities are apt to be regarded as regulators of conduct, as control agents whose domain of interest includes all the public life of the community. If this description is accurate, it helps explain why police behavior creates dissatisfaction. Dissatisfaction with the police may develop from the feeling that the police manage to control many aspects of the community's life, but fail to control that aspect which is of greatest concern—crime.

Prior to the massive urbanization of our society, people were probably more willing to assist the police in the enforcement of the law. As cities grew and strangers became a part of daily life, there developed what Karl Llewellyn has called "that attitude of an age of specialization: let the cop do the dirty work; what else are we paying him for?"[63] With perceptions of threatening crime rates, people turn to the police for help. In doing so, they often deny their own responsibility in the enforcement of the law, even to the point of being unwilling to report a crime to the police. This diminishes social control over potential criminals and may increase crime in a community if criminals consider the risk of apprehension prior to a crime and are aware that the chance they will be reported to the police is less in some communities than in others.

Communities can maintain criminogenic atmospheres by approving or tolerating criminal behavior. If this approval does not take the form of "thou shalt commit a crime," it may at least be present as an absence of a "thou shalt not commit a crime" norm. This is related to public unwillingness to report crime to the police and lack of support for the agents of law enforcement. Lack of such support can lead to higher crime rates, thus increasing public perception of crime and beginning again the cycle of reduced support for the law.

Footnotes

1. Karl Marx and Friedrich Engels, *The German Ideology*. New York: International Publishers, 1947.

2. Svend Ranulf, *Moral Indignation and Middle Class Psychology*. New York: Schocken Books, 1938, 1964.
3. James Marshall, *Intention in Law and Society*. New York: Funk and Wagnalls, 1968.
4. See G. M. Gilbert, "Crime and Punishment: An Exploratory Comparison of Public, Criminal and Penological Attitudes," *Mental Hygiene* XLII (October 1958), pp. 550–557; Arnold M. Rose and Arthur E. Prell, "Does the Punishment Fit the Crime? A Study in Social Valuation," *American Journal of Sociology* LXI (November 1955), pp. 247–259; Erwin O. Smigel, "Public Attitudes toward Stealing as Related to the Size of the Victim Organization," *American Sociological Review* XXI (June 1956), pp. 320–327; and Berl Kutschinsky, "Knowledge and Attitudes Regarding Legal Phenomena in Denmark," in Nils Christie, editor, *Scandinavian Studies in Criminology, Volume 2: Aspects of Social Control in Welfare States*. London: Tavistock Publications, 1968, pp. 125–160.
5. Rose and Prell, op. cit., p. 257; Smigel, op. cit., p. 322; and Douglas W. Knight, "Punishment Selection as a Function of Biographical Information," *Journal of Criminal Law, Criminology and Police Science* LVI (September 1965), pp. 325–327.
6. One attempt to do this is a study of public attitudes toward laws concerning parent-child relations. See Julius Cohen, Reginald A. H. Robson, and Alan Bates, *Parental Authority: The Community and the Law*. New Brunswick, N.J.: Rutgers University Press, 1958. The studies by Gilbert, Rose and Prell, and Kutschinsky cited in footnote 4 also employed variations on this method of testing attitudes toward the law or toward problem cases and then contrasting those attitudes with actual laws.
7. Donald P. Hartmann, Donna M. Gelfand, Brent Page, and Patrice Walder, "Rates of Bystander Observation and Reporting of Contrived Shoplifting Incidents," *Criminology* X (November 1972), pp. 247–267.
8. Hartmann et al., op. cit., also found that men reported shoplifting more than women. They suggest that this may be because women are more tolerant of shoplifting than men, but since other studies also show that women report crimes less than men, more factors are probably operating than just attitudes toward this one crime. Possibly socialization in passivity makes women, on the average, less likely to take the affirmative action of actually reporting an observed crime. Also, since more men than women hold jobs outside the home, they may be more threatened by such attacks on property.
9. We shall see examples of this method of research when we examine bystander response to crime in Chapter 9.
10. Most of the conclusions here are drawn from the national victim-

ization survey reported in Philip H. Ennis, Field Surveys II of the President's Commission on Law Enforcement and Administration of Justice, *Criminal Victimization in the United States: A Report of a National Survey*. Washington, D.C.: United States Government Printing Office, 1967. However, a study of a small Ohio town with a negligible crime rate found that only half of the crimes reported to interviewers were also reported to the police. Petty offenses often were not reported, but more serious ones usually were. See Simon Dinitz, "Progress, Crime, and the Folk Ethic: Portrait of a Small Town," *Criminology* XI (May 1973), pp. 3–21.

11. John E. Conklin, *Robbery and the Criminal Justice System*. Philadelphia: J. B. Lippincott Company, 1972, pp. 121–122.

12. Marshall B. Clinard and Daniel J. Abbott, *Crime in Developing Countries: A Comparative Perspective*. New York: John Wiley & Sons, 1973, pp. 23–24.

13. Albert J. Reiss, Jr., Field Surveys III, Part 1, of the President's Commission on Law Enforcement and Administration of Justice, *Studies in Crime and Law Enforcement in Major Metropolitan Areas*. Washington, D.C.: United States Government Printing Office, 1967, p. 69.

14. Herman Goldstein, "Citizen Cooperation: The Perspective of the Police," in James M. Ratcliffe, editor, *The Good Samaritan and the Law*. Garden City, N.Y.: Doubleday & Company, Inc., 1966, p. 205.

15. Cited in David Gottlieb and Charles E. Ramsey, *The American Adolescent*. Homewood, Ill.: The Dorsey Press, Inc., 1964, p. 109.

16. David A. Andelman, "Crime on the Campus Spreading Fear," *The New York Times*, April 19, 1971, pp. 39, 44.

17. Goldstein, op. cit., pp. 202–203.

18. Edwin M. Schur, *Crimes without Victims: Deviant Behavior and Public Policy*. Englewood Cliffs, N.J.: Prentice-Hall, Inc., 1965.

19. Harry Kalven, Jr., and Hans Zeisel, *The American Jury*. Boston: Little, Brown and Company, 1966, pp. 310–311.

20. Donald T. Campbell and H. Laurence Ross, "The Connecticut Crackdown on Speeding: Time-Series Data in Quasi-Experimental Analysis," in Lawrence M. Friedman and Stewart Macaulay, editors, *Law and the Behavioral Sciences*. Indianapolis: The Bobbs-Merrill Company, Inc., 1969, p. 391.

21. Edwin H. Sutherland, *The Professional Thief*. Chicago: The University of Chicago Press, 1937, pp. 122–126.

22. An authoritarianism scale was formed by summing responses to five items developed in T. W. Adorno, Else Frenkel-Brunswik, Daniel J. Levinson, and R. Nevitt Sanford, *The Authoritarian Personality*. New York: Harper and Row, Publishers, 1950. The

items, which were significantly intercorrelated in our samples, were: (a) Human nature being what it is, there will always be war and conflict. (b) He is, indeed, contemptible who does not feel an undying love, gratitude, and respect for his parents. (c) Every person should have a deep faith in some supernatural force higher than himself to which he gives total allegiance and whose decisions he does not question. (d) Sex crimes, such as rape and attacks on children, deserve more than mere imprisonment; such criminals ought to be publicly whipped. (e) Obedience and respect for authority are the most important virtues children should learn.

23. An anthropological study also found that there was consensus across cultures in condemning certain types of behavior, even where social norms were not codified and institutionalized in formal laws. See Julia S. Brown, "A Comparative Study of Deviations from Sexual Mores," *American Sociological Review* XVII (April 1952), pp. 135–146.

24. There is some evidence, however, that the influence of peer pressure on attitudes toward social behavior may be stronger than the effect of the law. See Leonard Berkowitz and Nigel Walker, "Laws and Moral Judgments," in Friedman and Macaulay, op. cit., pp. 198–211.

25. There are probably many reasons that the Belleville residents were less willing to report marijuana use, the only one of the thirteen offenses for which this was the case. Belleville residents may see marijuana use as adolescent experimentation with a consciousness-expanding substance and feel that its use will end with time. They may also define marijuana use as a mental health problem, a form of behavior requiring therapy and treatment rather than criminal punishment. This would fit with the findings that marijuana use is the only offense which fewer Belleville residents than Port City residents felt should be defined as illegal (see Appendix B, Table B-5). In general, suburban residents are probably more apt to see marijuana use as a casual activity of people who are otherwise noncriminal, whereas the residents of Port City are more likely to see marijuana as "just another drug" used by addicts who commit predatory crimes to support their habits.

26. The Spearman rank-order correlation between samples is a very high .95.

27. Rose and Prell, op. cit.; Thorsten Sellin and Marvin E. Wolfgang, *The Measurement of Delinquency*. New York: John Wiley & Sons, Inc., 1964, p. 268.

28. The Spearman rank-order correlation between the Port City ranking and the ranking by law was .68. The correlation between the Belleville ranking and the ranking by law was .64.

29. Gilbert, op. cit., also found general agreement between social

norms and the law in terms of comparable seriousness of offenses, although he also found some important discrepancies between the two rankings.

30. It was not possible to calculate scores on all perception of crime items and on willingness to report crime for all respondents, since some failed to answer questions. In fact, those for whom data on the perception of crime items were missing were least willing to report crime to the police, since the scores for the respondents in the table are higher than the overall scores for the samples from each community (9.75 versus 9.41 for Belleville, and 9.22 versus 8.41 for Port City).

31. One study found that perceived threat of crime—particularly of property (as opposed to personal) crime—was strongly related to reporting of crime. This study also discovered that reporting of crime was not significantly related to general attitudes about punishment, to attitudes toward the causes of human behavior, or to attitudes toward the police. Richard O. Hawkins, "Who Called the Cops? Decisions to Report Criminal Victimization," *Law and Society Review* VII (Spring 1973), pp. 427–444.

32. Clinard and Abbott, op. cit., p. 222.

33. Richard Sennett, "Middle-Class Families and Urban Violence: The Experience of a Chicago Community in the Nineteenth Century," in Stephan Thernstrom and Richard Sennett, editors, *Nineteenth-Century Cities: Essays in the New Urban History*. New Haven: Yale University Press, 1969, p. 397.

34. Albert D. Biderman, Louise A. Johnson, Jennie McIntyre, and Adrianne Weir, Field Surveys I of the President's Commission on Law Enforcement and Administration of Justice, *Report on a Pilot Study in the District of Columbia on Victimization and Attitudes toward Law Enforcement*. Washington, D.C.: United States Government Printing Office, 1967, p. 140.

35. Earl Johnson, Jr., "Organized Crime: Challenge to the American Legal System," *Journal of Criminal Law, Criminology and Police Science* LIII (December 1962), p. 422.

36. James Q. Wilson, "The Urban Unease: Community vs. City," *The Public Interest*, No. 12 (Summer 1968), p. 34.

37. Tony G. Poveda, "The Fear of Crime in a Small Town," *Crime and Delinquency* XVIII (April 1972), p. 149.

38. James P. Sterba, "Texas Toll of Boys Rises to 27 in Nation's Biggest Slaying Case," *The New York Times*, August 14, 1973, pp. 1, 18.

39. Biderman et al., op. cit., p. 157.

40. Cited in Tom A. Cullen, *When London Walked in Terror*. New York: Avon Books, 1965, pp. 135–136.

41. Frank F. Furstenberg, Jr., and Charles F. Wellford, "Calling the

Police: The Evaluation of Police Service," *Law and Society Review* VII (Spring 1973), p. 394.

42. Cited in John Darnton, "New Parks Head Insists Public Combat Vandalism," *The New York Times*, January 5, 1973, pp. 1, 28.

43. Richard C. Wade, Richard M. Clurman, "In Which Mr. Clurman, the New City Parks Administrator, Is Taken over the Coals for What He Said. He Then Says It Again," *The New York Times*, January 24, 1973, p. 41.

44. Edwin H. Sutherland and Donald R. Cressey, *Criminology*, eighth edition. Philadelphia: J. B. Lippincott Company, 1970, pp. 71–93.

45. Emile Durkheim, *The Division of Labor in Society*, translated by George Simpson. Glencoe, Ill.: The Free Press, 1933, pp. 102–110.

46. Ephraim H. Mizruchi and Robert Perrucci, "Norm Qualities and Differential Effects of Deviant Behavior: An Exploratory Analysis," *American Sociological Review* XXVII (June 1962), pp. 391–399.

47. See Clifford R. Shaw and Henry D. McKay, *Juvenile Delinquency and Urban Areas*, revised edition. Chicago: The University of Chicago Press, 1969.

48. Ramsey Clark, *Crime in America: Observations on Its Nature, Causes, Prevention and Control*. New York: Simon and Schuster, 1970, pp. 47–48.

49. Conklin, *Robbery and the Criminal Justice System*, pp. 59–78.

50. The subjects in this study were in the seventh through twelfth grades. They were classified as offenders or nonoffenders on the basis of both official arrest records and self-reported delinquencies. Gary F. Jensen, " 'Crime Doesn't Pay': Correlates of a Shared Misunderstanding," *Social Problems* XVII (Fall 1969), pp. 189–201.

51. Cited in Victor G. Strecher, *The Environment of Law Enforcement: A Community Relations Guide*. Englewood Cliffs, N.J.: Prentice-Hall, Inc., 1971, p. 18. Emphasis added here.

52. Charles Winick and Paul M. Kinsie, *The Lively Commerce: Prostitution in the United States*. Chicago: Quadrangle Books, 1971, pp. 144–145.

53. If such a third variable reduces support for the law as well as increases the amount and perception of crime, it may attenuate the strength of the actual inverse relationship between support for the law and salience of crime. This effect of a "suppressor variable" is discussed in Morris Rosenberg, *The Logic of Survey Analysis*. New York: Basic Books, Inc., 1968, pp. 84–94.

54. Walter B. Miller, "Lower Class Culture as a Generating Milieu of Gang Delinquency," *Journal of Social Issues* XIV (November 1958), p. 8.

55. Furstenberg and Wellford, op. cit., pp. 400–404.

56. Reiss, op. cit., pp. 16, 20.
57. George Goodman, Jr., "Relief Rooming House, Scene of Shootout, Is Feared by Residents and Police," *The New York Times*, November 24, 1972, p. 26.
58. Hawkins, op. cit., p. 439.
59. Biderman et al., op. cit., p. 141; Paul E. Smith and Richard O. Hawkins, "Victimization, Types of Citizen-Police Contacts, and Attitudes toward the Police," *Law and Society Review* VIII (Fall 1973), pp. 139–140.
60. Richard L. Block, "Fear of Crime and Fear of the Police," *Social Problems* XIX (Summer 1971), pp. 91–101; Richard L. Block, "Support for Civil Liberties and Support for the Police," *American Behavioral Scientist* VIII (July 1970), pp. 781–796.
61. Nearly the same proportions of samples from Australia and New Zealand—72 per cent and 71 per cent, respectively—said that the police are not helped enough by citizens in certain situations. D. Chappell and P. R. Wilson, *The Police and the Public in Australia and New Zealand*. St. Lucia, Queensland, Australia: University of Queensland Press, 1969, p. 49.
62. James Q. Wilson, "The Police and Their Problems: A Theory," in Carl J. Friedrich and Seymour Harris, editors, *Public Policy*, XII. Cambridge: Harvard University Press, 1963, pp. 189–216. The terms *proactive* and *reactive* are used in Albert J. Reiss and David J. Bordua, "Environment and Organization: A Perspective on the Police," in David J. Bordua, editor, *The Police: Six Sociological Essays*. New York: John Wiley & Sons, Inc., 1967, pp. 25–55.
63. Cited in Martin Mayer, *The Lawyers*. New York: Harper and Row, Publishers, 1967, p. 179.

Collective Response to Crime: Vigilante Movements and Civilian Patrol Groups

8

CRIME weakens the fabric of social life by increasing fear, suspicion, and distrust. It also reduces public support for the law, in terms of unwillingness to report crime and criticism of the police. However, under certain conditions people will engage in collective action to fight crime. They may work for a political candidate who promises to restore law and order. They may call meetings of community residents to plan an attack on crime.[1] Sometimes they may even band together in a civilian police patrol to carry out the functions that the police are not effectively performing for them. Since people who perceive high crime rates often hold the police responsible for crime prevention, we would expect such patrols to emerge where people feel very threatened by crime, believe that the police cannot protect them, and think from past experience with community groups that the people themselves can solve the problem.

Collective response to crime is relatively uncommon. People rarely mobilize for action to prevent crime, even when there is little cost or risk involved. For instance, a study of the impact on the public of the 1951 Kefauver Hearings·on government corruption and organized crime found that although the hearings caused much indignation and interest, they produced little in the way of direct action to combat corruption in government. Apathy was not the response, but neither was problem-solving behavior; such actions would have called for creativity and initiative "without benefit of precedent, simplicity or even the urging of general social approval."[2] Two months after the hearings ended, half of a sample expressed shock, anger, or a sense of betrayal at the committee's findings. When asked if they would like to help improve conditions, somewhat less than half said they would and 12 per cent more gave a qualified affirmative response. However, when asked what they would have done, only one-fourth of the suggestions were problem-solving in the sense that they might actually have contributed to reducing corruption. Only 13 per cent of the people engaged in some problem-solving behavior themselves—joining a committee, talking to someone in a position of power, writing to a politician, or trying to convince someone else to take action. Even fewer felt that what they did made any difference. There was thus a "disconcerting descent from vigorous arousal to a trickle of effective protest."[3] Concern was aroused, but the absence of any direct threat and a sense of social impotence inhibited any real problem-solving behavior.

At times, people may take an action they feel will have an impact on the crime problem, even though it actually has little effect. For example, a petition to reinstate the death penalty in Great Britain was signed by 24,000 residents of the area near the town of Hyde (population 31,000) after the brutal Moors murders.[4] This had no effect on the law in Great Britain nor did it prevent other murders; it may have been beneficial for the people, who felt that they were doing all they could to stop the apparently random violence.

Jane Jacobs cites an instance of the public being aroused to act against a local crime problem. After a series of robberies in a community where some drug addicts lived, citizens called the police a number of times; some even made the effort to learn that they should contact the Narcotics Bureau. People carefully supplied police detectives with detailed information about where heroin was being sold in the community, by whom and to whom it was being sold, and at what times the transactions were taking place. No action was taken by the police, who did not seem to care about the deterioration of the community.[5] If people go out of their way to try to stop crime but find that they have no effect on the problem, they may become resigned to crime or move to a safer area. Sometimes they may simply take the law into their own hands.

Vigilantes in Historical Perspective

Collective action in response to crime has a long history. The early Roman plebeians engaged in community self-help by throwing offenders from the Tarpeian rock; early Germans raised a hue and cry, took up arms and blew horns, chased offenders, and sometimes lynched them.[6] Vigilante actions to curb lawlessness have been particularly common where formal means of law enforcement are weak or nonexistent.

The history of vigilantism in the United States covers more than two hundred years. The first recorded movement was in South Carolina, where a group of about a thousand private citizens who were separated by great distance from formally constituted legal authority (the Crown) developed an organization called the Regulators to try to bring order to communities in the Back Country.[7] The group's attentions were focused on the "lower people and outlaws" in the area, those alienated people who engaged in anti-social and often violent criminal behavior. These people often lived in separate settlements, engaging in "arson, torture, and robbery" and challenging the order established by law-abiding citizens.[8] The Regulators sought to re-establish order and peace, although the fact that they were led by the community's elite and sought to control those at the bottom of the class structure makes it possible to interpret their actions as a means of preserving the class system and the advantages it offered to those with power and money. During the 1760's, the Regulators pursued and hanged outlaws. They did reduce the "wave of crime and riot" in the area, but over time their efforts were expanded to include the "supervision of morals and family life."[9] The lack of limits to their behavior evoked hostility against the Regulators, especially because of their "severe punishments . . . and increasingly rash selection of victims."[10] As a result, a group called the Moderators developed as a counter-movement in 1769, effectively curtailing the extreme activities of the Regulators, who had managed to bring some order to the community.

Vigilante movements differ from lynchings, which are responses to single incidents and have a shorter duration and less organization than vigilante groups. For example, after his conviction for the murder of a young girl in Georgia, Leo Frank was taken from prison and hanged by a lynch party comprised of twenty-five leading men of a nearby town.[11] This was not a vigilante group, since the party was small in size, organized for one particular action, and did not endure over time.

Frontier vigilante groups developed in response to a general lack of order rather than in response to a particular crime. New communities often lacked the resources to hire police officers and judges. Their isolation from large population centers that might provide such needs and the presence of open spaces to which criminals could flee led to self-help efforts.[12] If any formal criminal justice system existed in such communities, it was usually an "uneven judicial system" in which juries often acquitted defendants because of bribery or fear of reprisals.[13] Vigilante movements arose in response to the absence of formal means of social control and the feeling that only by taking action themselves could the people establish a stable and livable community.

One Western vigilante movement that led to a number of imitators is reported in Thomas J. Dimsdale's *The Vigilantes of Montana*. This movement was initiated to "repress disorder, punish crime, and prevent outrage."[14] It sought to protect life and property and to prevent leniency toward criminals. According to Dimsdale,

The face of society was changed, as if by magic; for the Vigilantes, holding in one hand the invisible yet effectual shield of protection, and in the other, the swift descending and inevitable sword of retribution, struck from his nerveless grasp the weapon of the assassin; commanded the brawler to cease from strife; warned the thief to steal no more; bade the good citizen take courage; and compelled the ruffians and marauders who had so long maintained the "reign of terror" in Montana, to fly the Territory, or meet the just rewards of their crimes.[15]

Although these claims are excessive, this vigilante movement did help create a more stable community, even if it only drove outlaws to nearby communities that had not yet established their own vigilante groups.

In many vigilante movements in this country, the leaders were "ambitious young men from the old settled areas of the East," upwardly mobile individuals who sought positions of power and prestige in the community and therefore wanted to establish an orderly community within which they could take positions of leadership.[16] As is true of today's civilian police patrols in large cities, frontiersmen wanted to protect themselves, their families, and their property, and they thus deferred to leaders who promised to establish law and order. As Richard Maxwell Brown says in his thorough examination of vigilantism in America,

Vigilante action was a clear warning to disorderly inhabitants that the newness of settlement would provide no opportunity for eroding the established values of civilization. Vigilantism was a violent sanctification of the deeply cherished values of life and property.[17]

The rank and file in such movements was often drawn from the middle classes; the leaders were usually from the upper strata. The lower classes, including but not limited to outcasts and criminals, were the target of the vigilantes, much as in nineteenth-century Paris the "laboring classes" as a whole were stigmatized as "dangerous classes" by those in positions of greater wealth and power.[18] Vigilantism can thus be viewed as a class conflict that becomes institutionalized, the fear of takeover of the new settlements by "riff-raff" being as much a spur to action as the fear of crime.[19]

Vigilante movements varied considerably in size, longevity, and organization. Institutionalization of the movement was necessary to maintain citizens' interest, to retain the manpower to cope with the continuing problems faced by the community, and to restrain the sadistic and vindictive people who sometimes joined the group. Brown found that the size of American vigilante groups ranged from only a dozen members to as many as 8,000; the number was usually a few hundred. Often the whole community would participate, and the group would be organized in terms of military command. Most movements lasted only a few weeks; not many endured for more than a year. Articles or a manifesto was often drawn up to state the functions and ideals of the group. Vigilantes would apprehend criminals and give them formal, but illegal or extra-legal, trials. A defense could be presented, but conviction and punishment usually followed.[20] Early movements often resorted to whipping or expelling an outlaw from the community, but later ones sometimes executed the offender. In 43 per cent of the movements studied by Brown, there was at least one execution. Few movements killed more than three or four people, since few had to be executed to instill terror in others. Potential offenders were thus induced to leave the community or conform with dominant social norms.[21]

Brown suggests that the philosophy of vigilantism includes three basic components. The movement seeks the *self-preservation* of its members through the protection of life and property. It proclaims the *right to revolution*, to strike against established authority when it fails to perform its functions, particularly the maintenance of public order. Finally, vigilantism includes a belief in *popular sovereignty*, the right of people to wield power in their own best interests.[22]

This philosophy may be carried out in two ways; a movement may be *socially constructive* or *socially destructive*.[23] Socially constructive movements deal with particular problems of disorder and instability, then disband after establishing order in the community. Brown suggests that such movements serve the ends of the community by representing "genuine community consensus" and by involving large numbers of local residents in the movement. Socially destructive movements, on the contrary, often encounter opposition from within the community and may produce "anarchic and socially destructive vigilante war."[24] These movements do not represent community consensus; as a result they lead to civil strife in an already fragile community. This conflict stems from personal or group feuds and from rivalry for political or economic power in the community. Brown gives an example of a vigilante group that had goals other than the reduction of crime and violence:

Allegedly concerned with a crime problem, the San Francisco vigilantes of 1856 were in actuality motivated by a desire to seize control of the municipal government from the Democratic political machine that found the nucleus of its support among the lower class Irish Catholic workers of the city.[25]

A vigilante movement may become socially destructive if its leaders fail to control violent or sadistic members. This occurred with the South Carolina Regulators. In such instances, a counter-movement may emerge and community violence may break out; any social solidarity that existed before the formation of the vigilante group or as a result of its efforts will be destroyed. Vigilante movements thus produced community-wide conflict when violent members were not controlled. They had a similar effect when the efforts of some people to gain or maintain political and economic power met with resistance from others with the same goals. The possibility that popular-based vigilante movements may become the battlegrounds for conflicts internal to the community is a reason to distrust such movements or even modern-day civilian police patrols, unless there are assurances that such movements actually represent a true community consensus and are accountable to the members of that community. Such consensus is especially difficult to define in the heterogeneous communities in today's large cities.

Vigilante movements were sometimes *substitutes* for effective systems of law enforcement and criminal justice. At other times they acted as *parallel structures* to supplement the functions of existing law-enforcement agents.[26] Civilian police patrols may emerge if people feel that the ineffectiveness of the local police requires citizen involvement. Collective actions such as citizen patrols and vigilante groups may reduce the cost of law enforcement, a point made by Brown about frontier communities but still true in today's cities. However, such movements actually enlist citizens to perform jobs without pay, so the cost to the community may be the same, even though no revenue is expended to pay citizens who help enforce the law. Oscar Newman has noted:

Block associations and tenant patrols in public housing have instituted a limited and useful kind of collective security. In these systems, designated individual residents take responsibility for watching over

191

the security of a building during high-crime hours. The person on patrol has to sit in the building lobby, usually at a makeshift desk, with some degree of risk to himself. In this role the tenant patrolman is a paraprofessional police officer, not a tenant who is concerned about the welfare of his neighbor. He is protecting the building in which he lives in the role of formal monitor, not as a natural extension of other, family-oriented and personally significant activities.[27]

Lack of paid, formally designated law-enforcement agents may cause citizens to undertake traditional law-enforcement functions, but this should not be taken to mean that the services of those people—whether a vigilante group, a tenant patrol, or a civilian police patrol—are free.

Many vigilante groups in the West took the law into their own hands by arresting, trying, and punishing outlaws. The "anti-horsethief societies" were another movement that was structurally like the vigilantes but functioned only to capture criminals and turn them over to formally constituted law-enforcement officials for trial and punishment. These groups were supplements to law enforcement, parallel structures that *assisted* the police and the courts rather than substituting for formal organizations. Many modern-day civilian police patrols function this way, as extensions or eyes and ears of the police rather than as substitutes for them.

Between organized vigilante groups and anti-horsethief societies, and purely individual responses to crime, lie actions taken against criminals by groups on an ad hoc basis. In other words, patterned responses to crime may emerge which are less formalized than vigilante movements but more predictable than the response of a particular individual. In fact, Brown says that *instant vigilantism* on the frontier did exist on a one-shot basis, although it usually occurred in communities where past experience with a more formal vigilante movement had produced a common understanding of how to react to a crime. Past experience permitted vigilante action without the ritual and formality ordinarily associated with the emergence of an organized group.[28] Instant vigilantism exists today in large cities. People chase and beat, sometimes even kill, offenders who arouse their anger.[29] Sometimes, such violence is supported by public officials. For example, after a series of fire-bombings in Syracuse, New York, the police chief told people that they had a legal right to use deadly force against arsonists, although they would later have to justify their actions to a grand jury.[30] Such official support of private actions against crime may make such behavior more likely.

Cases of instant vigilantism have also been reported in recent years in other nations. For example, a report from Kenya suggests that the government and the public both support harsh measures against offenders. The government favors capital punishment. Citizens often pursue thieves through the streets and beat them when caught; "[a]rrest and quick removal by the police are all that may save a man's life in some cases."[31] A report from Nigeria tells of the lynching of suspects after the government warned parents to beware of child abductors and the press reported a series of attempted kidnappings.[32] No formal vigilante group developed, but a pattern of self-help was evident. In fact, during 1972 more than a dozen suspected kidnappers were killed in Nigeria by crowds of private citizens.[33] In their study of crime in developing nations, Clinard and Abbott found:

> The traditions of the people underlie this custom. In village areas in which people are poor and their few possessions mean much to them apprehended thieves have always been beaten. Much personal satisfaction is derived from this performance, particularly if others are watching. It is also feared that offenders might not be dealt with severely enough if they were simply turned over to local authorities. In fact, it is generally the custom, at least in the urban areas, to beat a thief and then turn him over to the police.[34]

Some attribute these actions to traditional tribal norms of capture and punishment still held by people who have recently moved from rural tribal villages to large cities. Although such traditions do contribute to instant vigilantism, as they did in the western United States a century ago, attacks on offenders in American cities still occur today, even in communities where people have no past experience with self-help. In New York City a murderer was nearly beaten to death by a crowd.[35] In a separate incident in the same city, a crowd gathered outside a police station after a man who looked like the picture of a child murderer had been apprehended by the police. People demanded that the man be turned over to them for punishment.[36] Only fast work by the police got the suspect, who turned out not to be the killer, out of the station and away from the mob.[37]

Civilian Police Patrols in Urban Areas

Vigilante movements often helped frontier communities establish order and stability prior to the institutionalization of law-enforcement functions. Brown asserts that such movements are inappropriate in modern cities, where established agents of law enforcement already exist, although these agencies may be ineffective in providing the services they were established to perform. *Neovigilante* movements in today's cities are responses to the perception of a threat to life and property and a feeling that local law-enforcement agents cannot protect the people from crime. Similar views preceded the establishment of vigilante movements on the Western frontier.

An early example of urban vigilante action followed the Jack the Ripper murders in London in 1888. Residents of East London formed vigilante committees which patrolled the streets to prevent further crimes. The groups included laborers and college undergraduates. The people in the movement collected money to offer as a reward for the capture of the killer, to pay additional detectives to work on the case, and to pay unemployed men to patrol the streets. Surveillance of the community was so thorough that "some of the plainclothes men who were strange to the neighborhood were watched by members of the Whitechapel Vigilance Committee, while they in their turn came under the scrutiny of the detectives."[38] Women petitioned the government for action against the killer and against "fallen women" who brought such crimes upon themselves. Residents of East London sought to protect the reputation of their community by apprehending the murderer who had brought such unfavorable attention to their area.

East London in the latter part of the nineteenth century had the characteristics of a *defended neighborhood*, a community that is a distinct part of a city where informal social control regulates movement and behavior in order to avoid conflict between groups.[39] The means by which such a community differentiates itself from other areas include the actions of juvenile gangs, restrictive covenants, zoning regulations, sharply defined boundaries, a forbidding reputation, police enforcement of the law against outsiders, private guards and doormen, and citizen patrol groups.[40] Suttles suggests that the defended neighborhood is an urban phenomenon that emerges because cities are too large to exercise social control as a single unit. Defended neighborhoods develop partly as a response to the need for controls over the behavior of residents and outsiders, the latter being perceived as the greater threat even though most crime in the area is probably committed by residents.

To protect the community from outsiders, who are seen as predatory and disorderly, residents of a defended neighborhood develop various defensive measures, including civilian police patrols and juvenile gangs. To protect community and individual security, vigilante-like gangs develop for "dispensing homemade justice and exercising grass roots police power."[41] The gangs provide territorial defense. Fights between gangs are seen as conflict only if the gangs are from different neighborhoods; such fights are viewed as matters of lesser significance if they occur within the ethnic neighborhood. Suttles argues that such gangs serve a function for the whole neighborhood, although residents do not formally appoint the gangs as their protectors. The gangs control behavior in the community, thereby making the streets safer and protecting residents from the depredations of intruders. Reliance on juvenile gangs arises because of a profound distrust of the police and their ability to insure protection. However, the actions of the gangs and the perception that all outsiders intend harm fragment the city by driving barriers between people from different communities. By spreading fear of their community to other areas, the gangs cause outsiders to avoid their community. This may reduce informal social control that would exist if there were more people on the streets. Reduced human traffic in the area may also make it necessary for local businessmen to move or to close earlier, further reducing informal social controls in the area and thereby raising crime rates. The defended neighborhood may increase informal social control in some ways by the presence of vigilante-like juvenile gangs. However, this means of defense may also have negative effects, making the area more dangerous than it would be if outsiders were free to travel there.

Brown found that neovigilantism in large cities was most common in three types of communities: in black enclaves where residents felt they needed protection against violence by whites (including the police); in white areas where people felt threatened by the incursion of black criminals or rioters; and in urban communities where there was a high fear of crime. Urban vigilante groups seem more like the anti-horsethief societies than like the traditional Western vigilante groups, since they usually do not take the law into their own hands. Instead, they patrol the streets, try to prevent crime, and turn over apprehended suspects to the police. They try to deter crime by sighting and reporting street crimes to the police and by patrolling high-risk areas such as housing projects and apartment buildings. They attempt to provide social control over rowdy youths on the street and may try to protect the community from riot activity. They escort elderly citizens to insure their safety. Sometimes they work as police informants.[42] These citizen patrols thus serve many functions but the values of life and property that they seek to preserve are the same as the ones protected by the vigilante movements in the West. They thus provide inexpensive law enforcement and order maintenance for the community. One member of a patrol group says, "We're not vigilantes who are a law to themselves, but people from the community who realize that the city cannot any longer afford to give us the full measure of our tax dollar in crime prevention, sanitation, education and other areas."[43] As mentioned earlier, these services are not really free, since opportunity costs are involved when people have to spend their leisure time providing services that should be provided by the police. Taxes may be kept down, but the real cost to the community is no less.

A study of twenty-eight civilian police patrols in American cities by Gary T. Marx and Dane Archer found that these patrols developed because of a feeling that the police were ineffective in performing functions that were necessary to the maintenance of a stable community, such as cooling riots, providing surveillance, and educating residents about law enforcement and crime prevention. Two-thirds of the groups had contacts with the local police. Patrol members often sought police advice on the legal limits to their actions; in some cities such as Boston, the police even established guidelines for civilian patrol groups. The groups differed in their attitudes toward the police. All saw the police as failures to some extent. Some felt that the police themselves were the problem and had forced the people to defend themselves against the police, as well as against criminals. These *adversarial* groups differed from the *supplemental* groups in their assessment of the police, the latter feeling that court decisions and high crime rates had made police work difficult. Supplemental patrol groups did not blame the police for their ineffectiveness and were willing to help them. Of the groups studied by Marx and Archer, seven were anti-police and seventeen were pro-police; the other four were in-between in their attitudes toward the local police.[44]

A recent plan in New York City hopes to stimulate neighborhood crime prevention associations by having the city provide money to match contributions by local residents. The efforts of the groups are to be directed at better security for the community (through additional lighting, for example), but patrol activities are also encouraged. The associations are supervised and trained by the New York City Police Department, which may produce pro-police attitudes among members of the patrol groups.[45]

The youth patrols that emerged during the urban riots of the 1960's are another example of civilian groups whose major functions were supplemental rather than adversarial, although they did monitor police activity in the riot areas. In a study of twelve youth patrols, Terry Ann Knopf found that they generally had the approval of civil authorities and worked with the authorities to maintain order and security in the community.[46] The members of most patrols were young black males. They usually operated independently of the police and often distrusted

197

the police, but they did act largely to supplement regular police functions rather than to oppose the police. Ten of the twelve patrols were formed during riots; the number of participants varied from twenty to five hundred. They patrolled the streets, broke up crowds, reassured citizens, and stopped vandalism. They carried no weapons but relied instead on persuasion to meet their goals—the protection of life and property, the dissemination of information, the monitoring of police activities, and general assistance to the community. They also engaged in policing activities by telling people to stay calm and by reporting suspicious behavior to the police. At least half of the patrols developed either at the start of a disturbance or at a critical time during a riot. They were somewhat effective in curbing disturbances by convincing riot participants to cease their violence and by reducing tensions in the community. The patrol-group activity enhanced the self-esteem of the members by creating in them a sense of being able to help the community. However, after the riots, most of the patrols disbanded because of lack of organizational cohesion, the absence of a crisis, and the emergence of internal conflicts. There was also a lack of additional funding for the patrols and some political opposition to their continued existence. The youth patrols were generally supplemental, in that they sought to serve police functions for the community and help prevent riots.

Racial conflicts also provide examples of adversarial patrols. One group called the Defenders was studied by Harold A. Nelson, who examined its development and activities in a Southern community.[47] The group was comprised of blacks who sought to provide normal law enforcement and order maintenance for their community. In doing so, they had to challenge the dominant mores of the community and confront the power held by whites. The organization emerged in response to police brutality and the arrests of civil rights demonstrators. A leader of the local civil rights organization told the people not to riot or engage in anti-police violence, but rather to organize and plan a strategy that would benefit the community. Here we find that a man with prior organizational experience was able to create a new organization to provide law enforcement for the community, suggesting that prior experience with collective response to a social problem may later make a group reaction to a new problem more likely.

There were a number of meetings of black residents of this Southern town, and a decision was made to form a community patrol group. Men were carefully screened so that only those with high morals and those who were not heavy drinkers were chosen. An additional requirement which indicated the adversarial nature of the Defenders was that all members had to have served in the military "at least six weeks under active war combat conditions."[48] The Defenders carried weapons on their patrols. Their leaders felt that the police as well as the Ku Klux Klan would challenge their right to patrol their own community, and that intergroup violence would occur. One major function of the Defenders was to eliminate Klan activities in the black community and insure that the local police engaged in only their lawful duties. Eventually they were successful in reducing Klan and police oppression in the black community.

One reaction of the police to the Defenders was to stop *all* their own activities in the black community, including regular law enforcement. This gave the Defenders the opportunity to assume the normal functions of the police. They patrolled the streets of the community and talked to potential offenders. They protected civil rights activists from white crowds and investigated local opponents of the civil rights movement. The Defenders had not sought to completely replace the local police, but rather to restrict them to their legitimate policing functions and to prevent brutality, arbitrary arrests, and harassment. However, they were largely adversarial in nature, since they sought to protect the community against the police. The Defenders helped redistribute power in the community by diminishing white control over the black community and by increasing the acceptability and legitimacy of the more moderate civil rights organization. Through their activities, the participants in the Defenders and indeed the whole community developed a sense of pride and identity and a feeling that self-help was an effective way to change social conditions.

Another civilian patrol group that developed in a context of minority group relations was sponsored by the American Indian

Movement (AIM) in a Minneapolis community.[49] This patrol group was less concerned with social control than with being "a symbolic representation of the ideology of the social action-social change organization."[50] Members of the group walked a beat on Friday and Saturday nights, carrying a walkie-talkie and wearing red jackets with insignia. They watched police cars and helped drunks get home. They broke up fights and searched for missing teenagers. The group developed in response to what the Indians saw as a shift of the toughest police officers in the city to their community from the black community, where a black patrol group had brought pressure on the police. The Indian patrol group monitored the activities of police in their community, causing the police to charge them with interference. After about a year the group declined in strength because AIM shifted its resources to other programs and activities. The patrol did make the local police more responsive to the needs of the Indian community. The group was known to many residents of the community; however, few who were interviewed had either seen the group or had been in direct contact with it. Although the symbolic value of the group was its primary contribution, it probably introduced a somewhat greater degree of social control to the community.

Whether or not a civilian patrol group uses violence depends on its view of the local police and the encouragement or opposition it receives from the police. Youth patrols in urban riot areas did not use violence nor did the Indian patrol group, but the Defenders did. The police do not approve of all patrols, even the supplemental ones, since they believe that law enforcement should be left to trained professionals. The police do tolerate some adversarial groups if they help maintain order in the community; they also tolerate them in order to avoid overt conflict with the groups. However, the police view most adversarial groups negatively, either as spies on police activities or as challenges to their legitimate power. Marx and Archer found that if a patrol group is adversarial and if the police oppose the group (as was the case with the Defenders), the patrol group may use violence (and may also encounter violence from the police). This kind of patrol group is the type that is most likely to carry weapons, charge the police with brutality, and resist any police attempts to control their operations.[51]

Marx and Archer found more community support for supplemental patrol groups than for adversarial groups. This suggests that adversarial groups are usually less apt to reflect community consensus, either because people support the police in spite of their ineffectiveness or because they are unwilling to actively oppose the police. Brown's historical analysis suggests that supplemental groups, which better represent community consensus, would be less likely to divide a community by institutionalizing political and economic conflicts.

Community attitudes toward the police and crime help determine attitudes toward civilian police patrols and thus the likelihood that such patrol groups will be sustained over time. If attitudes toward the police are hostile and if the community has a high crime rate, people will be more likely to support a patrol group than if they are favorably disposed toward the police and do not feel threatened by crime. When people think the police are ineffective in protecting them, they may seek a greater control over their lives and their community by forming a patrol group. Another factor that may stimulate collective effort is prior experience with groups and associations aimed at solving community problems. Social solidarity and community identity may also spur the development of self-help groups.

Sometimes patrol groups develop without any clear mandate from the community. These groups are probably short-lived because they lack legitimacy in the eyes of their constituents. People may not give groups support if they fear that the legal restraints that exist for governmental law-enforcement agents will be lacking for these informal patrol groups. Also, the patrols sometimes represent cliques in the community rather than the population of the area as a whole. This creates fear of extortion and attempts to gain political power by using the patrol group as a power base. Sometimes local residents see the members of these groups as ordinary citizens rather than real police who have legitimacy and power.[52] To increase their acceptance by local residents, some patrol groups have become involved in welfare services and community programs.

One problem sometimes faced by civilian patrol groups, as well as by the frontier vigilante groups, is the recruitment of sadistic and violent members. Some groups include members with prior arrest records. Although these individuals might do a good job, their recruitment may reduce the favor with which the group is regarded by local residents.[53] Many groups do not screen their recruits effectively. Few are as rigorous in selecting members as the Defenders, although the Jewish Defense League in Boston has required members to undergo a psychiatric examination.[54] Another problem faced by patrol groups is that residents of the community may impersonate group members by wearing the badge or uniform of the patrol group in an attempt to gain and use power for personal ends.[55]

Patrol groups differ greatly in their activities. Some have used their power illegally. They have pressured known criminals to leave the community or cease their activities, and they occasionally have meted out summary punishment. Cities such as New York and Baltimore have recently had murders of known drug dealers. Some attribute these deaths to local juvenile gangs that patrol the streets to keep the area free of drugs; the motive for the murders is seen as a desire to build a better community. Others, including local police officers, view the murders as a form of gang warfare that just happens to involve drug dealers or as attempts by rivals to wrest control of local drug traffic from those who were murdered.[56] A report from Detroit indicates that a local vigilante group is "taxing" (extorting) money from local drug pushers to turn over to ghetto youth activities. This group employs Vietnam veterans who are experts in demolitions, thus intimidating those who refuse to pay.[57]

Another example of direct pressure on local criminals has occurred in Brazil. "Death squads" comprised of off-duty policemen have engaged in the beating and murder of known criminals. These patrol groups have meted out summary justice since 1964, but it was only in 1970 that the government acknowledged their existence.[58] The rationale for these squads is the frustration of local policemen at the slowness and uncertainty of justice in the courts and their anger at crimes by habitual criminals. They say they are ridding society of its worst elements without a long and troublesome investigation and trial.[59] Estimates of the number of people killed by these death squads range from 500 to 1,000 in the period from 1964 to 1970.[60] These patrols are quite similar to the vigilante groups in the American West, except that they exist in communities that have formal law-enforcement systems.

None of the patrol groups examined by Marx and Archer went to the extreme of the Brazilian death squads or the American gangs that killed drug pushers. However, these patrol groups have sometimes been used by the police to carry out actions that the police themselves cannot. A recent case in Boston involved a murder suspect in a crime in which the police had not been able to locate the victim's body. A local patrol group was allegedly told about the defendant. They then kidnapped him and held him overnight in a hunting lodge. The following day the police located the victim's body in a grave in a park. The offender was arrested and charged soon after. Here the police seemed to approve of the use of illegal measures (kidnapping and possibly torture) to gain information they could not legally gather.[61] Another instance of the police use of private citizens for similar purposes involved a group of fifteen New York City teenagers who, after attending a series of police lectures on narcotics, took a 27-year-old man who offered them marijuana to the police station.[62] Here the police information campaign had the effect of putting a group of unofficial undercover agents on the street, people who had no legal power of arrest but still took the man to the police station.

Most civilian patrols do not physically punish or kidnap suspects. They usually walk the streets of a community or the corridors of a building to "multiply the number of eyes and ears that police have at their disposal."[63] They hope to deter crime by their presence. In the rare event that they spot a crime in progress, they call the police to the scene to make an arrest. Patrol members have open communications with the police, who tell them not to make arrests because of the risk involved and because an arrest means lost time and pay if the patrol member has to testify in court. Patrols are generally routine, even dull; they rarely produce any contact with an offender. Saturation of an area provides surveillance and a real threat to the offender that he will be reported to the police or stopped during his crime. This surveillance is more likely to provide actual social control than is the more casual surveillance discussed in an earlier chapter, although the presence of the patrol group may only shift crime to nearby areas which are less carefully watched over by residents and patrol groups.

An examination of community patrols in Boston found that one of their major advantages is that they can quickly spot unusual behavior because they know the community and its residents.[64] In small towns the whole population can probably spot deviations from usual behavior patterns, but in a large and heterogeneous city a specialized group may be needed. Traditionally, beat patrolmen have performed this function, but with the use of patrol cars the officers are less able to carefully observe activities in the community and talk with local residents who could provide information about life in the area.[65]

The patrols in Boston were especially concerned with maintaining order in the community by controlling drunks, prostitutes, and young toughs. They took notes on such behavior, passed the notes to the police, and waited for action. If the police did nothing, they would report the activities again. Patrol groups sought to strengthen a sense of community by showing local residents that they could help themselves. By their presence they hoped to make people think the streets were safer, encouraging them to leave their television sets and meet their neighbors on the streets.[66] Patrol members told citizens to fight crime by leaving on their front porch lights to illuminate the streets and by taking precautions to prevent their own victimization. Patrol groups also lobbied for additional city policemen in their community. They served as buffers between the community and the police, helping to reduce mutual hostility and to negotiate between the two. The patrols suffered from lack of accountability and from the absence of training and screening of group members. However, with good leadership, community support, and the cooperation of the local police, some of the groups were able to curb crime and to improve people's sense of security.

Albert Fay Hill's *The North Avenue Irregulars* presents an interesting account of a patrol group in a suburb, a setting where patrols have increased in number as suburban crime rates have risen in recent years.[67] This rather unorthodox patrol group was led by a minister (Hill) and was comprised of twelve women. They sought to eliminate the influence of organized crime in New Rochelle and in Westchester County, New York. The group's activities were precipitated by a gangland slaying in which the body was dumped in New Rochelle and by State Investigation Commission hearings that revealed corruption by organized crime in the area. Hill describes the initial reaction of some local residents to these events as "massive indifference." Some people even attacked the Commission for drawing unfavorable attention to their community, rather than blaming those who had corrupted local government.

Under Hill's leadership, a dozen women began to follow local mobsters around town, trying to determine patterns of gambling activity in order to find the mob's central "bank." They remained as inconspicuous as possible in order to prevent reprisals and avoid the anger of local residents who gambled. They worked in shifts, using their own cars and communicating with each other by walkie-talkie. They occasionally employed informants who had inside information, but most of their activity was limited to the observation of behavior patterns. The work was physically exhausting and nerve-wracking; a number of the women took tranquilizers before beginning a shift. Their children also proved a problem at times, having to go to the bathroom when their mother was about to observe a critical transaction or telling their school friends about their mother's work.

The gangsters were outraged when they learned of the civilian patrol activity. Police could be bribed, but citizens working as morals enforcers were harder to influence. Threats were made against Reverend Hill, but work continued for months. The group's observations revealed police ties with local bookies and extensive gambling by local residents. The group succeeded in locating a major collection point for bets, but the central bank was never found. The Internal Revenue Service was contacted when the major collection point was discovered. Although *The New York Times* printed a story about the patrol group at a time when the publicity was harmful, group activities did produce indictments of a number of bookies and mobsters. Months of work had yielded some arrests, the discovery of a major collection point, information on patterns of gambling, and the establishment of a federal strike force in the area. Although the cases against the bookies and mobsters were dismissed in court when a federal betting tax stamp was declared unconstitutional, the group's work had helped to educate the public about the role of organized crime in the community. It had also demonstrated that amateurs could take effective action to improve the community when it was confronted with a social problem.

Another sort of patrol that has developed in recent years is the tenant patrol, an auxiliary force of monitors and guards that tries to keep housing projects, apartment buildings, and college dormitories free of intruders who might commit crimes.[68] Interestingly, police patrols on the streets have probably driven criminals off the streets and into buildings in search of victims, leading to a need for greater control of crime within the buildings. Tenant patrols check unfamiliar cars in the area, make sure that tenants' doors are locked, and check the roofs of buildings for strangers or stolen goods. They also screen people who enter the building and question people inside the building as to their intentions. Tenants may be instructed to watch and listen for unusual activities in or near their neighbors' apartments. As a result, people get to know each other and learn who does not live in the building. This breaks down barriers to social interaction among tenants, although it erects barriers between tenants and outsiders. Buildings may be designed to provide *defensible* space, but tenant patrols and mutual help agreements make more of the interior space of the buildings *defended* space. Tenants are thus united in the common cause of self-protection, although they may be so sensitized to potential dangers that excessive hostility toward strangers and outsiders develops. Distrust and suspicion may be even more harmful for the community than the small amount of crime that is prevented by those attitudes.

One aspect of civilian patrols about which we have little information is why they develop in some communities but not in others. To answer this question we would need detailed longitudinal data for a number of different kinds of communities.

Probably patrols are most apt to emerge where there is a high fear of crime, a sense that order and stability are necessary for the community but that legitimate authorities cannot or will not provide them, a homogeneous community with a degree of social solidarity, a past history of collective response to social problems, a critical mass of individuals who are willing to join a patrol group, and a charismatic leader to initiate and sustain the group.

A survey analyzed by Marx and Archer provides some information on the sources of support for civilian patrols.[69] In a sample of about 500 Boston residents, well over half of both blacks and whites favored civilian patrol groups. The feeling that such groups were a good idea was more prevalent among blacks than among whites, among the less educated than among the better educated, and among the young than among the old. Lower-class respondents were more apt to favor patrols as a means of crime control, but middle-class people leaned toward public meetings and political pressure to bring about a reduction in crime.[70] This is probably because middle-class people have had greater success in the past with public meetings and political pressure than have lower-class people. People favored patrol groups because they thought there was too much crime for the police to handle, because they saw community involvement and self-help as valuable, and because they felt that local residents could enforce the law more effectively than the city police. Those who disapproved of patrols thought that they would abuse their power, would not be accountable for their behavior, and would be poorly trained and equipped and would thus provide second-rate police service to the community. Some people simply stated that police activities should be left to the Boston Police Department.[71]

Respondents who opposed any patrol, whether adversarial or supplemental, were the most law-and-order oriented and the most apt to feel that the police were doing a good job. Those favoring supplemental patrols but opposing adversarial ones were supportive of the police but felt that they needed citizen cooperation to properly carry out their job. Blacks, the young, and the better educated were the most apt to support adversarial patrol groups. They felt that there was a need to check police abuse of power;

they were critical of police performance of their duties and felt that the police were discriminatory and brutal.

People were more apt to say that they would personally join a patrol group if they were black and young than if they were white and older. The less educated, Catholics and Protestants (as opposed to Jews and nonaffiliates), and Italians and Irish (as opposed to those with Northern European and English ancestry) were most apt to say that they would join a group. Willingness to join was not related to attitudes toward police performance, perceived importance of crime as a social problem, or the perceived need for more policemen in the community. Willingness to join a group was most strongly influenced by personal characteristics such as age and race.[72]

Marx and Archer found that for patrol groups to sustain themselves, they had to make the crisis to which they were responding continuously felt, they had to have a charismatic leader, and they had to be formally organized and financially supported.[73] These conditions were absent in the neighborhood youth patrols that existed in the riot areas, explaining the demise of the groups after riot activity subsided. Civilian patrol groups also have a better chance of survival if they have an ideology that states their goals in positive terms; vague targets such as "crime" and "disorder" may not sustain a group for long. Patrols will probably develop and last longer in communities where residents have prior experience in organizing and joining local groups and associations. Marx and Archer suggest that patrol groups have their greatest potential for use in fairly limited and well-defined settings where there are clear boundaries and homogeneous populations, such as housing projects and rock concerts. Nevertheless, they say that patrol groups face many problems in organizing and operating:

Self-defense groups often lack a clear mandate from the groups they wish to serve and their legal position regarding the use of force and citizen arrests is ambiguous. They may have trouble defining their task. The tendency of the groups to lack the resources for recruiting, screening,, and training appropriate manpower and for sustaining motivation beyond that which stems from a deeply felt crisis (along with the degree of autonomy some groups have) may contribute to ineffectiveness and abuses. And even if internal problems are solved, the groups may face harassment from the police.[74]

Some patrol participants feel that the most important aspects of their activities are symbolic and participatory. Although patrol groups may produce better police-community relations and may even deter some marginally committed offenders from crime, one of their major effects may be to enhance self-esteem and a sense of efficacy. They also make other residents feel that they too can reduce crime. If citizens feel that the patrols make the streets safer, they may be more willing to venture onto the streets at night. They may also be more willing to report suspicious behavior to the patrols or to the police. If the patrols have the effect of increasing surveillance, stimulating social interaction in public places, and eliciting support for the law, they may reduce crime indirectly, not by deterring offenders themselves but by increasing informal social control in the community.

Footnotes

1. A survey of high crime areas in Washington, D.C., found that only 12 per cent of the sample had gotten together with others or been a member of a group that had either talked about the crime problem or tried to fight crime in some way. Only about 17 per cent thought they could do something about the crime problem in their community. The President's Commission on Law Enforcement and Adminstration of Justice, *Task Force Report: Crime and Its Impact—An Assessment*. Washington, D.C.: United States Government Printing Office, 1967, p. 91.
2. G. D. Wiebe, "Responses to the Televised Kefauver Hearings: Some Social Psychological Implications," *Public Opinion Quarterly* XVI (Summer 1962), p. 179.
3. Ibid., p. 186.
4. Emlyn Williams, *Beyond Belief: A Chronicle of Murder and Its Detection*. New York: Random House, 1967, p. 339.
5. Jane Jacobs, *The Death and Life of Great American Cities*. New York: Vintage Books, 1961, pp. 123–124.
6. Roscoe Pound, "The Future of Criminal Law," *Columbia Law Review* XXI (January 1921), pp. 1–16.
7. Richard Maxwell Brown, *The South Carolina Regulators*. Cam-

bridge: The Belknap Press of Harvard University Press, 1963.

8. Ibid., pp. 27–29.

9. Ibid., p. 50.

10. Ibid., p. 90.

11. Leonard Dinnerstein, *The Leo Frank Case.* New York: Columbia University Press, 1968, p. 139.

12. Much of the following discussion of vigilante groups is based on Richard Maxwell Brown, "The American Vigilante Tradition," in Hugh Davis Graham and Ted Robert Gurr, editors, *Violence in America: Historical and Comparative Perspectives,* Volume 1. Washington, D.C.: United States Government Printing Office, 1969, pp. 121–180.

13. Ibid., p. 139.

14. Thomas J. Dimsdale, *The Vigilantes of Montana.* Norman, Okla.: University of Oklahoma Press, 1866, 1953, p. 14.

15. Ibid., p. 15.

16. Brown, "The American Vigilante Tradition," p. 138.

17. Ibid., p. 123.

18. Louis Chevalier, *Laboring Classes and Dangerous Classes in Paris during the Nineteenth Century,* translated by Frank Jellinek. New York: Howard Fertig, 1958, 1973.

19. In San Diego in 1912, a vigilante group supporting middle-class values of order and property harassed a group of radicals and prevented them from speaking and organizing in the community. See Laurence Veysey, editor, *Law and Resistance: American Attitudes toward Authority.* New York: Harper and Row, Publishers, 1970, pp. 208–234.

20. Brown, "The American Vigilante Tradition," p. 135.

21. Ibid., pp. 135–137.

22. Ibid., pp. 141–142.

23. Ibid., pp. 143–146.

24. Ibid., p. 143.

25. Ibid., p. 152.

26. Ibid., pp. 146–147.

27. Oscar Newman, *Architectural Design for Crime Prevention.* Washington, D.C.: United States Government Printing Office, 1973, pp. 16–17.

28. Brown, "The American Vigilante Tradition," p. 130.

29. For example, see John Sibley, "Mayor and Cawley Hail Citizens on Aid in Seizing Suspects," *The New York Times,* June 20, 1973, pp. 1, 40; Wolfgang Saxon, "Crowd Chases and Beats Slayer Unconscious Here," *The New York Times,* July 23, 1973, pp. 1, 28.

30. "Killing of Arsonists Is Sanctioned in Syracuse," *The New York Times,* August 6, 1971, p. 38.

31. Charles Mohr, "Crime a Growing Problem for Africa; Robbery

is Bringing Harsh Punishment," *The New York Times,* July 27, 1971, p. 2.

32. Thomas A. Johnson, "Crime Generates Nigeria Debate," *The New York Times,* August 20, 1972, p. 17.

33. "Mobs Take Law into Own Hands," *The New York Times,* October 9, 1973, p. 38.

34. Marshall B. Clinard and Daniel J. Abbott, *Crime in Developing Countries: A Comparative Perspective.* New York: John Wiley & Sons, 1973, p. 227.

35. Saxon, op. cit.

36. After another murder in the city at about the same time, one man remarked, "When the police find him, they'll just say he's a sick man and send him to a hospital for two years. . . . Then he'll be right back on the street. The only thing to do is to kill this man right away, quickly and quietly." Cited in Linda Greenhouse, "At the Precincts: Asking for Blood and Decrying It," *The New York Times,* August 26, 1973, p. 6.

37. Fred Ferretti, "Suspect in Boys' Slayings Cleared, Police Spirit Him past Angry Mob," *The New York Times,* August 22, 1973, pp. 1, 46.

38. Cited in Tom A. Cullen, *When London Walked in Terror.* New York: Avon Books, 1965, pp. 89–90.

39. Gerald D. Suttles, *The Social Construction of Communities.* Chicago: The University of Chicago Press, 1972, pp. 21–43, 189–229.

40. Ibid., p. 29.

41. Ibid., p. 190.

42. Gary T. Marx and Dane Archer, "The Urban Vigilante," *Psychology Today* VI (January 1973), pp. 45–50; Gary T. Marx and Dane Archer, "Citizen Involvement in the Law Enforcement Process: The Case of Community Police Patrols," *American Behavioral Scientist* XV (September–October 1971), pp. 52–72; and Gary T. Marx and Dane Archer, "Picking up the Gun: Some Organizational and Survey Data on Community Police Patrols." Paper presented at the Symposium on Studies of Public Experience, Knowledge and Opinion of Crime and Justice. Bureau of Social Science Research, Inc. Washington, D.C., March 1972.

43. Cited in Ronald Smothers, "Auxiliary Police Patrolling Broadway," *The New York Times,* September 27, 1972, p. 51.

44. Marx and Archer, "Citizen Involvement in the Law Enforcement Process," p. 57.

45. Murray Schumach, "City Puts Stress in Capital Budget on Fighting Crime," *The New York Times,* February 1, 1973, pp. 1, 44; Edward Ranzal, "Block-Security Program is Detailed by Lindsay," *The New York Times,* March 23, 1973, p. 41.

46. Terry Ann Knopf, *Youth Patrols: An Experiment in Community*

Participation. Waltham, Mass.: Brandeis University, Lemberg Center for the Study of Violence, 1969.

47. Harold A. Nelson, "The Defenders: A Case Study of an Informal Police Organization," *Social Problems* XV (Fall 1967), pp. 127–147.

48. Ibid., p. 132.

49. Fay G. Cohen, "The Indian Patrol in Minneapolis: Social Control and Social Change in an Urban Context," *Law and Society Review* VII (Summer 1973), pp. 779–786.

50. Ibid., p. 779.

51. Marx and Archer, "Picking up the Gun," p. 15.

52. Ibid., p. 18.

53. Marx and Archer, "Citizen Involvement in the Law Enforcement Process," pp. 64–65.

54. Marx and Archer, "Picking up the Gun," p. 19.

55. Marx and Archer, "Citizen Involvement in the Law Enforcement Process," p. 65.

56. Thomas A. Johnson, "Who Killed the 10 Drug Pushers?" *The New York Times*, January 23, 1972, p. 55.

57. "Vigilante Group 'Taxes' Detroit Dope Peddlers," *Boston Globe*, April 13, 1973, p. 2.

58. Joseph Novitski, "10 Petty Criminals Killed in Sao Paulo by a 'Death Squad,'" *The New York Times*, July 21, 1970, pp. 1, 6; Joseph Novitski, "Brazil Assails 'Death Squads,' Vigilantes Who Kill Criminals," *The New York Times*, July 25, 1970, pp. 1, 2.

59. Ibid.

60. Ibid.

61. Evelyn Keene, "Judge Says JDL Aided Bornstein Investigation," *Boston Globe*, December 23, 1972, p. 3; Alan H. Sheehan, "Discovery of Body Detailed by Friend," *Boston Globe*, June 13, 1973, p. 12.

62. "Youths Seize Man with Marijuana," *The New York Times*, July 31, 1973, p. 20.

63. Cited in Smothers, op. cit., p. 51.

64. Alan Lupo, "The Do-It-Yourself War against Street Crime," *Boston Magazine* LXV (May 1973), pp. 38–41, 72–81.

65. Ibid.

66. Lupo's suggestion that streets are less filled with people today than in the past because of television viewing is an interesting one, but it would not explain variation among communities in the amount of street life, since almost all American families now own televisions.

67. Albert Fay Hill, *The North Avenue Irregulars: A Suburb Battles the Mafia*. New York: Cowles Education Corporation, 1968.

68. There are an estimated 24,000 people in tenant patrols in New

York City alone. There are also an estimated 10,000 block-watchers who report suspicious behavior to the police, as well as 6,000 in an Auxiliary Police Force and 6,000 in a Civilian Patrol group. These 46,000 private law enforcers supplement the regular New York City Police Department force of 30,000. William L. Claiborne, "New Yorkers Fight Back: The Tilt toward Vigilantism," *New York* VI (October 15, 1973), p. 52.

69. Marx and Archer, "Picking up the Gun," pp. 25–47.
70. Marx and Archer, "The Urban Vigilante," p. 48.
71. Marx and Archer, "Picking up the Gun," pp. 29–30.
72. Ibid., pp. 31–39.
73. Ibid., pp. 49–50.
74. Marx and Archer, "Citizen Involvement in the Law Enforcement Process," p. 68.

9 Individual Response to Crime: Helping the Victim

T H E diminished social solidarity caused by the fear of crime creates an unwillingness to personally assist victims of crime. Staying home at night and avoiding strangers and neighbors reduces the chance that an individual will even see a crime in progress, much less be willing to help a victim in distress. The issue of public response to victims of emergencies has been called the Good Samaritan problem. There has been much concern with this problem in recent years. Since the mid-1960's, increasing crime rates and urban riots have created a heightened public fear of crime and violence. As violence and fear increased, so did discussion of the public's reluctance to help victims of violence and the police who confronted violence. The salience of this issue was further enhanced by the perception that the scene of crimes had shifted from ghettos to the city as a whole and from private places to public areas such as subways and parks.[1] Crime in these places was more threatening but also more subject to citizen observation, thus presenting people with decisions of whether or not to help victims in distress.

Probably the single event that has most influenced awareness of the Good Samaritan problem was the 1964 murder in Kew Gardens, Queens, of a young woman named Kitty Genovese. When the story appeared in *The New York Times* the next day, it was a brief four-paragraph story on an inside page. One reporter observed that if she had been killed on Park Avenue or Madison Avenue under the same circumstances, the story would have been on the front page; the story would have probably been longer if this white woman had been killed in Harlem, and it might have been shorter if she had been a black woman killed in Harlem. This journalist suggests that the amount of space devoted to a murder story varies with what has meaning for the paper's readers and what is of general interest.[2] However, the *Times'* brief treatment of the Genovese killing greatly underestimated the interest the story would generate.

The murder occurred in a middle-class neighborhood with a relatively low crime rate. As Miss Genovese was returning home from work at three o'clock in the morning, an assailant attacked her with a knife. She screamed. Lights went on in nearby apartments, and people looked out their windows. One witness to the violence shouted at the assailant to leave the woman alone. He left the scene but soon returned. Again lights went on, and again he left. He returned a third time and this time killed the woman. The three attacks took place over a period of thirty-five minutes, and at least thirty-eight witnesses knew of the violence. Only after the assaults were over did one man call the police, and he did that from a neighbor's apartment in order to avoid personal involvement.

When questioned later, witnesses offered various reasons for their failure to respond. Some said they thought the fight was a "lovers' quarrel." Others simply said they were too tired to do anything or did not want to get involved. A few said they were afraid, although it is not clear why their fear would prevent them from making an anonymous call to the police. Even professionals were unable to offer compelling reasons for the failure of thirty-eight people to respond. Some professionals simply said they could not understand why no one had helped. Others used jargon that avoided any real explanation, and a number of them sought a scapegoat (the police can't be trusted to respond to a call, or television violence inhibits direct response to real violence).[3]

Public response to the failure of the witnesses to help Miss Genovese was strong. Letters to newspaper editors recommended censuring the nonresponsive witnesses by printing their names in the paper. Most people said that *they* would have at least called the police; this view seems mistaken, given the actual reasons that people fail to respond to emergencies with help, reasons we shall soon examine. A number of letters to newspapers blamed the police; people said that New Yorkers were afraid or contemptuous of the police, and were therefore unwilling to report a crime to them. The *police* were thus criticized by the *public* for the *public*'s failure to respond. As in Port City, people blamed the police for the crime problem but denied any personal responsibility for helping to prevent crime, even for alerting the police that a crime was in progress.

The public could not understand why no help was given by anyone in a group as large as thirty-eight people. If only one person had seen the crime and had failed to respond, they could have attributed nonresponse to individual deviance or the risk that one person would have faced in intervening. When so large a group took no action, it seemed that something must be wrong with society as a whole. The cause that was fastened upon was apathy; people just no longer cared for their fellow man. This interpretation was unsettling, because it threatened the very basis of the moral and social order. In spite of the nearly universal condemnation of the unresponsive witnesses, the murder did not create a sense of solidarity among people. People did "wax indignant," as Durkheim suggested, but they did so in condemnation of the unresponsive bystanders who had violated social norms of helping rather than in condemnation of the murderer. People felt that others could not be trusted to render needed assistance. This reduced interpersonal trust and social solidarity; it did not increase the strength of social bonds.

The Genovese case and similar instances of bystander nonresponse have effects on crime itself. The assailant in the Genovese attack later said that he knew that no one would help his victim on that cold morning, making it less risky for him to commit the crime. If offenders think that bystanders will not help a victim in distress, they will not be deterred from committing crimes in public places. All they then have to do is to avoid the police, who are limited in the territory they can cover. People on the street and the design of buildings can increase surveillance of open spaces and possibly enhance informal social control, but without public willingness to respond to crimes by personally intervening or by calling the police, this surveillance will have little effect on potential offenders. Criminals who know they will be observed but not interfered with by witnesses will not be deterred by the mere presence of those witnesses. Offenders' awareness of public unwillingness to get personally involved will reduce social control and thus increase crime in a community. Senator Mike Mansfield has said, "In my judgment, this overt apathy or nonparticipation by citizens in regulatory functions of society is about to become a most critical and pressing problem. Today, citizens must recognize that through their plain apathy, they are committing crimes against society."[4]

Many people attribute nonresponse to public apathy. However, there are more adequate explanations of why people fail to help in some situations but help in others. In this chapter, we first look at the law in the United States that deals with the way individuals should behave in emergency situations. We then explore some empirical findings, particularly those obtained by Latané and Darley from a series of experiments, that bear on the problem of bystander response to emergencies.

Bystander Response and the Law

Anglo-American law does not generally require a witness to an emergency to help a victim whose predicament was not caused by the witness himself.[5] In fact, Anglo-American law warns witnesses that they face certain risks if they try to help a victim but fail; sometimes they may be sued for harming the victim as a result of errors they commit during their rescue attempt. Our legal system thus discourages bystander aid to victims. In contrast, the law in such countries as France and Germany requires affirmative action by witnesses under certain conditions. In France, the failure to help someone who could have been rescued from danger with no risk to the witness can be followed with a fine or a jail sentence for the nonresponsive bystander.[6] Laws in other nations provide compensation to the rescuer or his dependents if he suffers injury or death during a rescue attempt. Still other countries award money to those who help others.[7]

The American position on the duty to rescue is typified by the 1907 decision in *People v. Beardsley*.[8] Here the court stated that although citizens might have a moral duty to help others in

217

distress, such a moral duty does not imply any legal duty to rescue.[9] This decision probably met with public approval then, and it probably would now. In an earlier chapter we saw that residents of both Port City and Belleville felt that people do not help the police enough, but few of them favored laws that would *require* such assistance. Both in the law and in the public's view, helping victims and helping the police should be voluntary.

What impact on behavior would a law requiring affirmative action to help victims have? Although such a law might not influence behavior very much, it might be enough to affect some people who would otherwise hesitate to help victims in distress. In the long run, such a law might teach the public new norms of helping behavior. This didactic function of the law is difficult to document, but if people know that a law requires certain behavior, they may learn to view that behavior more positively. A study of university students' attitudes toward witnesses' obligation to help victims found that students in countries with no law requiring such assistance (Austria and the United States) were much less apt to say that the law in their nation required help in emergencies than were students in a nation with such a law (Germany).[10] In other words, the students knew what the law required. Such awareness was related to their support of punishment for someone who did not offer help to a victim; more students in Germany than in Austria or the United States said that a nonreponsive bystander should be punished. Apparently, the law affected social norms, although it is possible that the prior existence of those social norms made passage of the law feasible in the first place. However, the difference among the students in terms of how they thought *they* would behave if faced with an emergency was small. Roughly the same proportion in each country said that they would not have helped a victim in each of four hypothetical emergency situations. In Germany, 37 per cent said they would not have helped, compared to 39 per cent in Austria and 44 per cent in the United States. Although based solely on verbal responses to questionnaire items, this study suggests that laws requiring helping behavior will be known to the public (or at least those with more education) and will influence what people see as appropriate behavior. However, the law will probably have little impact on behavior. If people say they would not help in a hypothetical situation, they probably would not help if faced with an actual emergency and its attendant risks.

American law not only fails to require assistance by a witness to an emergency, but it also provides few means for an individual to collect for injuries he suffers during a rescue attempt.[11] It would be unfair to burden the victim with compensation of his rescuer, since the victim is often not to blame for his own suffering. However, government compensation of injured rescuers might at least remove one obstacle which could prevent a bystander from helping. Laws that absolve a rescuer from civil suit by a victim or his dependents in the event that a rescue attempt fails might eliminate another reason for failure to help. Since the potential rescuer has no assurance that his behavior will not later be interpreted in a way other than he intended, he might fail to act rather than risk legal problems that might cause him to suffer from his altruistic behavior. The law not only offers no incentives to help a victim, but it actually discourages such behavior because of possible legal repercussions for the unsuccessful helper.

Fear of legal involvement can inhibit willingness to help even if there is no threat of physical harm. In a study of bystander response to staged cases of shoplifting, 41 per cent of the witnesses who failed to report the crime to the shopkeeper mentioned either the possibility of being sued by the offender if they were mistaken in their accusations or the possibility of having to appear as a witness in court. Unwillingness to take chances with the legal system led to nonresponse. This attitude is reinforced by the absence of any positive reward or satisfaction to be gained by helping the victim.[12]

Although it might be too much to expect a witness to an emergency to act if he realistically feels that he might suffer harm, there seems to be no good reason for the law not to require a witness to call the police or an ambulance, even if he does so anonymously. Such a law could increase the frequency of Good Samaritan behavior. Laws that allow witnesses some latitude in their response might be more acceptable to the public than laws which require specific actions in particular situations. Rudzinski suggests the following law:

> Whoever, witnessing an obvious and imminent danger threatening the life of another person, fails to come to his aid either through his personal intervention or by providing aid by others or does not notify immediately the proper public officer or institution, although he could do one of those things without reasonable fear of danger to his person or to others, shall be punished by imprisonment of up to . . . , or a fine of up to . . . , or both.[13]

Even such a law would present a problem. There would be obvious difficulties in proving that a nonresponsive witness knew of the emergency and felt no reasonable fear and did not try to take any of the required actions. Lack of faith in the effectiveness of the police would have to be overcome to get people to report crimes. Public reliance on the police as crime-fighting specialists would have to be counteracted to make people realize that even specialists need public cooperation in order to learn about emergency situations. The public's attitudes toward specialists is sometimes reinforced by those specialists themselves; sometimes the police speak of Good Samaritans as intruders or intermeddlers, and doctors occasionally criticize citizens for their amateurish attempts to provide medical care. Before the above proposal for a law could be effective, the Good Samaritan would have to be seen as an altruist who is trying to help others rather than as an "officious intermeddler."[14]

Why has this country not enacted a law to require assistance by a witness to an emergency? One reason is probably that most people easily empathize with the dilemma faced by a bystander—whether to help the victim and risk harm or involvement with the law, or to ignore the emergency and insure harm to the victim. Most people would rather be live cowards than dead heroes. Alan Barth has said,

> Let us bear in mind, however, that the original Good Samaritan extolled by St. Luke was fortunate in not arriving on the scene until after the thieves had set upon the traveler, robbed him, and beaten him

half to death. The Samaritan cared for him and showed him great kindness, but he did not put himself in any peril by doing so. Perhaps this is about as much as can be reasonably asked of the ordinary mortal man.[15]

Witnesses fear reprisals from the offender if they interrupt the crime. They think that involvement will later cause them inconvenience in answering police questions and appearing in court. Just as witnesses will not help for these reasons, so the general public is unwilling to require citizens to help for the same reasons.

The urbanization and industrialization of our society, along with increased population density, have created a situation of role segmentalization and alienation of people from each other. The emphasis on reserve and privacy in large cities reduces individual commitment to the welfare of others and desensitizes people to the predicaments of their fellow men. This is reinforced by the traditional American value of rugged individualism, the idea that each person should be able to take care of himself and not have to depend on others for help. Television and media violence, even if fictionalized, may desensitize people to real emergencies, making it difficult for them to empathize with a victim who is suffering the same fate seen hundreds of times on television and in the movies. In a society in which people are highly mobile geographically, many are uprooted before they can establish firm ties to the community. As a result, they are strangers to other residents of the community to which they move. People who have recently moved to a community are less aware of what constitutes deviant behavior in the community and who is a stranger to the area, making them less likely to intervene should they observe something slightly unusual. Another characteristic of modern society that is related to the Good Samaritan problem is the specialization of function that accompanies increasing complexity of the social structure. In complex societies, people often assign responsibility for particular jobs to specialized agencies; for example, many people feel that preventing crime is the job of the police and not the general public. Reliance on the police may diminish public efforts to prevent crime or to intervene on behalf of a victim.

These structural characteristics have often been cited as reasons for the public unwillingness to help the victim of a crime. They also help to explain the absence of a law requiring such behavior. Although these features may characterize societies in which no help is forthcoming, they do not provide a very thorough explanation of why individuals in particular situations fail to help victims in distress while people in other situations do help. The assumption seems to be that if society were simpler, if people were less exposed to media violence, if people did not move about so much, then events such as the Kitty Genovese slaying would be less common. However, there is no evidence at all to suggest that if Miss Genovese had been attacked on the main street of Holcomb, Kansas, that the response of the neighbors would have been any different. In fact, evidence to be examined later indicates that the failure to respond is rooted in psychological and sociological forces that would inhibit response whether the crime occurred in a large city or a small town, in a complex society or a relatively simple one.

The absence of a law requiring Good Samaritan behavior may also be due to the lack of any organized interest group to lobby for such a law. Further, the relatively high crime rate in this country—in comparison with other industrialized nations—may make people feel that such a law would force them to intervene in risky situations that occur fairly often. If crime were less threatening, it might be possible to pass a law to require such assistance, although the effect of such a law on actual helping behavior would still be questionable.

Knowing that people are not legally obligated to help victims or to intervene in a crime may make potential offenders more likely to commit a crime. This will reinforce public fears and make Good Samaritan laws even more difficult to pass. Still, the absence of such laws is not the major reason that people do not respond to victims in distress, although such laws might occasionally influence behavior. The presence of a law, even if unenforced and lacking strong impact on behavior, might create confidence that *others* would help. This could increase social solidarity and make people more willing to walk the streets at night because of a feeling that they could depend on others to help in an emergency. This view might be inaccurate, but it still could be self-fulfilling if it led people to spend more time on the street, since potential criminals might be less willing to commit crimes in the sight of others. For such an effect to occur, a potential offender would have to feel that there was some chance of being interfered with or reported to the police by witnesses.

Reaction to an Observed Crime

How does a witness to a crime or an accident react? In the abstract, many of us feel that we would make an heroic rescue or at least call the police or an ambulance. People were very critical of the thirty-eight witnesses who failed to help Kitty Genovese because they dissociated themselves from the witnesses; they felt that they could never have behaved so callously in such a situation. We saw in an earlier chapter that a majority of the respondents in both Port City and Belleville said that they would at least call the police to report an attack on a woman outside their home. If their responses are to be believed, the residents of Port City and Belleville must be very different from those of Kew Gardens, Queens. A more likely explanation is that our respondents' answers were influenced by social norms about helping others in distress, but the witnesses to the Genovese murder were affected by forces other than the social norms to which they also would pay lip service when not confronted with an actual emergency.

Lawrence Freedman has examined some of the reasons for failure to respond to an emergency situation.[16] He suggests that an onlooker's initial reaction is usually *fear,* fear of being hurt and fear of reprisals. This bystander reaction is similar to the initial reaction of victims themselves; robbery victims often say that their first feeling about being held up was fear. A second reaction of witnesses is *acquiescence* to the situation. This results largely from a cognitive inability to perceive the unusual event as fitting into any familiar category of experience. People have a difficult time perceiving emergency situations as real. This may be due to the location of the event itself. Milgram and Hollander attribute the lack of witness response to Kitty Genovese's plight in part to the fact that the crime seemed "totally incongruous in a respectable neighborhood"; this "created a sense of unreality which inhibited rational action." [17]

People often have difficulty interpreting an observed event as a crime. This may result from rationalizations to justify their inaction; it may also be due to the ambiguity of the behavior. This is compounded by a cultural emphasis on privacy; people feel that an event must *clearly* be a crime before they dare intervene. Witnesses to the Genovese murder thought that the attack might have been a "lovers' quarrel"; they did not wish to intervene in a private matter, even if one "lover" killed the other. A number of witnesses to a man's "abduction" of a ten-year-old girl at a shopping center—an event staged by a Miami television station—failed to perceive the event as a crime. They thought it might merely have been the girl's father taking her home, although force was used. Other witnesses felt that whatever was happening was none of their business.

Whereas people sometimes acquiesce when faced with an emergency situation, another common reaction is to seek clarifying information about the event. This is especially common if there is no *direct* threat of harm to the witness and if the witness has time to seek information. [18] For instance, the assassination of President John F. Kennedy immobilized many people; more than half of one sample were unable to continue their normal activities. [19] Many people spent hours in front of their televisions or radios in search of information that would make the assassination comprehensible. Television

structured and clarified the extent of personal threat. . . . It gave timely reassurance by showing the existence and continuity of cherished institutions and values. It reinforced social prescriptions for correct behavior by showing the exemplary conduct of the nation's leaders. . . . And it helped narcotize behavior that might have been dangerous by exhausting the need for action. [20]

People also turned to family and friends to talk about the assassination and to learn more about it. One reason for such behavior is that this unusual event was particularly threatening because most people had no previous experience that allowed them to interpret it.

Another example of the search for information about a threatening event involved a mass murder in Japan of twelve political radicals by other members of the party. Public interest in the event was reinforced by extensive television coverage of a police attack to rescue a hostage from the radicals. After the murders and the police attack, people sought information to make sense of the events. Scholars spent much effort analyzing what had happened; a series of panel discussions was substituted for regular television programs, and the shows were widely watched by the Japanese public. These programs helped people clarify the unusual events and made it easier for them to interpret the crimes.[21]

When certain types of crime become commonplace, this need for clarifying and reassuring information is less strong. People reacted to the assassinations of Senator Robert F. Kennedy and Dr. Martin Luther King, Jr., with less confusion and uncertainty than they did to the assassination of President Kennedy. Condemnation of those crimes was still widespread, but political assassination was no longer as mysterious an event as it had been a few years before; people had a framework within which to place the more recent assassinations.

Freedman suggests that after fear and acquiescence, witnesses to an emergency often *fail to respond* appropriately and occasionally *deny* that anything so unusual could be happening. What may appear to be apathy is in fact a *massive inhibition*, a paralysis of consciousness that results from overwhelming internal conflicts. Failure to respond may also be due to excessive stimulation from the external environment. The impact of the unusual event on the individual's mind may diminish his ability to respond. Freedman concludes:

[I]n my view apathy and indifference are the least likely primary psychic vectors in response to [an emergency]. The sequence as I see it is, first, the intense emotional shock—characterized predominantly, but not exclusively, by anxiety; second, the cognitive perception and awareness of what has happened; third, an inertial paralysis of reaction, which as a non-act becomes in fact an act; and fourth, the self-awareness of one's own shock anxiety, non-involvement which is followed by a sense of guilt and intra-psychic and social self-justification.

I do not assume that these things happen in such neat sequence. For all practical purposes they seem to occur simultaneously.[22]

One way that a witness to a crime often justifies his inaction is to say to himself that there is probably some link between the victim and the offender, that the victim "got what he asked for." The ambiguity of many crimes allows witnesses to hold such a definition of the situation. This occurred when some witnesses saw the Genovese murder as a "lovers' quarrel" and when the Miami shoppers saw the girl's abduction as a father-daughter interaction. The notion of contributory fault by the victim, an idea supported by sociological research that shows that victim and offender often interact prior to a crime, makes the victim blameworthy in the eyes of the witness. This can reduce pressure to help the victim, since it makes the crime seem more "fair." The crime is also more understandable, hence less threatening to the witness, if the victim created his own predicament.

Kalven and Zeisel suggest that some concepts of tort law have been adopted by the criminal law. For example, the ideas of contributory negligence and assumption of risk often influence the outcome of a criminal case. Determination of the guilt of a rapist may be affected by assessing the life style of his victim and her relationship with him. Behavior by the woman which is seen as compromising, seductive, or suggestive may be used as an argument for acquittal, even though all other criteria for a rape conviction are present. In part, this is due to a common misperception that the criminal law is a contest between the victim and the offender, rather than between the state and the defendant.[23] Similarly, witnesses to a crime often interpret it as a struggle between offender and victim rather than an attack on social values. Instead of feeling closer to the victim because of the attack on shared values, the witness is more apt to see the victim as involved in a contest with the offender to which the victim may have contributed and which is of no concern to the witness. The victim may even be looked down upon by the witness if he or she loses the contest.[24]

People who observe a crime are more apt to render aid if they identify with the victim. If a witness disidentifies with the victim or sees the victim as different from himself, lack of direct action is more easily rationalized. One way witnesses do this is to think that the victim was previously involved with the offender; implicit is the feeling that the witness himself would never have gotten involved and would never find himself in a similar position requiring the aid of an onlooker. For example, a driver of a large car who passes an accident involving a small car may say to himself that small cars are unsafe and should not be on the open highway with larger cars.[25] If he had been driving a small car himself, the driver might have reasoned that the accident victim was a careless driver, or a young and inexperienced one, or in some other way contributed to the accident. A witness can most easily blame the victim, reduce the threat that he personally feels, and justify inaction if he can dissociate himself from the victim and his predicament.

People probably try harder to dissociate themselves from victims of highly threatening crimes. Seeking a prior relationship between a rapist and his victim helps place the crime in an understandable context and reduces an individual's fear of the same fate.[26] People do not necessarily absolve the offender of guilt, but their dissociation from a "willing" or "seductive" victim makes them feel that they would never have brought such a crime upon themselves or associated with anyone who would commit so heinous an offense. These perceptions need not be accurate in order to reduce anxiety and diminish the chance that a witness will help a victim.

People find it easier to accept harm to victims who occupy disvalued social roles. A national survey of attitudes toward violence found that "[e]xcluding people from groups to which one feels related can serve as a rationalization justifying violence toward them" or make violence inflicted on such people more easily acceptable.[27] If there is little identification with the victim, there is less need to extend compassion or assistance to him. For example, residents of a block in Queens, New York, tolerated vandalism of a local house because of rumors that the house had been sold to someone different from themselves. The story was that the house had been sold to blacks, or to Filipinos in a later version of the rumor. The new owners were in fact of Chinese ancestry, but all that mattered to the white residents of the community was that the people were members of a group that they held in lower esteem than their own. Vandalism was not strongly condemned because the victims were different; the new owners were Chinese, but someone had painted on the house "We Hate Niggers." [28]

An attempt to take advantage of local feelings toward the propriety of violent behavior against a certain stigmatized social group (homosexuals) was made by a sixteen-year-old boy who committed a murder in Arkansas. After the killing, he dressed the man's body in woman's clothing. He thought that a jury would blame the victim for his own murder because he appeared to be a homosexual and a transvestite. The ploy did not work; the boy was found guilty of first-degree murder and given a death penalty, although he has not been executed. [29]

The attitudes that some victims deserve their own victimization because of personal characteristics or behavior has occasionally been formalized. For example, the Criminal Injuries Compensation Board in Great Britain can reject for compensation anyone who has a criminal record or whose life style is considered "unsuitable." *The New York Times* reports on the Board as follows:

A man at a wrestling match who tapped a wrestler on the leg with a lighted cigar and got a broken jaw drew no sympathy from the board.

Nor did the young man at the office outing who got friendly with a girl he knew was married. They went to her place and were getting even friendlier when her husband arrived and slashed the young man.

But a man who is stabbed in a tavern brawl can expect to get some compensation, if he did not start the fight. [30]

This system formalizes the idea that victims vary in terms of blameworthiness. Those who have prior involvement in crime or contribute in some way to their victimization are not compensated for injuries suffered during a crime. Just as a witness may not help a victim he sees as blameworthy, even though the victim is actually suffering, so too do certain suffering victims receive little sympathy or compensation from the British government.

The amount of empathy a witness feels for the victim of a crime is critical in determining his reaction to the crime. Shils suggests that people see the sanctity of human life in degrees, feeling that those closest to and most like themselves are more important than those more distant from and less like themselves. Shils says there is a "gradation of 'sanctity' moving from the individual outward—first through his kinship and affectional attachments, then local, national, class, ethnic group, and culture, becoming more attenuated and patchier as it reaches into other countries, continents and races." [31] As personal affection and identification diminish, so also do the value placed on the life and the willingness to help preserve that life. [32] For example, experimental evidence shows that the *span of sympathy* felt by witnesses to another's plight is influenced by ethnic allegiances; whites are more apt to help other whites than to help blacks. [33]

Jane Jacobs claims that a primary requirement for successful city life is that people take responsibility for the welfare of strangers, since most social contacts in large cities are between people who do not know each other well. [34] She suggests that children learn to empathize with strangers less by pedagogical instruction than by first-hand experiences in which they see adults take responsibility for others with whom they do not have close ties. They learn to empathize by being the object of another's empathy or by seeing people react empathetically to others. [35] Jacobs says that the absence of this empathy in large and anonymous urban communities makes it difficult for children who grow up there to learn this trait. If this is true—and there is no solid evidence to support the idea—it might provide a partial explanation of why bystanders fail to respond to victims in distress. In a setting where people know each other and empathize with each other, whether this place be a small town or a closely-knit community, willingness to help others in distress may be widespread.

Pitirim A. Sorokin conducted a study a number of years ago which illustrates the way that identification with a victim determines assistance rendered to that individual. He found that the greater the distance between people and the victims of the hypothetical emergencies, the less likely those people would be to contribute to the solution of the victim's problem.[36] Sorokin used as a "thermometer of relative sociality" the amount of money that college students said they would contribute to three different causes. One cause was to buy equipment and material that would help the students themselves prepare for examinations. Another was to secure financial aid to help three students in their department stay in school, since their resources had been depleted by a natural disaster. The third was to help an "International Students' Relief" fund to support Chinese and Russian university students who were dying of starvation. Thus all victims were students, but they differed in terms of need and in terms of geographical and social distance from the subjects of the study. The amount of money that the subjects said they would donate decreased from the first cause to the third cause, although the severity of the problem increased. Sorokin concluded that "intensity of sociality [measured by monetary donation] decreases parallel as the social distance of the groups increases," even though the money was needed more by those who were more socially distant.[37] This study lends further support to the idea that willingness to help the victim of an emergency is influenced by the degree of identification between the witness and the victim.

Sorokin's study also raises the question of geographical distance between people as a determinant of reaction to crime. A crime that occurs close to home may elicit a greater response than one committed in a more distant place, although people in low crime areas may have difficulty at first in interpreting the crime as "real." What is probably most important is not the geographical distance involved, but rather the psychological and social distance. We need to know how an individual defines his community and with whom he identifies and interacts. The community of an individual is not easily defined in only geographical terms. Milgram suggests that people in cities do not make friends by physical proximity but have friends throughout the city, meaning they are unlikely to have friends close at hand if they need their help in an emergency.[38] However, people will be threatened by crimes in their area of the city or in areas with which they closely identify because of similarity to their own neighborhood or because they know people there. Still, in large cities, murders a few blocks away may elicit little reaction because those areas are not defined as part of one's own community. In contrast, people throughout the entire state of Kansas reacted sharply to the Clutter murders. Community in a psychological (or identificational) and sociological (or interactional and structural) sense is not always coterminous with community in geographical terms. This partly explains why New Yorkers may be little concerned with a murder a few blocks away, but Kansans become very upset about murders a few hundred miles away.

Failure to Help a Victim: Social Psychological Studies

Bibb Latané and John M. Darley dissent from the view that bystander nonresponse to a victim's plight is adequately explained by apathy or by the absence of social norms that expect helping behavior. They also disagree with the idea that the dehumanizing and alienating nature of large-city life is the primary cause of bystander failure to respond to a victim's cries. They do not think that there is less compassion in the city than in the small town, nor that there is less compassion today than in the past. Indeed, they argue that people who witness crimes such as the Genovese murder do react emotionally; they watch in "helpless fascination" but are unable to engage in active helping behavior.

In a series of experiments in the laboratory and in field settings, Latané and Darley sought to determine not the motivation of helping behavior, but rather what it is about a particular *situation* that determines whether or not help will be offered.[39] None of a series of *personality* variables that might plausibly be related to helping behavior was in fact related to such behavior.[40] The researchers suggest that the impact of situational factors confronting the witness to an emergency is so strong that he rarely has time to even think about helping in a conscious way; his personality traits are thus not a major influence on his response to the crisis. Latané and Darley conclude about explanations of helping behavior in terms of personality characteristics:

These explanations generally assert that people who fail to intervene are somehow different from the rest of us, that they are "alienated by industrialization," "dehumanized by urbanization," "depersonalized by living in the cold society," or "psychopaths."

These explanations serve a dual purpose for those who adopt them. First, they answer (if only in a superficial way) the puzzling and frightening question of why people watch others die without trying to save them. Second, they give individuals reason to deny that they too might fail to help in a similar situation.[41]

Latané and Darley found that the *biographical* characteristics of their experimental subjects were somewhat more closely related to helping behavior than the personality traits, although only two background measures were significantly related to such behavior. "The smaller the size of the community in which the subject grew up, the more likely she was to help the victim of the emergency."[42] There was also a slight tendency for lower-middle-class subjects to help victims more than upper-middle-class ones. Other background variables did not help explain whether or not a subject would offer assistance to the victim of an emergency.

The influence of *social norms* about helping in emergency situations is also questionable. Earlier we saw that many residents of Belleville and Port City said that they would help a victim of an assault, in spite of evidence that actual witnesses rarely do. This suggests that the social norm of helping may exist without having any real effect on the behavior of a person in a position to conform to or deviate from that norm. A study of the response of theology students to emergencies found that, although their role would seem to include helping norms, many of them failed to render assistance to victims in distress. Whether or not they helped was largely a function of whether or not they were in a hurry.[43] However, an experiment using fifteen police recruits and fifteen veteran policemen as subjects found that both groups were very likely to help victims in distress. In fact, 87 per cent of each group rendered aid. The researchers suggest that this high level of helping behavior may be due to the fact that the police role places them in the position of *active* helper, whereas ministers or theology students are *passive* helpers.[44] This study hints that if social norms of helping exist, *and* if an individual occupies a role in which affirmative action to help a victim is expected, help may be forthcoming. However, social norms do seem to play a relatively small part in determining whether or not most passersby will help a victim. Social norms are also contradictory. People are expected to help, but there is also a strongly held norm of respecting the privacy of others; this may conflict with an impulse to help. Also, norms are often stated in a vague and abstract way; helping a victim requires specific and definite action.[45]

Emergencies often entail risk of harm to the intervening bystander. At worst he may lose his life; the most he can hope for is to prevent harm to another. Positive rewards for the rescuer are rare. The situation is thus one of high risk and low reward. Emergencies are also unforeseen and unusual events for which most individuals are neither prepared nor trained. Consequently, they produce stress and uncertainty at a time when quick and assertive reactions are required.[46]

Latané and Darley suggest that before a bystander will intervene, he must make a series of decisions. A negative decision at any point takes him out of the field of potential helpers. First, he must *notice* the event. As we saw earlier, a large proportion of bystanders failed to notice crimes of shoplifting that were staged in a way to focus attention on the theft. Once the event is noticed, the bystander must *interpret it as an emergency*. We suggested earlier in this chapter that witnesses may redefine emergency situations to appear as non-emergencies. If the witness does define the situation as an emergency, he must then determine that he has *personal responsibility* to act. He may say that "it's none of my business," or he may feel unqualified to help (for example, he may not be able to swim to rescue a drowning person). He may think that the victim does not deserve his help ("it's his fault anyway"), or he may think that he only shares responsibility with other witnesses who are present.

If a bystander decides to help, he must next determine what *form of assistance* to render, whether it be what Latané and Darley call "direct intervention" to help the victim or "detour intervention" such as calling the police or an ambulance. Direct action is an obvious course but requires skill and bravery; detour intervention is circuitous and time-consuming but requires less courage or specialized ability.[47] Finally, the bystander must decide how to *implement the course of action* upon which he has decided. Stress associated with the emergency may make behavior that would otherwise be easily performed much more difficult. Clearly, there are a number of obstacles to providing help for a victim. A bystander may make a decision to help on the first four steps but then decide that there is no way to implement the mode of rescue upon which he has decided. He may then walk away and leave the victim to the care of other passersby.

Looking at the social context within which such decisions to help are made, Oscar Newman identifies the following factors as significant:

- Identification on the part of the observer with either victim or property.
- The extent to which the activity observed is understood to be occurring in an area within the sphere of influence of the observer.
- The extent to which the observer has actively developed proprietary feelings and is accustomed to defending his property.
- Identification of the observed behavior as being abnormal to the area in which it occurs and therefore warranting response.
- The extent to which the observer feels he can effectively alter the course of events being observed.[48]

We saw in an earlier chapter how the structure of a community and the design of its buildings could generate these preconditions for helping behavior.

One of the most frightening aspects about events such as the Genovese murder is the failure of *large numbers* of people to provide any help at all. People think that if more witnesses are present, there must be a greater probability that at least one of them will offer some assistance. We might also expect that pressure to conform to social norms of helping would be strongest in a large group. However, the experiments by Latané and Darley show that the presence of others actually *inhibits* helping behavior. They suggest that this may be because witnesses are embarrassed to engage in unusual (helping) behavior in public. Witnesses may also fear intruding on another's privacy when no aid is needed or desired. Norms of privacy may cause bystanders to keep their eyes to themselves so that they do not even notice emergencies. Even if an emergency is noticed, failure to help does not mean doing nothing; it means continuing the behavior that was already being performed when the emergency was noticed.

Lack of immediate reaction by any member of a group of witnesses can lead an individual to reason that since no one else took any action, his interpretation of the event as an emergency must be incorrect. Kitty Genovese's neighbors may have thought that if what they were witnessing was really a criminal attack upon an innocent victim, someone would have gone to her assistance or called the police by the time they could act. People in groups take their cues from others in the group; if those others seem unconcerned, an individual may feel that his original interpretation of the event was wrong. This creates a situation of *pluralistic ignorance* in which initial lack of action is taken as a sign that no emergency exists.[49] This inhibits action by any other member of the group. The interpretation of the situation is influenced by the group and determines the reaction of group members. Apathy and alienation contribute little to explaining why no one helps the victim in such a situation; in fact, the witnesses experience emotional arousal and inner conflict rather than apathy when confronted with a crisis, even if they fail to act.

In a series of staged emergencies, Latané and Darley varied the number of witnesses and the relationships among the witnesses. They found that if a person witnessed an emergency alone, he was more likely to respond by trying to determine the nature of the emergency, taking some action to help the victim, or reporting the crisis to someone who could help. When a confederate was present, it took the subject longer to notice signs of the emergency, and helping behavior was less common. Latané and Darley do suggest that under certain circumstances, as with an audience in a theater where smoke is noticed, the chance is increased that at least one person will act impulsively and destroy the unanimity of unconcern. This will lead others to react and may cause a panic.[50]

Witnesses were more apt to help a victim if they were alone than if they were with a stranger. Even if the other witness was a friend, helping behavior was inhibited by the presence of a second party. However, when aid was forthcoming, if the other witness was a friend, aid was given sooner than if the other witness was a stranger. This may be because friends are less embarrassed to help in front of each other, or because they are better able to show their concern nonverbally or to talk over the situation. Latané and Darley suggest that friends are less apt to develop pluralistic ignorance than strangers; still, they do inhibit each other from acting, in comparison to the likelihood that help would have been given had either friend observed the emergency alone. Witnesses later denied that they were influenced by the presence of others. Also, those who failed to help were not upset at their nonresponse, since their interpretation of the situation was consistent with their failure to help. It is unclear whether their perception of the emergency was influenced by their failure to act, or whether their failure to act was influenced by their interpretation of the situation. Many of those who failed to help were unsure as to exactly what had happened, others thought that the situation was not too serious, and still others said that they thought someone else would help.

One experiment by Latané and Darley involved a staged theft of money from a cashbox. Prior to this experiment, they thought that helping the victim of a crime might be more common if multiple witnesses were present—the threat of violence would be less than if a witness were alone, several witnesses might be able to overpower the criminal, each witness would be less easily singled out for reprisals by the offender, and each witness would be less apt to have to appear in court to testify than if he were the only one who saw the crime. The question that Latané and Darley asked was whether these factors would overcome the group inhibition of helping behavior that they had found in other experiments. They discovered that the presence of a second witness did not affect a person's noticing that a crime was being committed. However, witnesses in pairs did report the observed crime to someone *less* often than those witnesses who were alone. A wide variety of rationalizations, some ingenious, alleviated any stress that resulted from failure to report the crime. Witnesses who failed to report the theft said that they thought that the thief had been making change or that he "took the money by accident." Some said that there had not been much money to steal anyway.[51] Group inhibition of helping behavior (defined here as reporting the crime) was somewhat less strong when the emergency was a crime that had just been committed than it was in other types of emergencies, but witnesses were still less likely to act if they were with others than if they were alone.

A second staged crime, the theft of a case of beer from a liquor store, resulted in only 20 per cent of the witnesses (customers) spontaneously reporting the theft to the storekeeper, although others did so when asked by the proprietor what had happened to the men who had been in the store. Reporting this crime was not related to fear of reprisals, the number of thieves involved (one or two), or the sex of the witness to the crime. However, the crime was reported less often if two customers saw the crime than if only one did.[52]

A witness to a crime may experience *empathic distress* if he fails to help, feeling shame or the implied criticism of others. If he helps, however, he may suffer such costs as bodily harm or embarrassment at misinterpreting the situation. Latané and Darley suggest that internal stress may be reduced by distorting one's perception of an event, by interpreting the event as a non-emergency. Group influences may be especially strong because people want to believe that no emergency exists which requires them to act; seeing that others do not react is consistent with this desire and makes it easier to believe that nothing is really wrong. If a person is alone, there are fewer cues to define the situation as a non-emergency, and he is more likely to feel that he personally must take some action. Here responsibility is focused on the lone witness, rather than diffused over a number of onlookers.

Noticing an emergency is slightly less likely for witnesses in a group than for those who are alone, but *interpretation* of the event is considerably different. Witnesses in groups are much less likely to define situations as emergencies than are witnesses by themselves. In groups there is a *diffusion of responsibility;* people feel that *someone* should act but that it is not necessary that they themselves be that person. When a victim's cries are not directed at specific bystanders but at a group as a whole, help is less likely to be given, since no one feels a *personal* responsibility to assist the victim. When pleas are unfocused, witnesses assume that others will help or at least that if they do not help they will not be completely to blame for the fate of the victim. One social psychological experiment found that bystanders were most apt to help an asthma victim if they thought that only they could offer such aid; noninvolvement was more common if the witnesses thought that others were present to offer assistance.[53] In their discussion of the Genovese murder, Milgram and Hollander observe, "It is known that her cries for help were not directed to a specific person: they were general. But only individuals can act, and as the cries were not specifically directed, no particular person felt a special responsibility."[54] The diffusion of responsibility effect is related to the *number* of witnesses present at the scene. Latané and Darley found that help was less likely if two witnesses rather than one witnessed an event, but help was even less commonly given if there were five bystanders present.[55]

Another factor that can operate in groups of witnesses is the *social modeling* effect. This would have the opposite result from the group inhibition of helping behavior. If one bystander offers help, this may lead others to offer assistance as well. Those who initially help act as models who clarify the situation and help other bystanders to define it as an emergency. They also alert others to alternative means of dealing with the situation, leading them to revise their estimates of the risks and rewards involved.[56] One study shows that helping behavior is stimulated by watching others help victims. This may be because the behavior elicits sympathy for the victim, because multiple helpers reduce the risk faced by each one, or because it is easier to give aid if more than one is helping.[57] The social modeling effect works in a direction opposite to the diffusion of responsibility effect, by focusing attention on the event as an emergency and on the need to provide assistance. The problem is to determine under what circumstances the first helper will step forward. Latané and Darley's research suggests that such behavior is inhibited when many people witness a crisis situation. However, if someone breaks the ice, additional help may be forthcoming because of the modeling effect. One experiment discovered that if any help was received by a victim who needed assistance, *more* than one onlooker offered help in 60 per cent of the cases.[58] This indirectly suggests that the behavior of the first Good Samaritan may stimulate helping behavior in others. The question as to when the first person will step forward with help cannot be answered at this time, although experimental evidence indicates that the larger the group, the less likely that anyone will offer help.

Another influence on giving help may be familiarity with the setting. Latané and Darley discovered that four-fifths of the subjects who observed a young man in need of help offered to help in a subway, but half that proportion offered aid to a similar person in an airport terminal. They suggest that people may be more familiar with the subway setting and thus be more willing to help there.[59] In another experiment in a subway by Piliavin, Rodin, and Piliavin, help was more likely if the person in need of help appeared to be ill than if he appeared to be drunk.[60] This suggests that sympathy for the victim is related to bystander response. In this study, it was also found that men were more apt to help than women, especially in being the first to help the victim. There was only a slight tendency toward same-race helping behavior. There was no strong relationship between the number of bystanders and the speed with which help was offered in this experiment, although the experimental conditions (such as the number of bystanders) were not as carefully controlled as they were in the Latané and Darley studies.

Piliavin et al. suggest that the decision to respond to another's plight is influenced by the witness's perception of the costs of offering help (personal harm, expenditure of effort, social embarrassment), the costs of not helping (self-blame, censure from others), the rewards of helping (self-esteem, the gratitude of others), and the rewards of not helping (continuation of other activities). Helping depends less on an individual's altruism than on his desire to avoid an unpleasant emotional state.[61] Piliavin et al. conclude that helping behavior is determined by an onlooker's assessment of rewards and risks.[62] However, Latané and Darley provide evidence that the group context within which an emergency is observed is a primary determinant of helping behavior, even though most witnesses are not aware of the effect of the group on their behavior. These conclusions are not mutually exclusive; other witnesses may influence an individual's decision to help or not by affecting his calculation of costs and rewards. For example, the presence of others allows a witness to reduce the cost of not helping by allowing him to say that if others do not help, then he cannot be blamed for his failure to help. The presence of others may also increase the cost of helping; social embarrassment may arise if unwanted or unneeded help is offered. Carefully considered cost-benefit calculations are probably not made before helping or not helping a victim, but some crude consideration of risks and rewards may be made. That rough calculation is strongly influenced by the number of witnesses present at the scene of the emergency and by the extent to which responsibility is focused on a particular bystander.

The argument that help is less likely to be given in a large city than in a small town is consistent with some of Latané and Darley's findings. They discovered that people who thought that a friend was in a separate room also witnessing the emergency were more likely to help and were quicker to help than people who thought that a stranger was in a separate room.[63] This may be because people know they will later see their friends and have to justify to them their action or inaction. If there are social ties among the witnesses to an emergency, those people may feel that responsibility for helping falls on "us," on the group as a whole rather than on specific individuals. The cry for help may be focused on the entity of the group of which each person feels a part. As a result, the diffusion of responsibility effect may be less important and help may be given. Small and homogeneous communities—whether a small town or an urban neighborhood—are more likely to be characterized by such strong group ties and group identification than are large and heterogeneous communities.

Latané and Darley also found that if a subject who was soon to see an emergency had a brief encounter with the victim-to-be prior to the experiment, the witness was later much more willing to offer aid or seek help than if the witness and the victim had never met. This effect was even present in groups of bystanders. Witnesses in such groups said that when it became necessary to help the victim, they could picture in their minds the distress suffered by the victim.[64] Prior contact with a victim focused the victim's cries for help on the witness; the diffusion of responsibility was less significant. We might suggest that in small communities with close social ties, help might be more likely because there is a greater chance that a victim will have had prior contact with the witness than is true in a large and heterogeneous community where passersby are more likely to be strangers.

Another recent experiment also suggests that prior contact increases the likelihood of bystander intervention. On Jones Beach, Long Island, a "victim" placed a blanket near another bather. He turned on his portable radio and after a short time said, "Excuse me, I'm going up to the boardwalk for a few minutes. Would you watch my things?" The "witnesses" who were spoken to in this way were *committed*, in contrast to other *uncommitted* people who were only asked for a match by the victim. In a few minutes, a confederate "thief" picked up the radio, which was playing loudly, and walked away with it. Another confederate observed the reactions of the witnesses. The *only* witnesses who said that they had not even noticed the theft were in the uncommitted group. Of twenty uncommitted subjects who did notice the theft, only four tried to stop the thief. Of twenty committed bystanders, nineteen called to the thief to stop or chased him.[65] Thus the prior contact between victim and bystander focused responsibility on the bystander when the theft occurred, making his intervention more likely.

An actual case of bystander reaction to the victim of a crime in New York City also illustrates the effect of prior contact between victim and witnesses. Three men had just passed and greeted a neighbor. Soon after, he emerged from a building yelling that he had been attacked and robbed. Having had recent personal contact with the man, the three bystanders felt a personal responsibility to help; the same feeling would probably have been present, but much weaker and less likely to lead to action, if they had not just said hello to the man. The three witnesses chased and caught the robbers. A number of other residents of the community soon gathered around the offenders and prevented their escape. At least six people called the police to the scene. When the police arrived, the offenders actually took refuge with them because of fear of harm from the people.[66]

Another crime in New York a few days later involved people reacting to a twelve-year-old boy's cry for help after he found an intruder in his home. Neighbors overpowered the offender and beat him unconscious. Only the arrival of the police saved him.[67] In each case, witnesses had prior contact and familiarity with the victim. Also, in each case, after help was initially offered, many neighbors joined the effort. This suggests that social models do influence the number of people who will offer assistance, and that identification with the victim focuses responsibility and increases the likelihood of *some* help being offered. The Mayor and the Police Commissioner of New York both praised the citizens for the help they gave the victims, although the Police Commissioner expressed some doubts about the effect of people taking the law into their own hands.[68] Both stated that these instances of citizen involvement showed that the apathy which caused the lack of response to Kitty Genovese's plight was disappearing and that people were becoming more concerned with their neighbors. Such a conclusion indicates a misunderstanding of both the Genovese case and the two current ones. As we have seen in this chapter, more than apathy causes bystander nonresponse and more than altruism explains Good Samaritan behavior. The presence of others, the diffusion of responsibility, the perception of the events, and prior contact with the victim all lead us to believe that there might be no intervention in a crime like the Genovese murder if it occurred today, and that the two victims who received help more recently might well have been helped in 1964.

Latané and Darley's conclusions about helping behavior are well supported by their empirical evidence. The nonresponsive bystander is better described as "confused and conflicted, rather than alienated and depersonalized."[69] The longer it takes him to react to an emergency, the less likely he is to offer any help, since rationalizations for nonresponse develop quickly. He is particularly likely to interpret an event as not requiring him to act if others are present and if no one assists the victim immediately. The group inhibition of helping behavior may be especially strong in large and heterogeneous cities, because large numbers of people are present in public places and most of them are strangers to each other.[70] However, helping behavior will occur in urban communities where people know each other, identify closely with the community, and assume responsibility for the safety of the community. Such communities can be established in large cities. Some already exist in areas of ethnic homogeneity where strongly held traditions bind people together, although such communities are becoming less common with the assimilation of ethnic groups into the larger society.

People feel that safety lies in numbers, but experimental evidence indicates that assistance of a victim of an emergency may be more likely if responsibility for helping is focused on one person rather than diffused over a group. Criminals probably make the same assumption that the general public does in feeling that they run a greater risk if they commit a crime in the sight of a group of bystanders, even though their actual risk may be greater if only one witness sees their crime. Still, their misperception of when witnesses are most apt to offer help may deter some potential criminals from committing crimes in which they would actually run a relatively small risk of bystander intervention. However, their experience with nonresponsive crowds may increase their boldness and lead them to the conclusion that they actually run little risk even if they are observed committing an offense. To deter crime, people must not only be present in public places and observe what is going on there, but they must also accept responsibility for the protection of others by being willing to be the first to offer help to victims in distress.

Footnotes

1. Herman Goldstein, "Citizen Cooperation: The Perspective of the Police," in James M. Ratcliffe, editor, *The Good Samaritan and the Law*. Garden City, N.Y.: Doubleday & Company, Inc., 1966, pp. 200–201. Similar reasons for the public's concern with crime in nineteenth-century Paris are reported in Louis Chevalier, *Laboring Classes and Dangerous Classes in Paris During the First Half of the Nineteenth Century*, translated by Frank Jellinek. New York: Howard Fertig, 1958, 1973.

2. A. M. Rosenthal, *Thirty-eight Witnesses*. New York: McGraw-Hill Book Company, 1964, p. 16.

3. Ibid., pp. 48–52.

4. Cited in *Victims of Crime*, Hearing before the Subcommittee on Criminal Laws and Procedures of the Committee on the Judiciary, United States Senate, 92nd Congress, First Session. Washington, D.C.: United States Government Printing Office, 1972, p. 128.

5. Charles O. Gregory, "The Good Samaritan and the Bad: The Anglo-American Law," in Ratcliffe, op. cit., pp. 23–41.

6. André Tunc, "The Volunteer and the Good Samaritan," in Ratcliffe, op. cit., p. 47.

7. Ibid.; and Aleksander W. Rudzinski, "The Duty to Rescue: A Comparative Analysis," in Ratcliffe, op. cit., pp. 91–134.

8. *People v. Beardsley*, Supreme Court of Michigan, 1907. 150 Mich. 206, 113 N.W. 1128. Cited in Jerome Michael and Herbert Wechsler, *Criminal Law and Its Administration: Cases, Statutes and Commentaries*. Chicago: The Foundation Press, Inc., 1940, pp. 114–118.

9. A similar position was taken in the penal code prepared by the Indian Law Commissioners in 1838, namely that although it was desirable for men to help their neighbors as well as to abstain from harming them, the law had to be limited to keeping men from harming one another. *A Penal Code Prepared by the Indian Law Commissioners* (1838) Note M, 103–106. Cited in Michael and Wechsler, op. cit., pp. 120–123.

10. Hans Zeisel, "An International Experiment on the Effects of a Good Samaritan Law," in Ratcliffe, op. cit., pp. 209–212.

11. Gregory, op. cit.

12. Donald P. Hartmann, Donna M. Gelfand, Brent Page, and Patrice Walder, "Rates of Bystander Observation and Reporting of Contrived Shoplifting Incidents," *Criminology* X (November 1972), p. 264.

13. Rudzinski, op. cit., p. 123.

14. John P. Dawson, "Rewards for the Rescue of Human Life?" in Ratcliffe, op. cit., p. 63.

15. Alan Barth, "The Vanishing Samaritan," in Ratcliffe, op. cit., p. 163.

16. Lawrence Zelic Freedman, "No Response to the Cry for Help," in Ratcliffe, op. cit., pp. 171–182.

17. Stanley Milgram and Paul Hollander, "The Murder They Heard," in Renatus Hartogs and Eric Artzt, editors, *Violence: Causes & Solutions*. New York: Dell Publishing Company, Inc., 1970, p. 208.

18. Even if people perceive a direct threat of harm, they may seek clarifying information. Following the 1938 "Martian invasion" radio broadcast, communications systems were jammed as people called

the police, friends, and radio stations for verification of reports and for information about how to protect themselves. Howard Koch, *The Panic Broadcast: Portrait of an Event.* Boston: Little, Brown and Company, 1970.

19. Martha Wolfenstein and Gilbert Kliman, editors, *Children and the Death of a President: Multi-disciplinary Studies.* Garden City, N.Y.: Doubleday & Company, Inc., 1965, p. xx; Alfred Friendly and Ronald L. Goldfarb, *Crime and Publicity: The Impact of News on the Administration of Justice.* New York: The Twentieth Century Fund, 1967, pp. 318–321.
20. Wilbur Schramm, cited in Friendly and Goldfarb, op. cit., p. 321.
21. John M. Lee, "Japanese Shocked by Mass Murders," *The New York Times,* March 13, 1972, p. 13.
22. Freedman, op. cit., p. 175.
23. Harry Kalven, Jr., and Hans Zeisel, *The American Jury.* Boston: Little, Brown and Company, 1966, pp. 249–252.
24. Kurt Weis and Sandra S. Borges, "Victimology and Rape: The Case of the Legitimate Victim," *Issues in Criminology* VIII (Fall 1973), pp. 76–77.
25. This is an example used in Freedman, op. cit., pp. 172–174.
26. Menachem Amir, *Patterns in Forcible Rape.* Chicago: The University of Chicago Press, 1971, pp. 231–232.
27. Monica D. Blumenthal, Robert L. Kahn, Frank M. Andrews, and Kendra B. Head, *Justifying Violence: Attitudes of American Men.* Ann Arbor: Institute for Social Research, 1972, p. 137.
28. Fred Ferretti, "The Ugly Face of Race Hatred in Queens," *The New York Times,* June 12, 1971, p. 31.
29. Roy Reed, "Nation's Youngest Condemned Prisoner, 16, at Ease as He Waits," *The New York Times,* January 22, 1972, p. 14.
30. "Victims of Crime Paid in Britain," *The New York Times,* September 27, 1970, p. 10.
31. Edward Shils, "The Sanctity of Life," *Encounter* XXVIII (January 1967), p. 43.
32. A similar point is made by Jackson Toby about punitive attitudes toward rapists:

> Since the victims of rape are females, we might hypothesize that *women* would express greater punitiveness toward rapists than *men* and that degrees of hostility would correspond to real or imaginary exposure to rape. Thus, pretty young girls might express more punitiveness toward rapists than homely women. Among males, we might predict that greater punitiveness would be expressed by those with more reason to identify with the victim. Thus, males having sisters or daughters in the late teens

or early twenties might express more punitiveness toward rapists than males lacking vulnerable "hostages to fortune."

Jackson Toby, "Is Punishment Necessary?" *Journal of Criminal Law, Criminology and Police Science* LV (September 1964), p. 333.

33. Cited in Stanley Milgram, "The Experience of Living in Cities," *Science* CLXVII (March 13, 1970), p. 1463.
34. Jane Jacobs, *The Death and Life of Great American Cities.* New York: Vintage Books, 1961, pp. 82–83.
35. Ibid.
36. Pitrim A. Sorokin, with Mamie Tanquist, Mildred Parten, and Mrs. C. C. Zimmerman, "An Experimental Study of Efficiency of Work under Various Specified Conditions," *American Journal of Sociology* XXXV (March 1930), pp. 765–782.
37. Ibid., p. 773.
38. Milgram, op. cit., p. 1462.
39. Bibb Latané and John M. Darley, *The Unresponsive Bystander: Why Doesn't He Help?* New York: Appleton-Century-Crofts, 1970.
40. Ibid., pp. 113–116.
41. Ibid., p. 116.
42. Ibid., p. 117.
43. J. M. Darley and C. D. Batson, "Test of Samaritan Parable: Who Helps the Helpless," *The New York Times,* April 11, 1971, p. 25.
44. Arline R. Brenner and James M. Levin, "Off-Duty Policeman and Bystander 'Apathy,'" *Journal of Police Science and Administration* I (March 1973), pp. 61–64.
45. Latané and Darley, op. cit., pp. 19–21.
46. Ibid., pp. 29–31.
47. Ibid., pp. 34–35.
48. Oscar Newman, *Architectural Design for Crime Prevention.* Washington, D.C.: United States Government Printing Office, 1973, p. 60.
49. Latané and Darley, op. cit., pp. 38–42.
50. Ibid., pp. 52–54.
51. Ibid., pp. 70–74.
52. Ibid., pp. 74–77.
53. Charles Korte, "Group Influence on the Helpfulness of Accident Witnesses," *Law and Society Review* V (August 1970), pp. 7–19.
54. Milgram and Hollander, op. cit., p. 210.
55. Latané and Darley, op. cit., pp. 93–112.
56. Harvey A. Hornstein, "The Influence of Social Models on Helping," in J. Macaulay and L. Berkowitz, editors, *Altruism and Helping Behavior: Social Psychological Studies of Some Antecedents and Consequences.* New York: Academic Press, 1970, pp. 29–41.

57. James H. Bryan and Mary Ann Test, "Models and Helping: Naturalistic Studies in Aiding Behavior," *Journal of Personality and Social Psychology* VI (December 1967), pp. 400–407.
58. Irving M. Piliavin, Judith Rodin, and Jane Allyn Piliavin, "Good Samaritanism: An Underground Phenomenon?" *Journal of Personality and Social Psychology* XIII (December 1969), pp. 289–299.
59. Latané and Darley, op. cit., pp. 118–119.
60. Piliavin, Rodin, and Piliavin, op. cit.
61. Ibid.
62. The risks faced by a Good Samaritan are not always easily calculated. For instance, a passerby who stopped to help the victim of a car accident in Nigeria in 1973 was attacked and beaten to death by a crowd that thought he was the driver who had caused the accident. See "Mobs Take Law into Own Hands," *The New York Times*, October 9, 1973, p. 38.
63. Latané and Darley, op. cit., pp. 105–111.
64. Ibid.
65. From an experiment by Thomas Moriarity, reported in Patrice Horn and the editors of *Behavior Today*, "Newsline," *Psychology Today* VII (September 1973), p. 17.
66. Robert D. McFadden, "3 Residents Seize 2 Men in Mugging," *The New York Times*, June 17, 1973, p. 31.
67. John Sibley, "Mayor and Cawley Hail Citizens on Aid in Seizing Suspects," *The New York Times*, June 20, 1973, pp. 1, 40.
68. Ibid.
69. Latané and Darley, op. cit., p. 122.
70. Ibid., p. 127.

10 Epilogue

CRIMINOLOGISTS have proposed a number of theories of crime. They have attributed crime to biological factors, psycholog-ical predispositions, and social structure. Few have looked system-atically at the public's contribution to the crime problem. In this book we have seen that the reaction of people to crime can reinforce and exacerbate the crime problem.

Crime generates suspicion and distrust, thereby weakening the social fabric of a community. Viewing ex-convicts as outsiders makes it difficult for them to become reintegrated into society, forcing them back to a life of crime and enhancing the crime problem. Crime leads people to avoid others and to take self-protective security measures, both of which actions erect barriers between the residents of a community. By diminishing social interaction and reducing natural surveillance of public areas, in-formal social control over potential criminals may be weakened and crime rates may increase.

When people are faced with a crime problem, they often turn to the police. When the police are unable to curb crime, citizens blame them for their ineffectiveness. One consequence is that people are less willing to report crime to the police. This di-minishes the probability that offenders will be apprehended, since the police learn of most crimes from citizens. As the risk to offenders decreases, they may be more willing to commit crimes.

If people react to crime by denying personal responsibility for crime prevention and by becoming retreatist and defensive, they may be unwilling to assist victims of the crimes that they actually observe. If potential offenders become aware of citizen reluctance to become involved in the prevention of crime and the assistance of victims, social interaction and the surveillance of public spaces will have little effect on the crime problem.

A tightly knit community can minimize the problem of street crime. However, informal social control also poses a threat to the diversity of behavior that exists in a pluralistic society, even though it may curb violent crime. Still, street crime would decline if interpersonal relations were closer, if interaction among the residents of a community were more frequent, and if social bonds were stronger. A sense of responsibility for other citizens and for the community as a whole would increase individuals' willingness to report crime to the police and the likelihood of their intervention in a crime in progress. Greater willingness of community residents to report crime to the police might also obviate the need for civilian police patrols. More interaction in public places and more human traffic on the sidewalks would increase surveillance of the places where people now fear to go. More intense social ties would reinforce surveillance with a willingness to take action against offenders.

We propose no methods of creating such a society. We only hope that this book has provided some insight into the type of society that would reduce the crime problem.

Appendix A:
Port City and Belleville

THROUGHOUT this book we have referred to data collected in 1968 from two communities in the Boston area—Port City and Belleville. The main reason for selecting these two communities for study was the difference in their official crime rates, the suburb of Belleville having a low rate and the urban community of Port City having a comparatively high rate.[1] Using average crime rates per 100,000 people for the three years preceding our study, we see from Table A-1 that crimes against the person were *nine* times as common in Port City as in Belleville and that

Table A-1: Average Crime Rates Per 100,000 for 1965–1967 *

Crime	Belleville	Port City	United States	Boston area**
Murder	0	3	6	3
Rape	1	6	13	7
Robbery	2	44	83	59
Aggravated assault	12	79	119	62
Burglary	440	687	718	610
Larceny over $50	280	208	465	369
Auto theft	97	1424	290	725
Crimes against persons	15	132	221	131
Crimes against property	817	2319	1473	1704
Total crime rate	832	2451	1694	1835

* Three-year averages were used because these seven crimes were rare in each community and because the populations of the two communities were too small for rates based on a single year to be stable.

** Boston Standard Metropolitan Statistical Area, as defined by the United States Bureau of the Census.

crimes against property were *three* times as common in the urban community as in the suburb.[2] We also see that rates in the suburb were significantly lower for all crimes than either the rates in the Boston metropolitan area or the rates in the United States. The overall crime rate in the urban community was higher than either the rate in the Boston area or the rate in the nation, but much of the difference was due to the high rate of auto thefts in Port City. For other crimes, the rates in that community were about the same or slightly lower than the rates in the Boston area or the rates in the United States. Belleville is best described as a low crime-rate area and Port City as an area with an average crime rate, although in comparing the two communities we have sometimes referred to Port City as a high crime-rate area because its rates are greater than the rates in Belleville.

Sample Selection

In each community two hundred names were selected from a list of all residents over the age of twenty who lived there on January 1, 1968. State law requires all cities and towns to compile such lists every year for voting purposes. Using a random starting point and choosing every *n*th name, a sample that can be described as a systematic sample proportional to the population of each precinct was chosen from each community. The samples were systematic samples if one assumes that no statistical bias was introduced by the arrangement of names in the listings by street within each precinct, by number on each street, and by name of those residing at each address.

The two samples were selected in May 1968, and interviews were conducted between May and September. Between four and eight months elapsed from the time the voting lists were compiled to the time an initial attempt was made to interview an individual. A letter was sent to each of the four hundred subjects to explain the project. Each was then approached at the door by either the author or his wife. An interview and a self-administered Likert-item battery (agree-disagree items) were administered. The average time to complete the questioning was about forty-five minutes, an amount of time that did not seem excessive to the respondents.

In each community about one in ten of the original two hundred people could not be interviewed because he or she had moved or died. Some subjects who were found were not interviewed. In Belleville, 16 per cent gave outright refusals to be interviewed. A number of these refusals came from persons of high socioeconomic status, especially doctors and lawyers, who would not be interviewed because they felt their time was too valuable to spend on such activities. Some of the outright refusals in Belleville may have occurred because neighboring universities often used the community for surveys. A saturation effect may have produced an unwillingness to be interviewed once again. The refusals did not bias the sample of completed interviews in terms of age or sex. There was a very slight underrepresentation of the elderly due to the inability of some people to complete interviews because of infirmity or serious illness. There was no attrition due to lack of fluency in English. A total of one hundred thirty-eight residents of Belleville were interviewed.

In Port City, one hundred twenty-eight subjects were interviewed. Eleven per cent of the original two hundred refused to be interviewed, some because of general suspiciousness of surveys and others because they could not understand why anyone would want to know their opinions. At least two refusals came from people who had relatives in trouble with the law and did not want to speak with a stranger. No significant biases by sex or age resulted from these refusals, although there was again a slight underrepresentation of the elderly due to infirmity or illness and also due to lack of fluency in English.

Port City

Port City is geographically separated from the rest of the city by water. We might expect that this comparative isolation would produce stronger social bonds among the town's residents than if

253

boundaries were artificially drawn on a solid land mass. However, physical isolation can also produce alienation from the rest of the world. A scale measuring general alienation found that Port City residents were much more alienated than Belleville residents.[3] Class differences between the samples were largely responsible for the greater alienation of the urban residents, but physical separation from the mainstream of metropolitan life may also have contributed to the malaise.

The community of Port City has been losing population in recent years. In 1950 its population was 51,152, dropping to 42,926 in 1960 and to 35,826 in 1970. Expansion of the city's airport, which is located in Port City, has made this community a noisy and unpleasant place to live. Homes have been demolished because of airport expansion, depleting the town's population and reducing the number of available housing units in the area. Another factor responsible for the decline in population is that a number of postwar babies have reached the age to start families of their own. Many of these younger people have left their traditionalist community for areas they feel are better suited to a modern American way of life.

The population of Port City is almost entirely white, with less than one per cent being nonwhite at the time of the study. This was a consideration in selecting Port City as a place to conduct interviews. The survey was carried out during a time of political conventions and campaigning, when the major domestic issue was law and order. This phrase encompassed not only concern with the crime issue, but also concern with ghetto riots. We thus thought that a clearer picture of attitudes toward crime would emerge if there were no significant nonwhite population in the community. Another consideration was the fact that the two interviewers were white. This might have biased responses from nonwhite subjects, since surveys have found that cross-racial interviewing can influence the answers elicited from respondents.

Upon entering Port City, one is first struck by the large number of wooden, multiple-family dwellings which are placed close to each other and near the street. The 1970 Census found that 91 per cent of the structures in Port City were multiple-family units; 71 per cent housed three or more families. Physically, Port City is neither a slum nor an elegant residential area. The houses are considerably older than those in Belleville. More of Port City's dwelling units are classified as deteriorating or dilapidated. Population density is greater in Port City than in Belleville. Port City had about four times as many dwelling units with more than one person per room and about three times as many people per square mile as Belleville. The urban area is thus a community of greater population density, poorer housing, and more crowded conditions than the suburb.

Port City contains few recreational areas or parks where residents can congregate. This forces people onto the streets and streetcorners. On warm evenings, some people cluster on corners and on door stoops, at least until dark. However, there is also widespread fear for personal safety on the streets among the residents of Port City, suggesting that recent increases in the fear of crime may be disrupting traditional patterns of social interaction in the community.

The residents of Port City usually vote Democratic in Presidential elections. In fact, the degree of homogeneity is rather striking, with 87 per cent voting for Kennedy in 1960, almost 90 per cent for Johnson in 1964, 78 per cent for Humphrey in 1968, and 68 per cent for McGovern in 1972. This is not the only aspect in which the residents of Port City are homogeneous. Ethnically, 73 per cent of our sample was Italian, 12 per cent Irish, and the rest of various other groups. Related to this ethnic homogeneity was the predominantly Roman Catholic affiliation of the Port City residents, with more than nine-tenths of the sample being of this religion.

Educationally, only one-fifth of the residents had completed any college, and half had not finished high school. Eighty-five per cent of the sample came from families in which their father held a blue-collar job, and only 15 per cent had fathers who were white-collar workers. Two-thirds of the Port City respondents held blue-collar jobs themselves, and another one-fifth worked at clerical jobs. Only one in eleven held a managerial or professional position. With this educational and occupational background, we would expect the incomes of the Port City residents to be relatively modest. In fact, only one in six earned more than $10,000 in 1967; two-fifths earned less than $6,000. These figures are considerably below the incomes of Belleville residents and below national figures as well.

Port City is thus a relatively isolated, working-class community of substantial political, ethnic, and religious homogeneity. Residents hold blue-collar jobs, often have not completed high school, and earn comparatively low incomes.

Belleville

In contrast to Port City, Belleville is a middle-class residential suburb far enough from the city to avoid its problems but close enough to enjoy its benefits. Residents work in the central city and surrounding towns. They live in a community of many single-family dwellings, although a significant proportion (52 per cent) were multiple-family units in 1970. Population density is lower than in Port City both in terms of people per square mile and in terms of number of dwelling units with more than one person per room. Houses are spaced farther apart in Belleville, being set back from the road on lawns that border on wide, tree-lined streets. There are also a number of parks and recreational areas in the suburb. Belleville looks more green, more pleasant than Port City.

Whereas Port City has declined in population in the last two decades, the population of Belleville has remained constant— 27,381 in 1950, 28,715 in 1960, and 28,285 in 1970. Fewer than one per cent of the residents were nonwhite when the survey was conducted in 1968.

Belleville is not nearly as homogeneous a community as Port City. In contrast to the overwhelmingly Democratic vote by Port City residents in recent Presidential elections, the Belleville residents have more often split their votes between parties. In 1960 Kennedy received 51 per cent of their votes, in 1964 Johnson won 69 per cent, in 1968 Humphrey gathered 56 per cent, and in 1972 McGovern collected 49 per cent. Belleville is also more heterogeneous ethnically, with the Yankee-English group constituting the largest proportion (28 per cent) of our sample.

Twenty-five per cent of the respondents were Irish, 17 per cent were Italian, and various groups made up the rest. There was also less homogeneity of religious affiliation in Belleville, with half the residents being Catholic, a quarter Protestant, and a tenth Jewish.

The educational background of Belleville residents was comparatively high. Three-fifths had at least some college education, and only one-eighth had not completed high school. In contrast to Port City residents, more suburbanites came from families in which the father had held a white-collar job, 54 per cent coming from such backgrounds and 46 per cent coming from blue-collar families. The current occupations of many Belleville residents were white-collar and professional. Only 22 per cent held blue-collar jobs, 21 per cent worked at clerical jobs, and 45 per cent were employed in professional and managerial positions. Not surprisingly, given their educational and occupational characteristics, the residents of Belleville had higher incomes than the Port City residents. Half earned more than $10,000 in 1967, and only one-fourth earned less than $6,000.

Belleville is thus a physically attractive community with a population of stable size which occupies homes that are in good condition. The population is less homogeneous than that of Port City in terms of political affiliation, ethnicity, and religion. It is also less homogeneous in social-class background and in current socioeconomic status, containing larger proportions of people from white-collar backgrounds. Residents of Belleville are more highly educated, work in higher status jobs, and earn larger incomes than the residents of Port City.

Footnotes

1. Although official police records have numerous faults, they at least register the minimum amount of crime in a community, if no fictitious crimes are recorded. Because the proportion of crime that makes its way into official records varies from community to community, there are problems with comparing crime rates in different areas using official crime rates. However, in the selection of two communities for this study, it was felt that if two areas with

significantly different *official* rates were picked, there was probably a substantial difference in the *actual* amount of crime that occurred in each community.

2. Rates of property offenses would be even more similar in the two areas if auto thefts in Port City were discounted to allow for the numerous thefts from car rental agencies and public parking lots in the community. The larger difference for personal crimes than for property crimes is consistent with a finding in the *Report of the National Advisory Commission on Civil Disorders* (New York: Bantam Books, Inc., 1968, p. 267) that rates of property crimes are more constant for various communities than rates of personal crimes. Another national survey also found that "as one moves from the central city to the suburbs out into smaller towns and rural areas, the crime rates decline, but much more drastically for crimes against the person than for property rates. The metropolitan center, that is, has a violent crime rate about *five times* as high as the smaller city and rural areas but a property crime rate only *twice* as high." Philip H. Ennis, Field Surveys II of the President's Commission on Law Enforcement and Administration of Justice, *Criminal Victimization in the United States: A Report of a National Survey*. Washington, D.C.: United States Government Printing Office, 1967, pp. 29–30.

3. The eight Likert items summed in the general alienation scale are:

    a. Many times I feel that I have little influence over the things that happen to me.

    b. Most people in our society are lonely and unrelated to their fellow human beings.

    c. This country is run by politicians who do what they want, not what the people want.

    d. I have very little in common with most people I meet.

    e. There is nothing I can do to make anything better or worse in this country.

    f. The average citizen in this country can't have much effect on politics.

    g. I often feel lonely.

    h. I think that life, as most men live it, is meaningless.

Appendix B:
Statistical Tables

Table B-1: Mean Values on Perception of Crime Scale * and Number of Respondents in Each Category

Characteristic	Belleville	Port City
Sample Mean	1.14 (124)	1.63 (105)
Sex		
Male	1.15 (60)	1.61 (52)
Female	1.13 (64)	1.65 (53)
Age		
Young	1.16 (42)	1.77 (35)
Middle	1.17 (49)	1.50 (46)
Old	1.08 (33)	1.69 (24)
Ethnic Group		
Italian	1.19 (21)	1.63 (76)
Irish	1.14 (32)	2.53 (12)
Yankee or English	1.17 (35)	2.00 (4)
Religion		
Catholic	1.15 (62)	1.63 (98)
Protestant	1.18 (32)	2.00 (4)
Education		
Less than high school	1.15 (13)	1.54 (52)
Completed high school	1.09 (36)	1.75 (29)
Some college	1.16 (74)	1.71 (24)
Income		
Low	1.16 (30)	1.58 (39)
Medium	1.09 (26)	1.56 (39)
High	1.18 (54)	1.85 (18)
Prestige of occupation		
Low	1.15 (56)	1.65 (79)
Medium	1.19 (27)	1.54 (19)
High	1.11 (40)	1.71 (7)
Self-designated class		
Working class	1.15 (34)	1.57 (61)
Middle class	1.14 (86)	1.67 (42)
Father's occupation		
Working class	1.11 (58)	1.62 (89)
Middle class	1.16 (63)	1.73 (16)

* The range is from one to three, with one being less crime perceived and three being more crime perceived.

Table B-2: Mean Values on Perceived Safety Scale *

Characteristic	Belleville		Port City	
Sample mean	2.39	(138)	2.01	(128)
Sex				
Male	2.51	(64)	2.16	(62)
Female	2.28	(72)	1.87	(66)
Age				
Young	2.48	(44)	2.06	(41)
Middle	2.42	(56)	2.07	(56)
Old	2.24	(38)	1.86	(31)
Ethnic group				
Italian	2.36	(23)	1.99	(93)
Irish	2.53	(35)	2.05	(15)
Yankee or English	2.31	(39)	2.30	(5)
Religion				
Catholic	2.44	(69)	2.01	(120)
Protestant	2.31	(37)	1.96	(4)
Education				
Less than high school	2.41	(16)	1.97	(66)
Completed high school	2.34	(39)	1.99	(35)
Some college	2.41	(82)	2.15	(27)
Income				
Low	2.28	(32)	1.94	(48)
Medium	2.35	(28)	2.19	(46)
High	2.45	(61)	1.96	(19)
Prestige of occupation				
Low	2.33	(63)	1.97	(97)
Medium	2.38	(31)	2.14	(23)
High	2.47	(43)	2.17	(8)
Self-designated class				
Working class	2.44	(38)	2.06	(76)
Middle class	2.36	(96)	1.96	(50)
Father's occupation				
Working class	2.43	(62)	2.02	(108)
Middle class	2.36	(71)	1.97	(18)

* The range is from one to three, with one being less perceived safety and three being more perceived safety.

Table B-3: Mean Values on Trust Scale *

Characteristic	Belleville		Port City	
Sample mean	3.61	(136)	3.18	(127)
Sex				
Male	3.64	(64)	3.13	(62)
Female	3.59	(72)	3.23	(65)
Age				
Young	3.61	(44)	3.24	(40)
Middle	3.51	(56)	3.19	(56)
Old	3.77	(36)	3.10	(31)
Ethnic group				
Italian	3.50	(22)	3.14	(93)
Irish	3.65	(35)	3.37	(15)
Yankee or English	3.85	(38)	2.55	(5)
Religion				
Catholic	3.55	(68)	3.18	(120)
Protestant	3.76	(38)	3.33	(3)
Education				
Less than high school	3.38	(15)	3.07	(66)
Completed high school	3.47	(39)	3.28	(35)
Some college	3.73	(81)	3.33	(26)
Income				
Low	3.55	(32)	3.02	(47)
Medium	3.65	(27)	3.27	(46)
High	3.71	(60)	3.38	(19)
Prestige of occupation				
Low	3.47	(63)	3.11	(97)
Medium	3.76	(31)	3.40	(22)
High	3.72	(41)	3.40	(8)
Self-designated class				
Working class	3.50	(38)	3.23	(75)
Middle class	3.68	(94)	3.12	(50)
Father's occupation				
Working class	3.51	(62)	3.17	(108)
Middle class	3.72	(71)	3.22	(18)

* The range is from one to five, with one being the least amount of interpersonal trust and five being the most interpersonal trust.

Table B-4: Mean Values on Affect for Community Scale*

Characteristic	Belleville	Port City
Sample mean	2.61 (136)	2.14 (128)
Sex		
Male	2.63 (63)	2.13 (62)
Female	2.59 (73)	2.14 (66)
Age		
Young	2.38 (43)	1.96 (41)
Middle	2.68 (56)	2.16 (56)
Old	2.77 (37)	2.32 (31)
Ethnic group		
Italian	2.65 (23)	2.20 (93)
Irish	2.53 (34)	2.12 (15)
Yankee or English	2.69 (39)	1.60 (5)
Religion		
Catholic	2.59 (68)	2.18 (120)
Protestant	2.64 (37)	1.69 (4)
Education		
Less than high school	2.76 (16)	2.23 (66)
Completed high school	2.62 (38)	1.91 (35)
Some college	2.58 (81)	2.21 (27)
Income		
Low	2.65 (31)	2.13 (48)
Medium	2.56 (28)	2.16 (46)
High	2.58 (61)	1.96 (19)
Prestige of occupation		
Low	2.61 (63)	2.14 (97)
Medium	2.56 (29)	2.10 (23)
High	2.63 (43)	2.28 (8)
Self-designated class		
Working class	2.63 (37)	2.15 (108)
Middle class	2.61 (95)	2.11 (19)
Father's occupation		
Working class	2.62 (62)	2.15 (76)
Middle class	2.60 (71)	2.13 (50)

*The range is from one to three, with one being less positive affect for the community and three being more positive affect for the community.

Table B-5: Attitudes Toward Thirteen Crimes

Type of criminal behavior	Abbreviation
1. A man forcibly rapes a woman.	Rape
2. A man gets drunk at a bar and has an accident while driving home, killing another person in the accident.	Manslaughter
3. A man holds up another man with a gun and takes $100 from him.	Robbery
4. A man steals a car that he finds parked on the street.	Auto theft
5. A woman kills her husband by putting poison in his food.	Murder—poison
6. A man enters a bar, says he is going to kill another man, and attacks this man with a knife. He doesn't kill him, but he injures him seriously.	Aggravated assault
7. A man picks the pocket of another man and takes a wallet containing $100.	Larceny
8. An unarmed man breaks into an unoccupied house at night and steals $100 in cash.	Burglary
9. A leader in organized crime pays to have a leader of a rival gang killed.	Murder—gang
10. A bank manager steals $100 from the vault in the bank in which he works.	Embezzlement
11. A man buys and uses marijuana.	Marijuana use
12. A college student, with a group of other students, takes control of a university building as a means of protesting university policies.	Trespass—protest
13. A man takes bets for horse races in a downtown office.	Gambling

Table B-5 Continued

Type of criminal behavior	% Favoring Law		% Willing to Report Crime				Rank of Crime in State Law
	Belleville	Port City	Belleville	Rank	Port City	Rank	
* Rape	100.0%	99.2%	90.6%	2	86.7%	1	3.5
Manslaughter	98.6%	95.3%	90.6%	2	83.6%	2	5.5
* Robbery	100.0%	99.2%	89.1%	4	81.3%	3	3.5
* Auto theft	100.0%	98.4%	90.6%	2	80.5%	4	9
* Murder—poison	99.3%	97.7%	86.2%	7	79.7%	5	1.5
* Aggravated assault	100.0%	99.2%	87.0%	6	71.9%	6	8
* Larceny	98.6%	98.4%	81.9%	8	70.3%	7	10
* Burglary	100.0%	100.0%	88.4%	5	67.2%	8	5.5
* Murder—gang	99.3%	95.3%	76.1%	9	60.9%	9	1.5
Embezzlement	94.2%	89.1%	68.1%	10	56.3%	10	7
Marijuana use	71.0%	77.3%	40.6%	11	54.7%	11	12
Trespass—protest	69.6%	62.5%	39.1%	12	39.8%	12	13
Gambling	44.9%	31.3%	13.0%	13	7.8%	13	11

* One of the crimes in the Federal Bureau of Investigation's crime index.

Table B-6: Mean Number of Crimes Willing to Report

Characteristic	Belleville		Port City	
Sample mean	9.41	(138)	8.41	(128)
Sex				
Male	9.55	(65)	8.71	(62)
Female	9.29	(73)	8.12	(66)
Age				
Young	9.77	(44)	9.05	(41)
Middle	9.46	(56)	8.38	(56)
Old	8.92	(38)	7.61	(31)
Ethnic group				
Italian	9.52	(23)	8.24	(93)
Irish	9.23	(35)	9.33	(15)
Yankee or English	10.08	(39)	10.00	(5)
Religion				
Catholic	9.28	(69)	8.43	(120)
Protestant	9.86	(37)	7.50	(4)
Education				
Less than high school	8.88	(16)	8.23	(66)
Completed high school	9.62	(39)	8.11	(35)
Some college	9.46	(82)	9.22	(27)
Income				
Low	9.53	(32)	8.71	(48)
Medium	9.25	(28)	8.85	(46)
High	9.67	(61)	9.00	(19)
Prestige of occupation				
Low	9.37	(63)	8.28	(97)
Medium	10.06	(31)	8.57	(23)
High	9.23	(43)	9.50	(8)
Self-designated class				
Working class	9.34	(38)	8.18	(76)
Middle class	9.42	(96)	8.80	(50)
Father's occupation				
Working class	9.19	(62)	8.52	(108)
Middle class	9.64	(73)	7.58	(19)

Bibliography

ALDRICH, HOWARD, and ALBERT J. REISS, JR. "The Effect of Civil Disorders on Small Business in the Inner City. " *Journal of Social Issues* XXVI (Winter 1970), pp. 187–206.

ALEXANDER, CHRISTOPHER. "The City as a Mechanism for Sustaining Human Contact." In Robert Gutman, editor, *People and Buildings.* New York: Basic Books, Inc., 1972, pp. 406–434.

AMIR, MENACHEM. *Patterns in Forcible Rape.* Chicago: The University of Chicago Press, 1971.

"Are You Personally Afraid of Crime? Readers Speak Out." *Life* magazine LXXII (January 14, 1972), pp. 28–32.

BACHMUTH, RITA, S. M. MILLER, and LINDA ROSEN. "Juvenile Delinquency in the Daily Press." *Alpha Kappa Delta* XXX (Spring 1960), pp. 47–51.

BARNARD, CHARLES N. "The Fortification of Suburbia against the Burglar in the Bushes." *Saturday Review of the Society* I (May 1973), pp. 34–40.

BARTH, ALAN. "The Vanishing Samaritan." In James M. Ratcliffe, editor, *The Good Samaritan and the Law.* Garden City, N. Y.: Doubleday & Co., Inc., 1966, pp. 159–169.

BERKOWITZ, LEONARD, and NIGEL WALKER. "Laws and Moral Judgments." In Lawrence M. Friedman and Stewart Macaulay, editors, *Law and the Behavioral Sciences.* Indianapolis: The Bobbs-Merrill Company, Inc., 1969, pp. 198–211.

BIDERMAN, ALBERT D., LOUISE A. JOHNSON, JENNIE McINTYRE, and ADRIANNE WEIR. Field Surveys I of the President's Commission on Law Enforcement and Administration of Justice, *Report on a Pilot Study in the District of Columbia on Victimization and Attitudes toward Law Enforcement.* Washington, D.C.: United States Government Printing Office, 1967.

BLOCK, M. K., and G. J. LONG. "Subjective Probability of Victimization and Crime Levels: An Econometric Approach." *Criminology* XI (May 1973), pp. 87–93.

BLOCK, RICHARD L. "Fear of Crime and Fear of the Police." *Social Problems* XIX (Summer 1971), pp. 91–101.

———. "Support for Civil Liberties and Support for the Police." *American Behavioral Scientist* VIII (July 1970), pp. 781–796.

BLUMENTHAL, MONICA, ROBERT L. KAHN, FRANK M. ANDREWS, and KENDRA B. HEAD. *Justifying Violence: Attitudes of American Men.* Ann Arbor: Institute for Social Research, 1972.

BOGGS, SARAH L. "Formal and Informal Crime Control: An Exploratory Study of Urban, Suburban, and Rural Orientations." *The Sociological Quarterly* XII (Summer 1971), pp. 319–327.

BRENNER, ARLINE R., and JAMES M. LEVIN. "Off-Duty Policeman and Bystander 'Apathy.' " *Journal of Police Science and Administration* I (March 1973), pp. 61–64.

BROWN, JULIA S. "A Comparative Study of Deviations from Sexual Mores." *American Sociological Review* XVII (April 1952), pp. 135–146.

BROWN, RICHARD MAXWELL. "The American Vigilante Tradition." In Hugh Davis Graham and Ted Robert Gurr, editors, *Violence in America: Historical and Comparative Perspectives*, Volume 1. Washington, D.C.: United States Government Printing Office, 1969, pp. 121–180.

———. *The South Carolina Regulators.* Cambridge: The Belknap Press of Harvard University Press, 1963.

BRYAN, JAMES H., and MARY ANN TEST. "Models and Helping: Naturalistic Studies in Aiding Behavior." *Journal of Personality and Social Psychology* VI (December 1967), pp. 400–407.

CAMPBELL, DONALD T., and H. LAURENCE ROSS. "The Connecticut Crackdown on Speeding: Time-Series Data in Quasi-Experimental Analysis." In Lawrence M. Friedman and Stewart Macaulay, editors, *Law and the Behavioral Sciences.* Indianapolis: The Bobbs-Merrill Company, Inc., 1969, pp. 374–393.

CAPOTE, TRUMAN. *In Cold Blood: A True Account of a Multiple Murder and Its Consequences.* New York: Random House, 1965.

Chamber of Commerce of the United States. *Marshaling Citizen Power against Crime.* Washington, D.C.: Chamber of Commerce of the United States, 1970.

CHAMBERS, CARL D., and JAMES A. INCIARDI. "Deviant Behavior in the

Middle East: A Study of Delinquency in Iraq." *Criminology* IX (August-November 1971), pp. 291–315.

CHAMBLISS, BILL, editor. *Box Man: A Professional Thief's Journey.* New York: Harper and Row, Publishers, 1972.

CHAPMAN, DENNIS. *Sociology and the Stereotype of the Criminal.* London: Tavistock Publications, 1968.

CHAPPELL, D., and P. R. WILSON. *The Police and the Public in Australia and New Zealand.* St. Lucia, Queensland, Australia: University of Queensland Press, 1969.

CHEVALIER, LOUIS. *Laboring Classes and Dangerous Classes in Paris during the Nineteenth Century,* translated by Frank Jellinek. New York: Howard Fertig, 1958, 1973.

CIPES, ROBERT M. *The Crime War.* New York: The New American Library, 1968.

CLAIBORNE, WILLIAM L. "New Yorkers Fight Back: The Tilt toward Vigilantism." *New York* VI (October 15, 1973), pp. 49–63.

CLARK, RAMSEY. *Crime in America: Observations on Its Nature, Causes, Prevention and Control.* New York: Simon and Schuster, 1970.

CLINARD, MARSHALL B., and DANIEL J. ABBOTT. *Crime in Developing Countries: A Comparative Perspective.* New York: John Wiley & Sons, 1973.

COATES, ROBERT B., and ALDEN D. MILLER. "Neutralization of Community Resistance to Group Homes." In Yitzhak Bakal, editor, *Closing Correctional Institutions.* Lexington, Mass.: D. C. Heath and Company, 1973, pp. 67–84.

COBB, RICHARD. *The Police and the People: French Popular Protest 1789–1820.* London: Oxford University Press, 1970.

COHEN, FAY G. "The Indian Patrol in Minneapolis: Social Control and Social Change in an Urban Context." *Law and Society Review* VII (Summer 1973), pp. 779–786.

COHEN, JULIUS, REGINALD A. H. ROBSON, and ALAN BATES. *Parental Authority: The Community and the Law.* New Brunswick, N.J.: Rutgers University Press, 1958.

COMSTOCK, CRAIG. "Avoiding Pathologies of Defense." In Nevitt Sanford and Craig Comstock, editors, *Sanctions for Evil: Sources of Social Destructiveness.* Boston: Beacon Press, 1971, pp. 290–301.

CONKLIN, JOHN E., editor. *The Crime Establishment: Organized Crime and American Society.* Englewood Cliffs, N.J.: Prentice-Hall, Inc., 1973.

————. "Criminal Environment and Support for the Law." *Law and Society Review* VI (November 1971), pp. 247–265.

————. "Dimensions of Community Response to the Crime Problem." *Social Problems* XVIII (Winter 1971), pp. 373–385.

————. *Robbery and the Criminal Justice System.* Philadelphia: J. B. Lippincott Company, 1972.

———— and EGON BITTNER. "Burglary in a Suburb." *Criminology* XI (August 1973), pp. 206–232.

———— and ERWIN O. SMIGEL. "Norms and Attitudes toward Business-related Crimes." Paper presented at the Symposium on Studies of Public Experience, Knowledge and Opinion of Crime and Justice. Bureau of Social Science Research, Inc. Washington, D.C., March 1972.

"A Connoisseur's Catalogue of Modern Protective Aids." *Saturday Review of the Society* I (May 1973), pp. 41–44.

COOK, FRED J. "There's Always a Crime Wave." In Donald R. Cressey, editor, *Crime and Criminal Justice.* Chicago: Quadrangle Books, 1971, pp. 23–37.

CRAIG, JONATHAN, and RICHARD POSNER. *The New York Crime Book.* New York: Pyramid Books, 1972.

CULLEN, TOM A. *When London Walked in Terror.* New York: Avon Books, 1965.

DAVIS, F. JAMES. "Crime News in Colorado Newspapers." *American Journal of Sociology* LVII (January 1952), pp. 325–330.

DAWSON, JOHN P. "Rewards for the Rescue of Human Life?" In James M. Ratcliffe, editor, *The Good Samaritan and the Law.* Garden City, N.Y.: Doubleday & Co., Inc., 1966, pp. 63–89.

DIMSDALE, THOMAS J. *The Vigilantes of Montana.* Norman, Okla.: University of Oklahoma Press, 1866, 1953.

DINITZ, SIMON. "Progress, Crime, and the Folk Ethic: Portrait of a Small Town." *Criminology* XI (May 1973), pp. 3–21.

DINNERSTEIN, LEONARD. *The Leo Frank Case.* New York: Columbia University Press, 1968.

DOW, THOMAS E., JR. "The Role of Identification in Conditioning Public Attitude toward the Offender." *Journal of Criminal Law, Criminology and Police Science* LVIII (March 1967), pp. 75–79.

DURKHEIM, EMILE. *The Division of Labor in Society,* translated by George Simpson. Glencoe, Ill.: The Free Press, 1933.

————. *The Rules of Sociological Method,* translated by Sarah A. Solovay and John H. Mueller and edited by George E. G. Catlin. New York: The Free Press, 1938.

EDGERTON, ROBERT B. *Deviant Behavior and Cultural Theory*. Reading, Mass.: Addison-Wesley Publishing Company, Inc., 1973.

ENNIS, PHILIP H. Field Surveys II of the President's Commission on Law Enforcement and Administration of Justice, *Criminal Victimization in the United States: A Report of a National Survey*. Washington, D.C.: United States Government Printing Office, 1967.

ERIKSON, KAI T. *Wayward Puritans: A Study in the Sociology of Deviance*. New York: John Wiley & Sons, Inc., 1966.

ESZTERHAS, JOE. *Charlie Simpson's Apocalypse*. New York: Random House, 1973.

FARIS, ELLSWORTH. "The Origin of Punishment." *International Journal of Ethics* XXV (October 1914), pp. 54–67.

FEAGIN, JOE R. "Home-Defense and the Police: Black and White Perspectives." *American Behavioral Scientist* XIII (May 1970), pp. 797–814.

"Fortress on 78th Street." *Life* magazine LXXI (November 19, 1971), pp. 26–35.

FRADY, MARSHALL. "The Continuing Trial of Jesse Hill Ford." *Life* magazine LXXI (October 29, 1971), pp. 56–68.

FRANKE, DAVID, and HOLLY FRANKE. *Safe Places*. New Rochelle, N.Y.: Arlington House, 1972.

FREEDMAN, LAWRENCE ZELIC. "No Response to the Cry for Help." In James M. Ratcliffe, editor, *The Good Samaritan and the Law*. Garden City, N.Y.: Doubleday & Co., Inc., 1966, pp. 171–182.

FRIENDLY, ALFRED, and RONALD L. GOLDFARB. *Crime and Publicity: The Impact of News on the Administration of Justice*. New York: The Twentieth Century Fund, 1967.

FURSTENBERG, FRANK F., JR. "Fear of Crime and Its Effects on Citizen Behavior." Paper presented at the Symposium on Studies of Public Experience, Knowledge and Opinion of Crime and Justice. Bureau of Social Science Research, Inc. Washington, D.C., March 1972.

———. "Public Reaction to Crime in the Streets." *The American Scholar* XL (Autumn 1971), pp. 601–610.

——— and CHARLES F. WELLFORD. "Calling the Police: The Evaluation of Police Service." *Law and Society Review* VII (Spring 1973), pp. 393–406.

GEIS, GILBERT and TED L. HOUSTON. "Charles Manson and His Girls: Notes on a Durkheimian Theme." *Criminology* IX (August–November 1971), pp. 342–353.

GERASSI, JOHN. *The Boys of Boise: Furor, Vice and Folly in an American City*. New York: Macmillan Publishing Co., Inc., 1966.

GILBERT, G. M. "Crime and Punishment: An Exploratory Comparison of Public, Criminal and Penological Attitudes." *Mental Hygiene* XLII (October 1958), pp. 550–557.

GLASER, DANIEL. "Criminology and Public Policy." *The American Sociologist* VI (June 1971), pp. 30–37.

GLAZER, NATHAN. "When the Melting Pot Doesn't Melt." *The New York Times Magazine*, January 2, 1972, pp. 12–13, 27–31.

GOLDSTEIN, HERMAN. "Citizen Cooperation: The Perspective of the Police." In James M. Ratcliffe, editor, *The Good Samaritan and the Law*. Garden City, N.Y.: Doubleday & Co., 1966, pp. 199–208.

GREGORY, CHARLES O. "The Good Samaritan and the Bad: The Anglo-American Law." In James M. Ratcliffe, editor, *The Good Samaritan and the Law*. Garden City, N.Y.: Doubleday & Co., Inc., 1966, pp. 23–41.

HARTMANN, DONALD P., DONNA M. GELFAND, BRENT PAGE, and PATRICE WALDER. "Rates of Bystander Observation and Reporting of Contrived Shoplifting Incidents." *Criminology* X (November 1972), pp. 247–267.

HAWKINS, RICHARD O. "Who Called the Cops? Decisions to Report Criminal Victimization." *Law and Society Review* VII (Spring 1973), pp. 427–444.

HILL, ALBERT FAY. *The North Avenue Irregulars: A Suburb Battles the Mafia*. New York: Cowles Education Corporation, 1968.

HOFFMAN, RICHARD B. "Performance Measurements in Crime Control." *Journal of Research in Crime and Delinquency* VIII (July 1971), pp. 165–174.

HORNSTEIN, HARVEY A. "The Influence of Social Models on Helping." In J. Macaulay and L. Berkowitz, editors, *Altruism and Helping Behavior: Social Psychological Studies of Some Antecedents and Consequences*. New York: Academic Press, 1970, pp. 29–41.

JACOBS, JANE. *The Death and Life of Great American Cities*. New York: Vintage Books, 1961.

JEFFERY, C. RAY. *Crime Prevention through Environmental Design*. Beverly Hills: Sage Publications, 1971.

JENSEN, GARY F. " 'Crime Doesn't Pay': Correlates of a Shared Misunderstanding." *Social Problems* XVII (Fall 1969), pp. 189–201.

Joint Commission on Correctional Manpower and Training, *The Public Looks at Crime and Corrections*. Washington, D.C.: Joint Commission on Correctional Manpower and Training, 1968.

KALVEN, HARRY, JR., and HANS ZEISEL. *The American Jury*. Boston: Little, Brown and Company, 1966.

KLEINMAN, PAULA H., and DEBORAH S. DAVID. "Victimization and Perception of Crime in a Ghetto Community." *Criminology* XI (November 1973), pp. 307–343.

KNIGHT, DOUGLAS W. "Punishment Selection as a Function of Biographical Information." *Journal of Criminal Law, Criminology and Police Science* LVI (September 1965), pp. 325–327.

KNOPF, TERRY ANN. *Youth Patrols: An Experiment in Community Participation.* Waltham, Mass.: Brandeis University, Lemberg Center for the Study of Violence, 1969.

KOCH, HOWARD. *The Panic Broadcast: Portrait of an Event.* Boston: Little, Brown and Company, 1970.

KORTE, CHARLES. "Group Influence on the Helpfulness of Accident Witnesses." *Law and Society Review* V (August 1970), pp. 7–19.

KUTSCHINSKY, BERL. "Knowledge and Attitudes Regarding Legal Phenomena in Denmark." In Nils Christie, editor, *Scandinavian Studies in Criminology, Volume 2: Aspects of Social Control in Welfare States.* London: Tavistock Publications, 1968, pp. 125–159.

LATANÉ, BIBB, and JOHN M. DARLEY. *The Unresponsive Bystander: Why Doesn't He Help?* New York: Appleton-Century-Crofts, 1970.

LEJEUNE, ROBERT, and NICHOLAS ALEX. "On Being Mugged: The Event and Its Aftermath." Paper presented at the Twenty-third Annual Meeting of the Society for the Study of Social Problems, New York City, August 1973.

LEMERT, EDWIN M. *Social Pathology: A Systematic Approach to the Theory of Sociopathic Behavior.* New York: McGraw-Hill Book Company, Inc., 1951.

LESY, MICHAEL. *Wisconsin Death Trip.* New York: Pantheon Books, 1973.

LIND, ANDREW W. "Some Ecological Patterns of Community Disorganization in Honolulu." *American Journal of Sociology* XXXVI (September 1930), pp. 206–220.

LINGEMAN, RICHARD R. "Writer Is Mugged, Denies Being 'Victim.'" *The New York Times Magazine,* October 22, 1972, pp. 12–20.

LINSKY, ARNOLD S. "Who Shall Be Excluded: The Influence of Personal Attributes in Community Reaction to the Mentally Ill." *Social Psychiatry* V (July 1970), pp. 166–171.

"Living with Crime, U.S.A." *Newsweek* LXXX (December 18, 1972), pp. 31–36.

LOGAN, ANDY. *Against the Evidence: The Becker-Rosenthal Affair.* New York: The McCall Publishing Company, 1970.

Lupo, Alan. "The Do-It-Yourself War against Street Crime." *Boston Magazine* LXV (May 1973), pp. 38–41, 72–81.

Maccoby, Eleanor E., Joseph P. Johnson, and Russell M. Church. "Community Integration and the Social Control of Juvenile Delinquency." *Journal of Social Issues* XIV (June 1958), pp. 38–51.

Malinowski, Bronislaw. *Crime and Custom in Savage Society.* Paterson, N.J.: Littlefield, Adams & Company, 1926, 1964.

Marx, Gary T., and Dane Archer. "Citizen Involvement in the Law Enforcement Process: The Case of Community Police Patrols." *American Behavioral Scientist* XV (September–October 1971), pp. 52–72.

————. "Picking up the Gun: Some Organizational and Survey Data on Community Police Patrols." Paper presented at the Symposium on Studies of Public Experience, Knowledge and Opinion of Crime and Justice. Bureau of Social Science Research, Inc. Washington, D.C., March 1972.

————. "The Urban Vigilante." *Psychology Today* VI (January 1973), pp. 45–50.

Mays, John Barron. *Crime and the Social Structure.* London: Faber and Faber Ltd., 1963.

McIntyre, Jennie. "Public Attitudes toward Crime and Law Enforcement." *The Annals of the American Academy of Political and Social Science* CCCLXXIV (November 1967), pp. 34–46.

Mead, George Herbert. "The Psychology of Punitive Justice." *American Journal of Sociology* XXIII (March 1918), pp. 577–602.

Milgram, Stanley. "The Experience of Living in Cities." *Science* CLXVII (March 13, 1970), pp. 1461–1468.

————, and Paul Hollander. "The Murder They Heard." In Renatus Hartogs and Eric Artzt, editors. *Violence: Causes & Solutions.* New York: Dell Publishing Company, Inc., 1970, pp. 206–212.

Miller, Walter B. "Ideology and Criminal Justice Policy: Some Current Issues." *Journal of Criminal Law and Criminology* LXIV (June 1973), pp. 141–162.

————. "Lower Class Culture as a Generating Milieu of Gang Delinquency." *Journal of Social Issues* XIV (November 1958), pp. 5–19.

Mizruchi, Ephraim H., and Robert Perrucci. "Norm Qualities and Differential Effects of Deviant Behavior: An Exploratory Analysis." *American Sociological Review* XXVII (June 1962), pp. 391–399.

Morin, Edgar. *Rumour in Orléans,* translated by Peter Green. New York: Pantheon Books, 1969, 1971.

MORRIS, TERENCE. "The Social Toleration of Crime." In Hugh J. Klare, editor, *Changing Concepts of Crime and Its Treatment*. Oxford: Pergamon Press, 1966, pp. 13–34.

NELSON, HAROLD A. "The Defenders: A Case Study of an Informal Police Organization." *Social Problems* XV (Fall 1967), pp. 127–147.

NEWMAN, OSCAR. *Architectural Design for Crime Prevention*. Washington, D.C.: United States Government Printing Office, 1973.

———. *Defensible Space: Crime Prevention through Urban Design*. New York: Macmillan Publishing Co., Inc., 1972.

People v. Beardsley, Supreme Court of Michigan, 1907. 150 Mich. 206, 113 N.W. 1128. Cited in Jerome Michael and Herbert Wechsler, *Criminal Law and Its Administration: Cases, Statutes and Commentaries*. Chicago: The Foundation Press, Inc., 1940, pp. 114–118.

PILIAVIN, IRVING M., JUDITH RODIN, and JANE ALLYN PILIAVIN. "Good Samaritanism: An Underground Phenomenon?" *Journal of Personality and Social Psychology* XIII (December 1969), pp. 289–299.

PLATT, ANTHONY M. *The Child Savers: The Invention of Delinquency*. Chicago: The University of Chicago Press, 1969.

POVEDA, TONY G. "The Fear of Crime in a Small Town." *Crime and Delinquency* XVIII (April 1972), pp. 147–153.

The President's Commission on Law Enforcement and Administration of Justice, *The Challenge of Crime in a Free Society*. Washington, D.C.: United States Government Printing Office, 1967.

———. *Task Force Report: Crime and Its Impact—An Assessment*. Washington, D.C.: United States Government Printing Office, 1967.

QUINNEY, RICHARD. *The Social Reality of Crime*. Boston: Little, Brown and Company, 1970.

RAINWATER, LEE. "Fear and the House-as-Haven in the Lower Classes." In Robert Gutman, editor, *People and Buildings*. New York: Basic Books, Inc., 1972, pp. 299–313.

RANULF, SVEND. *Moral Indignation and Middle Class Psychology*. New York: Schocken Books, 1938, 1964.

REISS, ALBERT J., JR. Field Surveys III, Part 1, of the President's Commission on Law Enforcement and Administration of Justice. *Studies in Crime and Law Enforcement in Major Metropolitan Areas*. Washington, D.C.: United States Government Printing Office, 1967.

Report of the National Advisory Commission on Civil Disorders. New York: Bantam Books, Inc., 1968.

Report of the President's Commission on Crime in the District of Columbia. Washington, D.C.: United States Government Printing Office, 1966.

RHODES, WILLIAM C. *Behavioral Threat and Community Response.* New York: Behavioral Publications, Inc., 1972.

ROSE, ARNOLD M., and ARTHUR E. PRELL. "Does the Punishment Fit the Crime? A Study in Social Valuation." *American Journal of Sociology* LXI (November 1955), pp. 247–259.

ROSENTHAL, A. M. *Thirty-Eight Witnesses.* New York: McGraw-Hill Book Company, 1964.

ROSENTHAL, JACK. "The Cage of Fear in Cities Beset by Crime." *Life* magazine LXVII (July 11, 1969), pp. 16–23.

ROSS, SID. "The Thief Who Was Awarded $30,000." *Parade* magazine, December 13, 1970, pp. 7–9.

RUDZINSKI, ALEKSANDER W. "The Duty to Rescue: A Comparative Analysis." In James M. Ratcliffe, editor, *The Good Samaritan and the Law.* Garden City, N.Y.: Doubleday & Co., Inc., 1966, pp. 91–134.

SCHUR, EDWIN M. *Crimes without Victims: Deviant Behavior and Public Policy.* Englewood Cliffs, N.J.: Prentice-Hall, Inc., 1965.

SCHWARTZ, RICHARD D. "Social Factors in the Development of Legal Control: A Case Study of Two Israeli Settlements." In Lawrence M. Friedman and Stewart Macaulay, *Law and the Behavioral Sciences.* Indianapolis: The Bobbs-Merrill Company, Inc., 1969, pp. 509–522.

———, and JEROME H. SKOLNICK. "Two Studies of Legal Stigma." In Richard D. Schwartz and Jerome H. Skolnick, editors, *Society and the Legal Order: Cases and Materials in the Sociology of Law.* New York: Basic Books, Inc., 1970, pp. 568–579.

SELLIN, THORSTEN, and MARVIN E. WOLFGANG. *The Measurement of Delinquency.* New York: John Wiley & Sons, Inc., 1964.

SENNETT, RICHARD. "Middle-Class Families and Urban Violence: The Experience of a Chicago Community in the Nineteenth Century." In Stephan Thernstrom and Richard Sennett, editors, *Nineteenth-Century Cities: Essays in the New Urban History.* New Haven: Yale University Press, 1969, pp. 386–420.

SHEATSLEY, PAUL B., and JACOB J. FELDMAN. "The Assassination of President Kennedy: A Preliminary Report on Public Reactions and Behavior." *Public Opinion Quarterly* XXVIII (Summer 1964), pp. 189–215.

SHILS, EDWARD. "The Sanctity of Life." *Encounter* XXVIII (January 1967), pp. 39–49.

SMIGEL, ERWIN O. "Public Attitudes toward Stealing as Related to Size of the Victim Organization." *American Sociological Review* XXI (June 1956), pp. 320–327.

SMITH, PAUL E., and RICHARD O. HAWKINS. "Victimization, Types of Citizen-Police Contacts, and Attitudes toward the Police." *Law and Society Review* VIII (Fall 1973), pp. 135–152.

SOROKIN, PITIRIM A., with MAMIE TANQUIST, MILDRED PARTEN, and MRS. C. C. ZIMMERMAN. "An Experimental Study of Efficiency of Work under Various Specified Conditions." *American Journal of Sociology* XXXV (March 1930), pp. 765–782.

STRECHER, VICTOR G. *The Environment of Law Enforcement: A Community Relations Guide.* Englewood Cliffs, N.J.: Prentice-Hall Inc., 1971.

SUTHERLAND, EDWIN H. "The Diffusion of Sexual Psychopath Laws." In William J. Chambliss, editor, *Crime and the Legal Process.* New York: McGraw-Hill Book Company, 1969, pp. 74–81.

———. "The Sexual Psychopath Laws." In Albert Cohen, Alfred Lindesmith, and Karl Schuessler, editors, *The Sutherland Papers.* Bloomington: Indiana University Press, 1956, pp. 185–199.

———, and DONALD R. CRESSEY. *Criminology*, eighth edition. Philadelphia: J. B. Lippincott Company, 1970.

SUTTLES, GERALD D. *The Social Construction of Communities.* Chicago: The University of Chicago Press, 1972.

———. *The Social Order of the Slum: Ethnicity and Territory in the Inner City.* Chicago: The University of Chicago Press, 1968.

TOBY, JACKSON. "Is Punishment Necessary?" *Journal of Criminal Law, Criminology and Police Science* LV (September 1964), pp. 332–337.

TUNC, ANDRÉ. "The Volunteer and the Good Samaritan." In James M. Ratcliffe, editor, *The Good Samaritan and the Law.* Garden City, N.Y.: Doubleday & Co., Inc., 1966, pp. 43–62.

VEYSEY, LAWRENCE, editor. *Law and Resistance: American Attitudes toward Authority.* New York: Harper and Row, Publishers, 1970.

Victims of Crime. Hearing before the Subcommittee on Criminal Laws and Procedures of the Committee on the Judiciary, United States Senate, 92nd Congress, First Session. Washington, D.C.: United States Government Printing Office, 1972.

Viliborghi v. State, Supreme Court of Arizona, 1935. 45 Ariz. 275, 43 P.(2d) 210. Cited in Jerome Michael and Herbert Wechsler, *Criminal Law and Its Administration: Cases, Statutes and Commentaries.* Chicago: The Foundation Press, Inc., 1940, pp. 70–75.

WARREN, DONALD I. "Neighborhood Structure and Riot Behavior in Detroit: Some Exploratory Findings." *Social Problems* XVI (Spring 1969), pp. 464–484.

WEIS, KURT, and SANDRA S. BORGES. "Victimology and Rape: The

Case of the Legitimate Victim." *Issues in Criminology* VIII (Fall 1973), pp. 71–115.

Westin, Jeane. "A Novel Way to Stop School Vandals." *Parade* magazine, January 20, 1974, pp. 12–14.

Whitman, Howard. *Terror in the Streets.* New York: The Dial Press, 1951.

Wiebe, G. D. "Responses to the Televised Kefauver Hearings: Some Social Psychological Implications." *Public Opinion Quarterly* XVI (Summer 1962), pp. 181–200.

Wilkins, Leslie T. *Social Deviance: Social Policy, Action, and Research.* Englewood Cliffs, N.J.: Prentice-Hall, Inc., 1965.

Williams, Emlyn. *Beyond Belief: A Chronicle of Murder and Its Detection.* New York: Random House, 1967.

Wilson, James Q. "The Police and Their Problems: A Theory." In Carl J. Friedrich and Seymour Harris, editors, *Public Policy*, XII. Cambridge: Harvard University Press, 1963, pp. 189–216.

———. "The Urban Unease: Community vs. City." *The Public Interest*, No. 12 (Summer 1968), pp. 25–39.

———. *Varieties of Police Behavior: The Management of Law and Order in Eight Communities.* Cambridge: Harvard University Press, 1968.

Winick, Charles, and Paul M. Kinsie. *The Lively Commerce: Prostitution in the United States.* Chicago: Quadrangle Books, 1971.

Wolfenstein, Martha, and Gilbert Kliman, editors. *Children and the Death of a President.* Garden City, N.Y.: Doubleday & Company, Inc., 1965.

Wolfgang, Marvin E. *Patterns in Criminal Homicide.* Philadelphia: University of Pennsylvania Press, 1958.

———. "Urban Crime." In James Q. Wilson, editor, *The Metropolitan Enigma.* Garden City, N.Y.: Doubleday & Co., Inc., 1970, pp. 270–311.

Zeisel, Hans. "An International Experiment on the Effects of a Good Samaritan Law." In James M. Ratcliffe, editor, *The Good Samaritan and the Law.* Garden City, N.Y.: Doubleday & Co., Inc., 1966, pp. 209–212.

Zimbardo, Philip G. "The Human Choice: Individuation, Reason, and Order versus Deindividuation, Impulse, and Chaos." In William J. Arnold and David Levine, editors, *1969 Nebraska Symposium on Motivation.* Lincoln: University of Nebraska Press, 1969, pp. 237–307.

———. "Vandalism: An Act in Search of a Cause." Unpublished manuscript.

Index

n indicates entry is found in footnote on page cited.
t indicates entry is in table on page cited.

Abbott, Daniel J., 46*n*, 141, 152*n*, 180*n*, 182*n*, 193, 211*n*
Accidents, 6, 227
Addicts, drug, 36, 40, 78, 101*n*, 172, 181*n*, 186, 202–203
Adorno, T. W., 180*n*
Affect for the community, 9, 76, 85, 91–93, 142, 262*t*
  scale, 92–93, 99, 142, 262*t*
Africa, 140
Age, 11*n*, 36–37, 40, 57, 66, 80, 83–84, 92, 95, 98–99, 108–110, 120, 122, 164, 196, 207–208, 253, 259*t*, 260*t*, 261*t*, 262*t*, 265*t*
Aggravated assault, *see* Assault
Airport, 239, 254
Alarms
  burglar, 4–6, 9, 90, 93–94, 105–107, 115–117, 119, 121, 125
  false alarms, 116–117
  types of, 116
Alcoholism, *see* Drunkenness
Aldrich, Howard, 12*n*, 127*n*
Alex, Nicholas, 100*n*
Alexander, Christopher, 104*n*, 138, 151*n*
Alienation, 21, 102*n*, 187, 221, 231–232, 235, 242, 254, 258*n*
Allport, Gordon W., 72*n*
Altruism, 239, 242·
Ambulances, 40, 110, 219, 223, 233
American Indian Movement, 199–200
Amir, Menachem, 13*n*, 49*n*, 72*n*, 245*n*
Andelman, David A., 103*n*, 180*n*
Anderson, Jack, 128*n*
Andrews, Frank M., 129*n*, 245*n*

Angell, Robert Cooley, 69*n*
Anti-horsethief societies, 192, 196
Anti-Semitism, 35–36
Anxiety about crime, 2, 8, 21, 24, 33, 37, 45*n*, 59, 62, 74–75, 83, 87, 94, 125, 148, 168, 225, 227
Apartment buildings, 85, 105, 110, 196, 206, 215
Apathy, 9–10, 185, 205, 216–217, 225, 231, 235, 242
Archer, Dane, 196–197, 200–201, 203, 207–208, 211*n*, 212*n*, 213*n*
Architecture, 96, 118–119, 145–149, 216, 234
Argentina, 125
Arkansas, 228
Armored cars, 5
Armstrong, Barbara, 126*n*
Arnold, William J., 14*n*, 153*n*
Arson, 78, 187, 193
Artzt, Eric, 244*n*
Assassination, 70*n*, 224–225
Assault, 2–3, 6, 13*n*, 15, 29, 37, 64–65, 83, 99, 107–108, 110–111, 117–118, 129*n*, 161, 165, 173, 180*n*, 192–193, 200, 202, 215–216, 220–221, 223, 228, 232, 235, 241–242, 247*n*, 251, 263*t*, 264*t*
Atlanta, 36
Australia, 184*n*
Austria, 218
Authoritarian submission, 160
Authoritarianism, 160–161, 163, 180*n*
Automobiles, 3, 6, 31, 86–88, 97–98, 106–107, 113, 116–117, 119, 121, 145, 149, 159, 205–206, 227,

279

Automobiles (Cont.)
247*n*, 263*t*, 264*t*
theft of, 3, 6, 15–16, 28, 88, 161,
251–252, 258*n*, 263*t*, 264*t*
Autonomy-withdrawal syndrome,
138, 145
Avoidance behavior, 73, 88, 94–96,
99, 105, 107, 109–111, 114–115,
118, 214, 248
Ayres, B. Drummond, 71*n*, 151*n*
Ayres, James, 49*n*

Bachmuth, Rita, 45*n*
Baghdad, 28
Bailey, L. H., 151*n*
Bakal, Yitzhak, 49*n*
Baltimore, 76–77, 81, 94, 114–115, 202
Barmash, Isadore, 127*n*
Barnard, Charles N., 126*n*, 128*n*
Barth, Alan, 220–221, 244*n*
Bates, Alan, 179*n*
Batson, C. D., 246*n*
Belleville, 21, 24–25, 31, 73, 76–80,
82–85, 89–94, 97–99, 101*n*, 102*n*,
103*n*, 159–167, 173, 175–177,
181*n*, 182*n*, 218, 223, 232, 251–
257, 258*n*, 259*t*, 260*t*, 261*t*, 262*t*,
263*t*, 264*t*, 265*t*
interveiws with residents of, 252–
254
sample selected from, 252–253
Berkowitz, Leonard, 150*n*, 181*n*, 246*n*
Biderman, Albert D., 8, 12*n*, 13*n*,
43*n*, 44*n*, 45*n*, 103*n*, 128*n*, 182*n*,
184*n*
Binder, David, 46*n*
Biographical characteristics, *see* So-
cial background factors
Bittner, Egon, 101*n*, 128*n*
Blacks, *see* Race
Block, M. K., 44*n*, 100*n*
Block, Richard L., 184*n*
Block-watchers, 60, 110, 191, 212*n*
Blue-collar workers, *see* Occupation
Blumenthal, Monica D., 122, 129*n*,
245*n*
Blumenthal, Ralph, 71*n*
Boggs, Sarah L., 13*n*, 138–139, 151*n*
Boise, 62–63
Bombing, 34–35
Bookmakers, 101*n*, 205–206

see also Gambling
Bordua, David J., 184*n*
Borges, Sandra S., 100*n*, 245*n*
Boston, 21, 32, 71*n*, 77–78, 81, 84
96–97, 101*n*, 107–109, 112, 118,
134, 137, 145, 152*n*, 160, 172,
197, 202–204, 207, 251–252
Boston Police Department, 203, 207
"Box man," 135–136
Brazil, 202–203
Brenner, Arline R., 246*n*
Briarcliffe (New York), 88
Bribery, 188, 205
see also Corruption, government
Bronx, 149
Brooklyn, 113, 168
Brothels, 172–173
Brown, Julia S., 181*n*
Brown, Richard Maxwell, 189–192,
194, 196, 201, 209*n*, 210*n*
Brutality, police, 158, 198–199, 201,
207–208
Bryan, James H., 247*n*
Burglaries, 3–5, 15, 35, 54, 64, 77–78,
82–83, 85–86, 88, 101*n*, 106,
113–119, 124, 129*n*, 135–136,
138, 161, 167, 172, 242, 251,
263*t*, 264*t*
Burnham, David, 151*n*
Businesses, closing, 5, 6, 59, 73, 96,
105, 111–112, 143, 195–196
Businessmen, 125, 169, 175, 195–196
Bystanders
compensation to, 217, 219
injury to, 233
number of, 215–216, 234–240, 242–
243
response to crime, 9–10, 65–66, 74,
85.–86, 116, 131, 136, 139, 141–
142, 146–149, 151*n*, 156–157,
159, 165, 169, 177, 179*n*, 204,
214–243, 244*n*, 248–249
costs and rewards of, 238–240
detour intervention, 233
direct intervention, 233
law regarding, 177, 217–223, 244*n*

Caldwell, Earl, 100*n*
California, 86, 149, 152*n*
Cambridge (Massachusetts), 141, 152*n*
Campbell, Donald T., 180*n*

Capital Punishment, *See* Death penalty
Capote, Truman, 50, 54–59, 70*n*, 118, 128*n*
Carmody, Deirdre, 70*n*
Carron, Andrew, 49*n*
Catholics, *see* Religion
Chamber of Commerce of the United States, 100*n*
Chambers, Carl D., 149*n*
Chambliss, William J., 71*n*, 150*n*
Change of venue, 58, 70*n*, 135
Chapman, Dennis, 47*n*
Chappell, D., 184*n*
Charlestown (Boston), 145
Chevalier, Louis, 2, 12*n*, 34, 45*n*, 47*n*, 210*n*, 243*n*
Chicago, 21, 34–35, 48*n*, 74, 101*n*, 118, 143, 167
Children, number of, 95, 132
Chinese, 228, 230
Ching, Frank, 127*n*
Christie, Nils, 48*n*, 179*n*
Church, Russell M., 142, 152*n*
Cipes, Robert M., 13*n*
Cities, *see* Urban-suburban-rural differences
Civil liberties, 176
Civil rights movement, 198–199
Civilian police patrols, 10, 185, 189, 191–192, 194–209, 212*n*, 249
accountability, 201, 204, 207
adversarial patrol groups, 197–201, 207
crises, responding to, 198, 208
funding of, 198, 208
ideology of, 208
leadership of, 204, 207–208
legitimacy, 201, 208
organization of, 198, 208
patrolling, 194, 196–200, 202–203
police and, 197–200, 203, 204, 209
recruitment of members to, 199, 202, 204, 207–208
sadistic members in, 202
self-esteem of members, 198–199, 209
supplemental patrol groups, 197–201, 203, 207
support for, 201, 204, 207–208
youth patrols, 197–198, 200, 208

Civilian review boards, 176
Claiborne, William L., 213*n*
Clare, Myrt, 54–55, 57, 114
Clark, Ramsey, 22, 44*n*, 171, 183*n*
Class, *see* Social class
Clinard, Marshall B., 46*n*, 141, 152*n*, 180*n*, 182*n*, 193, 211*n*
Clothing styles, 52, 69*n*
Clubs, as weapons, 118
Clurman, Richard M., 183*n*
Clutter family, 54–59, 85, 93, 114, 118, 138, 231
Clutter, Arthur, 55
Clutter, Herb, 54
Coates, Robert B., 42, 49*n*
Cobb, Richard, 47*n*
Cohen, Albert, 70*n*
Cohen, Fay G., 212*n*
Cohen, Julius, 179*n*
Collective conscience, 51, 56–57, 64, 132–133
Colorado, 23–24, 56, 58, 101*n*
Columbia University, 118
Communism, 25
Comstock, Craig, 105, 125*n*
Concern with crime, 26, 45*n*, 76–78, 81, 94
Concerts, rock, 208
Confessions, 52
Conflict
generational, 52–53, 108–109
social, 52–53, 66, 108, 187, 189–191, 195, 198–201
Conklin, John E., 11*n*, 49*n*, 72*n*, 73*n*, 100*n*, 101*n*, 102*n*, 103*n*, 104*n*, 128*n*, 129*n*, 154*n*, 180*n*, 183*n*
Connecticut, 87, 110, 119, 159
Contributory negligence, 226
Cook, Fred J., 47*n*
Corrections, community-based, 39
Corruption, government, 11*n*, 12*n*, 185–186, 188, 205
Coser, Lewis, 52, 69*n*
"Cosmopolitans," 98, 104*n*
Courts, 4, 16, 59, 106, 123, 131, 155, 157–159, 174, 197, 202–203, 206, 219, 221, 236
Craig, Jonathan, 151*n*
Cressey, Donald R., 47*n*, 70*n*, 152*n*, 170–171, 183*n*

Crime
  causes of, 25–26, 38, 41, 53, 121,
    123, 168, 248
  collective response to, 10, 52, 57,
    61–63, 67–68, 97, 112, 185–209
  costs of
    direct, 3–6, 8, 10, 27, 42, 113
    indirect, 3–6, 8, 10, 42
  displacement of, 9–10, 48n, 105,
    111, 117, 124, 188, 204, 206
  functional theory of, 50–55, 60–61,
    65
  location of, 8, 19, 26, 111, 214, 223–
    224, 239
  perceived seriousness of, 16, 77–78,
    101n, 164–166, 180n, 181n
  reclassification of, 29–30
  reporting of, 9–10, 15–17, 43n, 86,
    88, 131, 137–138, 142, 145, 149,
    155–160, 162–176, 178, 180n,
    186, 196, 203–204, 209, 215–216,
    219–220, 222–223, 233, 235–237,
    241–242, 248–249, 264t, 265t
  reasons for failure to report
    crime, 16–17, 156–159, 174,
    215–216, 236–237
Crime against business, 5–6
Crime Index, 3, 15, 78, 161–163, 264t
Crime as a political issue, 1, 18, 20,
  25–30, 36, 46n, 76, 94, 169–170,
  185–186, 198, 254
Crime rates
  actual, 3, 15–18, 20–21, 43n, 84,
    170, 257n
  falling, 28–30
  reported, 3, 15–18, 21, 23–24, 30,
    43n, 79, 82, 137, 251–252, 257n
  rising, 1, 10, 16–18, 20–21, 23–24,
    28, 30, 37, 44n, 66, 104n, 115,
    131, 170–171, 173–174, 178, 196,
    205, 214, 248
Crime reduction, 9, 10, 27–29, 40–42,
  48n, 53–54, 67, 93, 105, 136–137,
  148, 152n, 155, 169–170, 174–
  176, 185, 187, 190, 196–197,
  204, 207, 209, 221, 248
Crime as a social problem, 17, 76–78,
  115, 155, 166, 206–208
Crime statistics, 2, 29, 45n, 76, 169
Crime waves, 1, 3, 19–24, 37, 86
Crimes without victims, 16, 158

Criminal environment, 20, 25, 79–80,
  83, 91, 101n, 102n, 155, 164,
  166, 170, 174
Criminal Injuries Compensation
  Board (Great Britain), 228
Criminal justice system, 4, 10, 27,
  131, 135, 155–159, 178, 188, 191,
  202–203
  see also Courts; Police; Prisons
Criminals as outsiders, 7, 28, 30–42,
  52, 55, 61, 65–66, 69n, 70n, 166,
  195–196, 206, 248
Cullen, Tom A., 48n, 182n, 211n

Danziger, Martin, 153n
Dark figure, 15–17, 43n, 257n
Darley, John M., 217, 231–240, 242,
  246n, 247n
Darnton, John, 182n
David, Deborah S., 45n
Davis, F. James, 45n, 101n
Dawson, John P., 244n
Daylight savings time, 143
Death penalty, 27, 36, 59, 159, 186,
  190, 193, 228
"Death squads," 202–203
Deeley, Peter, 45n
Defended neighborhood, 194–195
Defenders, the, 198–200, 202
Defensible space, 146, 206
Defensive measures, 93–94, 105–125
  see also Protective measures
Definitions favorable to violation of
  the law, 152n, 171
Delaney, Paul, 11n, 100n
Democratic Party, 46n, 190–191, 255–
  256
Demonstrations, 1, 122–123, 161–163,
  263t, 264t
  see also Universities, students
Denmark, 39, 41
De Onis, Juan, 46n
Deterrence, 10, 52–53, 106, 143, 145–
  146, 148–149, 172–173, 178, 196,
  203, 209, 216, 222, 243, 248
Detroit, 202
Developing nations, 27–28, 140–141,
  193
Deviant behavior, 8, 19, 30–32, 37–
  38, 52, 63, 107, 131–134, 136–
  137, 140, 142–145, 148–149,

171, 204, 216, 221, 232, 234
and boundaries, 19, 51–52, 61–63,
171
Differential association, theory of,
152n, 170
Dimsdale, Thomas J., 188, 210n
Dinitz, Simon, 13n, 33, 44n, 47n, 99n,
101n, 180n
Dinnerstein, Leonard, 48n, 210n
Discrimination, 25, 27, 41, 123, 159,
208
Discussion groups, 37, 61–62, 67, 185–
186, 207, 209n
see also Organizations, social
Dissociation, see Identification
Distance, geographical, 229–231
Distance, social, 31, 35, 229–231
Division of labor, 132
see also Societies, simple and complex
Dogs, see Watchdogs
Dorchester, 32, 81
Dormitories, 97, 123–124, 206
Dow, Thomas E., Jr., 47n
Drinking, 4, 199
underage, 78, 158
Drugs, 40, 109, 112, 186, 202–203, 205
addiction, 16, 36, 40, 158
addicts, 36, 40, 78, 101n, 172, 181n,
186, 202–203
education, 61–62
raids, 11n, 104n, 113, 129n
rehabilitation, 40–41, 61
sale of, 176, 186, 202–203
use of, 61–62, 77–78, 126n, 161–163,
168, 181n, 263t, 264t
Drugstores, 112
Drunkenness, 32, 200, 204, 239, 263t
Durkheim, Emile, 8, 50–54, 58, 60–
64, 68, 68n, 69n, 75–76, 99,
132–133, 151, 171, 183n, 216

Edgerton, Robert B., 150n
Education, 38, 41–42, 44n, 77, 80–81,
83, 89, 95, 98, 110, 120, 122–124,
163–164, 196–197, 204, 206–208,
218, 255–257, 259t, 260t, 261t,
262t, 265t
Elderly, 36–37, 66, 84, 108–110, 196,
253
see also Age

Embezzlement, 158, 161, 163, 263t,
264t
Empathic distress, 237
Empathy
with bystanders, 220–221
with offenders, 33
with strangers, 229
with victims, 221, 227–231, 234,
240–241
Employment agencies, 39
Engels, Friedrich, 154–155, 178n
English, the, 208, 257
See also Ethnic groups
Engraving, 116–117, 124
Ennis, Philip H., 13n, 42n, 43n, 103n,
179n, 258n
Erikson, Kai T., 19, 38, 44n, 48n, 49n,
51–52, 69n, 134, 150n
Escorts, 18, 66, 73, 107–110, 124, 196
Eszterhas, Joe, 71n
Etching, 116–117, 124
Ethnic groups, 26, 34–36, 64–68, 80,
83, 89, 120–121, 142, 148, 164,
195, 208, 227–230, 243, 255–257,
259t, 260t, 261t, 262t, 265t
Ex-convicts, 33, 36, 39, 41–42, 54, 248
Executions, see Death penalty
Exposure-to-crime index, 24, 45n
Extortion, 124, 201–202

Fait accompli effect, 161
Faris, Ellsworth, 150n
Fauconnet, Paul, 68n
Feagin, Joe R., 120–122, 129n
Fear, 1–10, 22–26, 28–29, 31, 34–37,
39, 41, 45n, 50, 53, 55–59, 61–
62, 64–67, 73–75, 81–87, 90–91,
93, 95–99, 99n, 100n, 105–106,
109–115, 117, 119–121, 129n,
131, 137, 142–143, 145–146, 167–
168, 176, 185, 189, 195–196, 201,
207, 214–215, 219–220, 222–
223, 225, 227, 242, 249, 255
see also Safety, feelings of
Fear of victimization, 26, 45n, 74, 77,
81, 90, 98, 114, 157, 168
Federal Bureau of Investigation, 3,
15, 30, 43n, 78, 161–162, 264t
Felcher, Barry, 128n
Feldman, Jacob J., 70n
Fences, 101n, 116

Feron, James, 152*n*
Ferretti, Fred, 211*n*, 245*n*
Filipinos, 227
Firearms, 6, 9, 59, 66, 83, 86–87, 94, 105–107, 114–115, 117–123, 125, 139, 158, 198–199, 201, 263*t*
Focal concerns, 174
Ford, Jesse Hill, 67, 87, 118–119
Forest Hills (New York) housing dispute, 66
Forgery, 53
Frady, Marshall, 72*n*, 129*n*
France, 18, 34–35, 52–53, 109, 217
Frank, Leo, 35–36, 188
Franke, David, 150*n*
Franke, Holly, 150*n*
Freedman, Lawrence Zelic, 223, 225, 244*n*, 245*n*
Frenkel-Brunswick, Else, 180*n*
Friedman, Lawrence M., 150*n*, 151*n*, 180*n*, 181*n*
Friedrich, Carl J., 184*n*
Friendly, Alfred, 45*n*, 150*n*, 245*n*
Friendships, pattern of, 98, 124
Furstenberg, Frank F., Jr., 46*n*, 76–77, 81, 94–95, 99, 100*n*, 103*n*, 104*n*, 114–115, 128*n*, 169, 182*n*, 183*n*

Gallup, George, 46*n*
Gallup poll, 158
Gambling, 25, 101*n*, 133, 161–163, 205–206, 263*t*, 264*t*
Gangs, 112, 122, 147, 195–196, 202
Gangsters, *see* Organized crime
Garden City (Kansas), 55
Gardiner, John A., 11*n*, 12*n*
Geis, Gilbert, 127*n*
Gelfand, Donna M., 151*n*, 179*n*, 244*n*
Genovese, Kitty, 136, 165, 214–216, 222–224, 226, 231, 234–235, 238, 242
Georgia, 35–36, 188
Gerassi, John, 62–63, 71*n*
Germans, 187
Gilbert, G. M., 179*n*, 181*n*
Glaser, Daniel, 132, 149*n*
Glazer, Nathan, 47*n*, 66, 72*n*
Goldfarb, Ronald L., 45*n*, 49*n*, 150*n*, 245*n*
Goldstein, Herman, 180*n*, 243*n*

Good Samaritans, 214, 219–222, 239, 242, 247*n*
Goodman, George, Jr., 183*n*
Gordon, C. Wayne, 47*n*
Gottlieb, David, 180*n*
Graham, Fred P., 49*n*
Graham, Hugh Davis, 210*n*
Great Britain, 23, 70*n*, 159, 186, 228
Greenhouse, Linda, 211*n*
Gregory, Charles O., 244*n*
Grenade, 86
Griffin, Senator Robert, 11*n*
Guards, security, 5, 110, 124–125, 129*n*, 195, 206
Gurr, Ted Robert, 210*n*
Gutman, Robert, 103*n*, 151*n*, 153*n*

Halfway houses, 30, 41–42, 61
Hamden (Connecticut), 87, 110
Handicapped people, 36–37
Hangings, 52, 59, 159, 187
Harlem (New York), 29, 214
Harris, Richard, 45*n*
Harris, Seymour, 184*n*
Hartmann, Donald P., 151*n*, 179*n*, 244*n*
Hartogs, Renatus, 244*n*
Hawkins, Richard O., 182*n*, 183*n*, 184*n*
Haymarket Square (Chicago) bombing, 34
Head, Kendra B., 129*n*, 245*n*
Herbers, John, 71*n*
Heroin, *see* Drugs
Hill, Reverend Albert Fay, 204–206, 212*n*
Hippies, 62, 69*n*, 126*n*
Hitchhiking, 107–108
Hoffman, Richard B., 152*n*
Hofmann, Paul, 46*n*
Holcomb (Kansas), 54–59, 61, 93, 222
Hollander, Paul, 223–224, 238, 244*n*, 246*n*
Home defense, 117–123, 129*n*
Homicide, *see* Murder
Homosexuality, 16, 31, 62–63, 158, 168, 228
Honolulu, 131
Hooliganism, 27
Hoover, J. Edgar, 30

Horn, Patrice, 247*n*
Hornstein, Harvey A., 246*n*
Horowitz, Irving Louis, 150*n*
Hospitals, mental, 37–38, 60, 211*n*
Housing, 67, 91, 96, 146–147, 254–257
   design of, 96, 145–149, 216, 234
Housing projects, 32–33, 68, 110, 119, 137, 145–149, 191–192, 196, 206, 208
   interior spaces of, 146
   zones of influence in, 146–147
Houston, 168
Houston, Ted L., 127*n*
Human traffic, 5–7, 9–10, 73, 78, 98–99, 104*n*, 112–113, 124–125, 142–148, 152*n*, 173, 195, 212*n*, 216, 222–223, 249, 255
Humphrey, Senator Hubert H., 27, 255–256
Hyde (Great Britain), 186

Identification
   with offender, 33, 35, 109, 117
   with victim, 57, 60, 107–109, 227–231, 234, 240–242, 245*n*
   with witness, 223
Ik tribe, 140
Immigration, *see* Moving
Impersonal domains, 143
Inciardi, James A., 149*n*
Income, 11*n*, 41–42, 57, 79–80, 83, 89–90, 95, 97, 114, 164, 189, 255–257, 259*t*, 260*t*, 261*t*, 262*t*, 265*t*
India, 157, 244*n*
Indian Law Commissioners, 244*n*
Indians, 199–200
Inflation, 76–77
Informants, 196, 203, 205
Inmates, 4, 7, 33, 39–40, 65
Insurance, 5–6, 16–17, 157
Interest groups, 222
   see also Lobbying
Internal Revenue Service, 205
Inventory shrinkage, 158
Iowa, 64, 106, 136
Iraq, 28, 132
Irish, 191, 208, 255, 257
   see also Ethnic groups
Isolation, geographic, 31–32, 40, 55–56, 98, 187–188, 253–254, 256

Israel, 139–140
Italians, 208, 255, 257
   see also Ethnic groups
Italy, 27, 126*n*

Jack the Ripper murders, 36, 169, 194–195
Jacobs, Jane, 7, 13*n*, 70*n*, 127*n*, 142–143, 148, 152*n*, 153*n*, 186, 209*n*, 229, 246*n*
Japan, 225
Jefferey, C. Ray, 153*n*
Jensen, Gary F., 183*n*
Jewish Defense League, 66, 202
Jews, 35–36, 66–67, 208, 257
Jobs, *see* Occupation
Johnson, Earl, Jr., 182*n*
Johnson, Joseph P., 142, 152*n*
Johnson, Louise A., 12*n*, 43*n*, 103*n*, 128*n*, 182*n*
Johnson, President Lyndon B., 46*n*, 255–256
Johnson, Thomas A., 211*n*, 212*n*
Johnston, Laurie, 125*n*
Joint Commission on Correctional Manpower and Training, 44*n*, 49*n*
Judges, 188
Juries, 159, 188, 193, 228
Juvenile delinquency, 19, 24, 32–33, 78, 101*n*, 112, 132–133, 141–142, 147–148, 168, 183*n*, 196, 202, 204

Kahn, Robert L., 129*n*, 245*n*
Kalven, Harry, Jr., 180*n*, 226, 245*n*
Kampala (Uganda), 141
Kandell, Jonathan, 130*n*
Kansas, 54–59, 138, 222, 231
Karate, 107
Kaufman, Michael T., 129*n*
Kayakachoian, Gary, 127*n*
Keene, Evelyn, 212*n*
Kefauver hearings, 185–186
Kelley, Clarence M., 12*n*, 72*n*
Kennedy, President John F., 70*n*, 224–225, 255–256
Kennedy, Senator Robert F., 225
Kenya, 193
Kew Gardens (Queens, New York), 214–215, 223

Kidnappings, 23, 52–53, 61, 87, 109, 125, 193, 203, 224, 226
King, Dr. Martin Luther, 225
King, Wayne, 127n
Kinsie, Paul M., 127n, 183n
Klare, Hugh J., 69n
Kleinman, Paula H., 45n
Kliman, Gilbert, 245n
Knight, Douglas W., 179n
Knight, Michael, 43n
Knives, 6, 59, 117–118, 165, 215, 228, 263t
Knopf, Terry Ann, 197, 211n
Koch, Howard, 245n
Koestler, Arthur, 69n
Kondoism, 28
Korte, Charles, 246n
Ku Klux Klan, 199
Kutschinsky, Berl, 48n, 179n
Kvutza, 139–140

Labeling, 19, 30–31, 154
Larceny, 3, 5–6, 15, 18, 28–30, 64, 75, 88, 99, 110, 116, 124, 141, 158–159, 161, 188, 236–237, 241, 251, 263t, 264t
by employees, 158
Latané, Bibb, 217, 231–240, 242, 246n, 247n
Law enforcement, 4, 27, 39, 60–61, 158–159, 161, 178, 191–192, 194–199, 201, 203
cost of, 187, 191–192, 196
proactive, 177, 184n
reactive, 177–178, 184n
Law and order, 1, 25–27, 95, 177, 185, 189, 207, 254
Laws, 19, 131–132, 139–141, 154–178, 181n, 217–223, 226, 244n
attitude toward violation of, 160–161, 163
development of, 60
didactic function of, 161, 218
public opinion and, 60, 135, 154–155, 159, 177, 179n, 218, 226
Lee, John M., 245n
Lejeune, Robert, 100n
Lemert, Edwin M., 19–20, 44n
Leningrad, 69n
Lesy, Michael, 136, 151n

Levin, James M., 246n
Levine, David, 14n, 153n
Levinson, Daniel J., 180n
Liberia, 140–141
Libraries, 6, 96, 110, 143
Lichtenstein, Grace, 43n
Liddy, G. Gordon, 118
Life magazine, 117
Lights, 6, 9, 56, 59, 64, 114, 116–117, 143, 147, 197, 204, 215
Likert items, 252, 258n
Lincoln (Nebraska), 59
Lind, Andrew W., 131, 149n
Lindesmith, Alfred, 70n
Lingeman, Richard R., 100n
Linsky, Arnold S., 38, 48n
Llewellyn, Karl, 178
Loan sharks, 78, 101n
Lobbying, 204, 222
"Locals," 98, 104n
Locks, 6, 9, 18, 57, 59, 64, 93–94, 105, 107, 110, 114–116, 119, 121, 123–124
Lockwood, Charles, 12n
Logan, Andy, 11n, 150n
Loitering, 8, 78
London, 36, 169, 194–195
Long, G. J., 44n, 100n
Long Island, 241
Los Angeles, 108
Lukas, J. Anthony, 100n
Lupo, Alan, 212n
Lynching, 36, 65, 69n, 187–188, 193

Macaulay, J., 246n
Macaulay, Stewart, 150n, 151n, 180n, 181n
Maccoby, Eleanor E., 142, 152n
Mace, 121
McFadden, Robert D., 247n
McGovern, Senator George, 255–256
McIntyre, Jennie, 9, 12n, 14n, 43n, 103n, 128n, 182n
McKay, Henry D., 183n
Mafiosi, 126n
see also Organized crime
Malcolm, Andrew H., 104n, 127n, 129n
Malinowski, Bronislaw, 132–133, 150n

Malt, Harold Lewis, Assoc., 127*n*
Manchester (Pittsburgh), 40–41
Mansfield, Senator Mike, 217
Manslaughter, 161, 163, 263*t*, 264*t*
Manson, Charles, 108–109
Marijuana, 61–62, 161–163, 181*n*, 203, 263*t*, 264*t*
    see also Drugs
Marital status, 95
Markham, James M., 71*n*
Marshall, James, 154–155, 179*n*
"Martian invasion" broadcast, 244–245*n*
Marx, Gary T., 196–197, 200–201, 203, 207–208, 211*n*, 212*n*, 213*n*
Marx, Karl, 154–155, 178*n*
Maryland, 108
Massachusetts, 42, 165, 264*t*
Massachusetts Bay Colony, 19, 38, 134
Mayer, Martin, 184*n*
Mays, John Barron, 53, 69*n*
Mead, Gorge Herbert, 53, 69*n*
Media, *see* Press
Merton, Robert K., 104*n*
Methadone clinics, 40
Miami, 224, 226
Michael, Jerome, 126*n*, 244*n*
Migration, *see* Moving
Milgram, Stanley, 137, 151*n*, 223–224, 230, 238, 244*n*, 246*n*
Military experience, 199, 202
Miller, Alden D., 42, 49*n*
Miller, S. M., 45*n*
Miller, Walter B., 26–27, 46*n*, 174, 183*n*
Mills, C. Wright, 150*n*
Minneapolis, 200
Missouri, 62, 138–139
Mizruchi, Ephraim H., 183*n*
Mobility, geographical, 7, 47*n*, 114, 124, 141, 144, 221
    see also Moving
Mobility, social, 189
Mobilization measures, 94, 114–115, 121
Moderators, the, 187
Mohr, Charles, 210*n*
Montana, 188
Montgomery, Paul L., 47*n*, 48*n*, 127*n*
Moors murders, 70*n*, 186

Moriarity, Thomas, 247*n*
Morin, Edgar, 35, 44*n*, 48*n*, 52, 69*n*, 109, 127*n*
Morris, Terence, 69*n*
Moscow, 69*n*
Moshav, 139–140
Movies, 4, 221, 235
Moving, 6, 32–36, 91–93, 104*n*, 110, 112, 125, 141, 144, 152*n*, 186, 189, 193, 221–222, 254
    from a high crime-rate area, 6, 12*n*, 56, 60, 64, 67, 71*n*, 91–92, 104*n*, 112, 134, 186
Mugging, *see* Robbery
Murder, 2–4, 6, 12n, 13*n*, 15, 22, 28, 34–36, 39, 54–61, 65, 67, 71*n*, 86–87, 97, 99, 101*n*, 106–109, 112, 114, 117–119, 123, 133, 136, 138, 161, 165, 168–169, 186, 192–195, 202–203, 205, 211*n*, 214–216, 223–226, 228, 230–231, 234, 242, 247*n*, 251, 263*t*, 264*t*

Narcotics, *see* Drugs
National Advisory Commission on Civil Disorders, 1, 10*n*, 258*n*
National Commission on the Causes and Prevention of Violence, 11*n*
National Crime Commission, *see* President's Commission on Law Enforcement and Administration of Justice, The
National Guard, 59
Nebraska, 59, 172
Negroes, *see* Race
Nelson, Harold A., 198–199, 211*n*
Neo-Fascists, 27
New Jersey, 117
New Rochelle (New York), 205
New York City, 2, 29, 36–37, 59–61, 65, 110–112, 119, 124, 133, 146, 149, 165, 170, 175–176, 193–194, 197, 202–203, 214–215, 227–228, 231, 241–242
New York City Police Department, 15, 29–30, 197
New York *Daily News*, 24
New York State Investigation Commission, 205

New York State Special Commission on Attica, The, 49*n*
New York Times, The, 24, 205, 214–215, 228
New Zealand, 184*n*
Newman, Oscar, 47*n*, 145–148, 152*n*, 153*n*, 191–192, 210*n*, 234, 246*n*
Newspapers, *see* Press
Nigeria, 193, 247*n*
Nixon, President Richard M., 27–28, 46*n*
Nordheimer, Jon, 100*n*
Norfolk (Virginia), 129*n*
Norms, social, 8, 51–53, 60, 63, 68, 83, 95, 131–133, 139–140, 144, 158, 161, 165, 171–172, 174, 179*n*, 181*n*, 193, 216, 218, 223, 231–235, 239
    of noninvolvement, 138, 156–157, 215, 221
    prescriptive, 171–172
    proscriptive, 171–172
North End (Boston), 96, 137
Novitski, Joseph, 212*n*

Occupation, 27, 67, 91, 95–96, 98, 123, 179*n*, 255–257
    father's, 80, 83, 164, 255, 257, 259*t*, 260*t*, 261*t*, 262*t*, 265*t*
    prestige of, 80, 83, 89, 120, 164, 189, 253, 259*t*, 260*t*, 261*t*, 262*t*, 265*t*,
O'Donnell, Richard W., 126*n*
Oelsner, Lesley, 71*n*, 72*n*, 127*n*
Ohio, 33, 101*n*, 180*n*
Omaha (Nebraska), 172
Opportunity cost, 4–5, 196
Opportunity for crime, 135–136, 143, 146
Organizations, social, 6, 92, 96, 98, 104*n*, 110, 141, 185–186, 189, 192, 198–199, 201, 208–209, 209*n*
Organized crime, 25, 30, 46*n*, 100*n*, 101*n*, 126*n*, 168, 185, 205–206, 263*t*, 264*t*
Orléans (France), 18, 35, 52–53, 109

Pace, Eric, 126*n*
Page, Brent, 151*n*, 179*n*, 244*n*

Paris, 2, 34, 45*n*, 189, 243*n*
Parks, 6, 96, 110–111, 143–144, 147, 170, 203, 214, 255–256
Parliament, 31
Parsons, Talcott, 69*n*
Parten, Mildred, 246*n*
Participation in social organizations, *see* Organizations, social
Pathologies of defense, 105–106
Pencil, as weapon, 118
Pennsylvania, 129*n*
People v. Beardsley (1907), 217–218, 244*n*
Perception of crime, 17–25, 28, 45*n*, 47*n*, 50, 56, 66–67, 74, 76–81, 84–85, 88, 90–94, 98, 100*n*, 101*n*, 106, 111, 115, 123, 125, 138, 144, 155, 164, 166–167, 170–171, 174–176, 178, 182*n*, 183*n*, 185, 208, 214, 224, 237, 242, 244*n*, 259*t*
    scale 79–80, 84–85, 90, 92–93, 98, 102*n*, 166, 182*n*, 259*t*
Perception of criminals, 30–42, 85–86, 166
Perrucci, Robert, 183*n*
Perry (Iowa), 64, 136
Personality variables and helping behavior, 231–232
Phalon, Richard, 128*n*
Phoenix, 108
Pick-pocketing, 111, 263*t*
Piliavin, Irving M., 239, 247*n*
Piliavin, Jane Allyn, 239, 247*n*
Pittman, David J., 47*n*
Pittsburgh, 40–41
Platt, Anthony M., 150*n*
Playgrounds, *see* Parks
Pluralistic ignorance, 235–236
Police, 4, 9–10, 16, 20, 22, 25, 27–30, 32, 34, 37, 41, 59, 61, 63–65, 85–88, 101*n*, 108, 111–112, 116–117, 119–124, 129*n*, 133, 135, 137, 139, 142–143, 145, 154–159, 167–170, 173–178, 185, 187–188, 192–209, 212*n*, 214–216, 219–221, 223, 225, 233, 241–242, 244*n*, 248
    attitudes toward, 120–123, 151*n*, 158, 168–169, 175–178, 182*n*, 184*n*, 208, 218, 220

brutality, 158, 198–199, 201, 207–208
corruption, 176, 205
and crime prevention, 10, 117, 119, 123, 151n, 155, 167–169, 174, 176–177, 185–186, 248
criticism of, 63, 112, 120–122, 151n, 157–158, 167–170, 175–176, 185, 191, 193–198, 200–201, 204, 207–208, 215–216, 248
as helpers, 232–233
political pressure on, 28–30
professionalism, 17
recording of crimes, 16–17, 28–30, 43n
and reporting of crime, 15–17, 23, 28–30, 43n, 85–86, 88, 137, 155–159, 162–168, 171–173, 177, 186, 219, 223, 233, 241–242, 248–249, 257n
violence, 122–123, 202–203, 225
Political views, 26–27, 95, 255–257
Population
density, 136, 221, 255–256
size, 22, 254, 256–257
Port City, 21, 24–25, 31–32, 55, 73, 76–80, 82–85, 89–94, 97–99, 101n, 102n, 103n, 159–167, 173, 175–177, 181n, 182n, 216, 218, 223, 232, 251–257, 258n, 259t, 260t, 261t, 262t, 263t, 264t, 265t
interviews with residents of, 252–254
sample selected from, 252–253
Posner, Richard, 151n
Pound, Roscoe, 2, 11n, 209n
Poveda, Tony G., 61, 71n, 168, 182n
Poverty, 16–17, 25, 38, 77, 123
Power, political, 7–8, 46n, 154, 169–170, 172–173, 189–191, 198–199, 201–202, 207
Prejudice, 34–35, 67, 85, 95
Prell, Arthur E., 179n, 181n
President's Commission on Crime in the District of Columbia, The, 13n
President's Commission on Law Enforcement and Administration of Justice, The, 6, 11n, 12n, 13n, 15–17, 24–25, 31–32, 42n, 43n, 44n, 45n, 47n, 74–75, 100n,

101n, 103n, 126n, 128n, 136, 150n, 179n, 180n, 182n, 209n, 258n
Press, 2, 18–20, 22–25, 27, 29, 45n, 58, 61–62, 69n, 71n, 76, 81, 107, 136, 145, 169, 193, 205, 214–215
Primary groups, 132, 138–141
Prisonization, 40
Prisons, 4, 27, 37–40, 65, 159, 188
Privacy, 8–9, 37, 85, 113, 136, 138, 146–147, 177–178, 214, 221, 224, 233–235
Private police, see Guards, security
Prostitution, 52, 109, 111, 172–173, 204
Protection money, 112
Protective measures, 3–6, 9, 18, 37, 53, 59–62, 64, 68, 81, 90, 93–94, 96–97, 105–106, 108, 110–125, 139, 151n, 167, 191–192, 195, 197, 204, 206, 248
Protest, see Demonstrations; Universities, students
Protestants, see Religion
Public characters, 54–55, 144
Puerto Ricans, 65
Puerto Rico, 60
Punishment, 2, 23, 27, 51–53, 68n, 117, 123, 131–133, 135, 154, 158–159, 161–162, 165, 171, 182n, 187–188, 190, 192–194, 202–203, 218, 220, 245n
of bystanders, 217–218, 220
disinterested tendency to inflict, 154
Puritans, 38
Purse-snatches, 108, 111

Queens (New York), 88, 214–215, 223, 227–228
Quinney, Richard, 8, 13n, 44n

Race, 8, 16–17, 26, 34, 36, 38, 40–41, 44n, 45n, 49n, 64–68, 69n, 71n, 72n, 76–77, 81, 83, 85, 87, 91, 95, 103n, 111, 115, 118, 120–123, 151n, 158–159, 175, 196–200, 207–208, 214, 227–229, 239, 254, 256
Radicals, political, 35, 86, 210n, 225

Radios, 22, 70*n*, 224, 241, 244*n*
Rainwater, Lee, 96, 103*n*, 104*n*, 147–148, 153*n*
Ramsey, Charles E., 180*n*
Ranulf, Svend, 154–155, 178*n*
Ranzal, Edward, 211*n*
Rape, 3, 6, 8, 13*n*, 15–16, 22, 24, 67, 69*n*, 75, 83, 107–108, 119, 158, 161, 180*n*, 226–227, 245*n*, 251, 263*t*, 264*t*
Ratcliffe, James M., 180*n*, 243*n*, 244*n*
Reed, Roy, 245*n*
Regional variations, 35–36, 120, 123
Regulators, the, 187, 191
Rehabilitation, 38, 40
Reintegration of deviants and criminals, 7, 33, 38–42, 53, 248
Reiss, Albert J., Jr., 12*n*, 13*n*, 44*n*, 47*n*, 101*n*, 102*n*, 103*n*, 104*n*, 127*n*, 128*n*, 180*n*, 183*n*, 184*n*
Religion, 11*n*, 35–36, 80, 83, 141, 164, 191, 208, 255–257, 259*t*, 260*t*, 261*t*, 262*t*, 265*t*
Reporting of crime, *see* Crime, reporting of
Reprisals, 16, 155–158, 174, 188, 205, 221, 223, 236–237
Residence
of criminals, 31–34, 166
length of, 92, 95–96
preferred, 134
Responsibility
for crime prevention, 10, 119–120, 151*n*, 155, 167–170, 174–178, 185, 216, 220–221, 233, 248–249
diffusion of, 10, 237–243
for helping, 237–238, 243, 249
Restitution, 159
Restrictive covenants, 195
Retribution, 53, 123, 188
Rhodes, William C., 13*n*, 48*n*
Riots, 1, 5, 112, 121–123, 131, 168, 196–198, 200, 208, 214, 254
Risk
assumption of, 226
to offender, 9–10, 136, 145, 148–149, 172–173, 178, 203, 216, 222, 243, 248
to public, 8, 18–19, 40, 61, 75, 80–81, 94–95, 99, 105, 107–108, 110–115, 117, 124, 146, 185, 192, 216–217, 219–220, 222, 226, 233, 238–240, 247*n*
Robbery, 3, 15, 27–30, 35, 37, 41, 43*n*, 49*n*, 53, 59, 64–65, 67, 74–75, 83, 88, 95–96, 100*n*, 105, 110–114, 118–119, 121–122, 156–157, 161, 172–173, 186–187, 220, 223, 241, 251, 263*t*, 264*t*
Robson, Reginald A. H., 179*n*
Rodin, Judith, 239, 247*n*
Role segmentalization, 221
Rome, 187
Rose, Arnold M., 179*n*, 181*n*
Rosen, Linda, 45*n*
Rosenberg, Morris, 183*n*
Rosenthal, A. M., 244*n*
Rosenthal, Jack, 12*n*, 81, 100*n*, 103*n*, 104*n*, 150*n*
Ross, H. Laurence, 180*n*
Ross, Sid, 126*n*
Roxbury, 32, 81
Rudzinski, Aleksander W., 220, 244*n*
Rumors, 18, 35, 52–53, 56–57, 59, 62, 109, 227–228
Runaways, 168, 200
Russians, 230

Safecracker, 135–136
Safety
feelings of, 1, 9, 25, 27, 29, 32, 54, 66, 76, 80–88, 90–91, 93, 111, 115, 123, 125, 139, 142–144, 146–148, 150*n*, 204, 209, 222, 243, 255, 260*t*
islands, 61
in own neighborhood, 8, 47*n*, 67
scale, 83, 260*t*
zones, 144
St. Croix (Virgin Islands), 73
St. Louis, 96, 147
Salerno, Ralph, 46*n*
San Diego, 210*n*
San Francisco, 190–191
Sanford, R. Nevitt, 125*n*, 180*n*
Saxon, Wolfgang, 210*n*, 211*n*
Scapegoats, 58, 215
Scheib, Durwood, 64
Schelling, Thomas C., 4–5, 12*n*
Scherl, Donald J., 100*n*
Schofield, Michael, 47*n*

School, 6, 59–61, 67, 71*n*, 87, 91–92, 104*n*, 110, 148, 152*n*
Schramm, Wilbur, 245*n*
Schuessler, Karl, 70*n*
Schumach, Murray, 103*n*, 127*n*, 130*n*, 211*n*
Schur, Edwin M., 43*n*, 180*n*
Schwartz, Richard D., 48*n*, 139–140, 151*n*
Security, feelings of, *see* Safety, feelings of
Security measures, *see* Protective measures
Segregation, housing and school, 34, 65–66, 71*n*
Seigel, Max H., 48*n*
Self-defense, 117–125, 129*n*
Sellin, Thorsten, 181*n*
Sennett, Richard, 11*n*, 34–35, 48*n*, 182*n*
Sex, 8, 11*n*, 24, 37–38, 44*n*, 57, 80, 83–84, 89, 95, 98, 108–109, 115, 120, 137, 164–165, 179*n*, 194, 205, 237, 239, 245*n*, 253, 259*t*, 260*t*, 261*t*, 262*t*, 265*t*
Sexual psychopath laws, 60
Shaw, Clifford R., 183*n*
Sheatsley, Paul B., 70*n*
Sheehan, Alan H., 212*n*
Shils, Edward, 229, 245*n*
Shopkeepers, 18, 35, 52–53, 109, 111–112, 143–144, 151*n*, 155, 219, 237
Shoplifting, 156, 179*n*, 219, 233
Sibley, John, 47*n*, 210*n*, 247*n*
Simmel, Georg, 52
Singer, Linda R., 49*n*
Size of community, 134–135, 140, 142, 232
    see also Population size
Skolnick, Jerome H., 48*n*
Smigel, Erwin O., 11*n*, 179*n*
Smith, Hedrick, 69*n*
Smith, Paul E., 184*n*
Smothers, Ronald, 71*n*, 211*n*, 212*n*
Social background factors, 11*n*, 25, 79–80, 83, 89–90, 92, 122–123, 141, 154–155, 163–164, 207, 232, 253, 259*t*, 260*t*, 261*t*, 262*t*, 265*t*
Social class, 26, 39, 41, 57, 66, 98, 154–155, 161–162, 164, 167, 172–173, 187, 189, 191, 207, 232, 256–257
    conflict, 33–35, 187, 189–191
    dangerous classes, 34, 189
    laboring classes, 189
    self-designated, 80, 83, 164, 259*t*, 260*t*, 261*t*, 262*t*, 265*t*
Social cohesion, *see* Solidarity
Social control
    formal, 9, 53, 122–123, 131, 137–140, 143, 151*n*, 168, 170, 178, 188
    informal, 9–10, 50, 53, 87, 99, 107, 125, 131–149, 150*n*, 151*n*, 168, 170, 172–173, 178, 195–196, 200, 204, 209, 216–217, 248–249
Social disorganization, 59, 99, 136, 142, 150*n*, 159, 173
    see also Solidarity
Social integration, *see* Solidarity
Social interaction, 4, 7, 9, 42, 50, 68, 93–99, 105–107, 110–111, 113, 124–125, 131–132, 135, 137–141, 144–147, 204, 206, 209, 229–230, 240–241, 248–249, 255
    between victim and bystander, 240–242
Social modeling effect, 238–239, 242
Social status, *see* Social class
Social stratification, 154–155
Socialization, 132, 171, 179*n*, 229
Societies, simple and complex, 132–135, 138, 140, 221–222
Solidarity, 7–9, 21, 35, 50–60, 62–68, 76, 85–88, 93, 99, 105–106, 112, 131, 133, 136–137, 140–142, 144–145, 147–148, 185, 190–191, 201, 204, 206–207, 214, 216, 222, 226, 240, 243, 248–249, 253–254
    functional, 68
    normative, 68
South, the, 65, 68*n*, 122, 198–199
South Carolina, 187, 191
Sovetsky Sport, 69*n*
Soviet Union, 27, 69*n*
Span of sympathy, 229
Spearman rank-order correlation, 181*n*
Special Senate Committee on Aging, 109–111
Specialization, 73, 178, 221

Speck, Richard, 74
Starkweather, Charles, 59
Steffens, Lincoln, 23, 45n
Sterba, James P., 182n
Stereotypes
  of criminals, 30–31, 34–35, 37–38, 86
  of ethnic groups, 35
  of the poor, 34
Stigmatization, 7, 15, 27, 38–39, 63, 189, 228
Strangers, 1, 6–7, 9, 13n, 18, 29, 31–34, 36, 46n, 50, 53, 56–60, 62, 64–65, 73, 85–88, 92, 94–96, 107, 110–111, 114, 133, 137–138, 141, 144–147, 168, 178, 206, 214, 221, 229, 235, 241, 243, 253
Strecher, Victor G., 11n, 183n
Street life, see Human traffic
Strike force, 206
Stun guns, 121, 129n
Subcultures, 40, 69n, 158, 174
Subway, 105, 214, 239
Suicide, 6
Sullivan, Ronald, 128n
Support for the law, 148, 154–178, 183n, 185, 201, 209
Suppressor variable, 173–175, 183n
Supreme Court, 27, 123
Surveillance, 9–10, 99, 124, 132, 134–136, 139–141, 143–149, 152n, 168, 173, 191–192, 194, 197, 200, 203–204, 206, 209, 214, 216, 222, 248–249
Suspicion, see Trust
Sutherland, Edwin H., 60, 70n, 152n, 170–171, 180n, 183n
Sutherland, Sandra, 100n
Suttles, Gerald D., 34, 47n, 143–144, 152n, 195, 211n
Sympathy
  with offender, 33
  with victim, 238–239
Syracuse (New York), 193

Talbot, Warren H., 127n
Tanquist, Mamie, 246n
Target-hardening, 4, 93
Tarpeian rock, 187
Taxes, 170, 196, 206
Taxicabs, 107, 110, 113

Tear gas sprays, 118, 121
Telephones, 59, 137, 157, 244n
Television, 22, 25, 45n, 117, 124, 204, 212n, 215, 221–222, 224–225
Tenafly (New Jersey), 117
Tenant patrols, 37, 67, 118, 191–192, 206, 212n
Tennessee, 67
Territoriality, 146, 148, 195
Test, Mary Ann, 247n
Theft, see Larceny
Thernstrom, Stephan, 11n, 48n, 182n
Threshold effect, 84–85, 90, 93, 176
Toby, Jackson, 245n
Tolchin, Martin, 127n
Tolerance of crime, 132, 142, 171–172, 178, 179n
Tolerance quotient, 19–20
Tompkins, John S., 46n
Tort law, 226
Torture, 187, 203
Tourism, 73, 100n, 126n
Towns, 51, 54–59, 61–64, 101n, 132–141, 147, 150n, 177, 193, 204, 222, 229, 231, 240–241
  see also Urban-suburban-rural differences
Transportation, public, 97–98, 107
Trespassing, 161–163, 263t, 264t
Tribes, 68n, 132, 140–141, 147
  see also Societies, simple and complex
Trouble as a focal concern, 174
Trust, 1, 7, 9, 18, 21, 38, 50, 52–64, 66, 68, 75–76, 85–91, 93–97, 99, 105, 107, 115, 123–125, 131, 133, 137–138, 144–145, 158, 185, 195, 197–198, 206, 216, 248, 253, 261t
  scale, 89–90, 261t
Tunc, André, 244n
Turnbull, Colin M., 151n
Turner, Ralph H., 47n

Uganda, 28, 141, 157, 167
Ukraine, 69n
Unemployment, 5, 38, 76–77, 194
Uniform Crime Reports, 30
United States Bureau of the Census, 251n, 254
Universities, 97, 107, 123–124, 149, 253

students, 33, 97, 158, 162, 194, 218, 230, 232, 263t, 264t
Urban-suburban-rural differences, 8, 40, 58, 63–64, 73, 77, 91, 104n, 120, 123, 133–142, 145, 147, 151n, 177–178, 193, 204, 222, 229–232, 240, 243, 251–252, 254–256, 258n
Urbanization, 178, 221, 231–232

Values, 26, 33, 35–36, 51, 54, 56–57, 68, 68n, 75, 114, 122, 131, 140, 154, 189–190, 193–194, 196, 210n, 224, 226, 229
Vandalism, 5, 67, 78, 101n, 116, 149, 152n, 170, 198, 227–228
Vassar College, 29–30
Vecsey, George, 126n
Veysey, Laurence, 210n
Victimization, 6, 8, 18, 20, 24, 26–27, 39, 43n, 45n, 57, 65, 74–77, 80–81, 83, 85, 94–96, 98–99, 104–105, 107–109, 112, 114–115, 117, 121, 124–125, 142, 146, 159–160, 168, 176, 204, 228, 245n
anticipatory, 93
direct, 75–76, 112
survey, 15–17, 43n, 85, 156, 159, 179n
Victims, 20, 45n, 60, 113, 115, 142, 160, 176, 187, 203, 206, 214, 219, 222–223, 226–230, 245n
and attitudes toward the police, 176
compensation to, 228
confrontation with bystander, 240–242
confrontation with offender, 117–119, 121–122
contribution to the crime, 3–4, 12n, 13n, 99, 108–109, 194, 215, 224, 226–227
injury to, 117, 121–122, 228
perception of crime, 18–19, 24, 74–75, 80–81, 159
relation to offender, 7, 34, 39, 41, 49n, 65, 71n, 156, 226–227
resistance, 74, 121–122
Vietnam war, 77, 202
Vigilante groups, 10, 62, 167, 187–196, 201–202, 210n
accountability of, 191
articles and manifestoes of, 189
costs of, 191–192
counter-movements to, 187, 191
instant vigilantism, 192–194
longevity, 187, 189, 200
neovigilantism, 194, 196
organization of, 188–189, 192, 198–199
philosophy of, 190
sadistic members in, 189, 191, 202
size of, 188–190, 198
socially constructive, 190
socially destructive, 190
trials by, 189–190, 192
Viliborghi v. State (1935), 106, 126n
Villena, J., 151n
Violence for Social Control, 123, 129n
Virgin Islands, 73
Virginia, 86, 117
Voting, 252, 254–257
Vulnerability, 6–7, 37, 50, 57, 75, 91, 93–94, 96, 107–110, 113–115, 124

Wade, Richard C., 183n
Walder, Patrice, 151n, 179n, 244n
Walker, Christopher, 45n
Walker, Nigel, 150n, 181n
Walkie-talkies, 124, 200, 205
Wallace, Christopher, 48n
Warren, Donald I., 149n
Washington, D. C., 91, 112, 118, 209n
Washington Square Park (New York City), 111
Watchdogs, 6, 9, 64, 105–107, 114–115, 124, 139
Watergate burglary, 118
Weapons, see Clubs, as weapons; Firearms; Grenade; Knives; Pencil, as weapon
Wechsler, Herbert, 126n, 244n
Weir, Adrianne, 12n, 43n, 103n, 128n, 182n
Weis, Kurt, 100n, 245n
Welfare hotels, 36–37, 48n, 175–176
Wellford, Charles F., 169, 182n, 183n
West Germany, 27, 217–218
Westchester County (New York), 32, 205

Westin, Jeane, 152n
White slavery, 18, 35, 52–53, 109
    see also Prostitution
Whitechapel Vigilance Committee, 194
White-collar crime, 11n, 158
White-collar workers, see Occupation
Whites, see Race
Whitman, Howard, 12n, 127n
Wiebe, G. D., 209n
Wilkins, Leslie T., 21, 44n
Williams, Emlyn, 209n
Willingness to report crime, 9–10, 15–16, 158, 160, 162–170, 172–178, 182n, 185, 249, 264t, 265t
Wilson, James Q., 11n, 13n, 44n, 150n, 177–178, 182n, 184n
Wilson, P. R., 184n
Winick, Charles, 127n, 183n
Wisconsin, 136

Witnessing a crime, 15, 20, 24, 136, 155–156, 165, 169, 203, 214–243, 248
Wolfenstein, Martha, 245n
Wolfgang, Marvin E., 12n, 18–19, 44n, 49n, 72n, 181n
Wooten, James T., 103n
Work-release, 40

Yeye or mod culture, 53
Youth patrols, 197–198, 200, 208
Youths, 41–42, 61–63, 65, 69n, 71n, 98–99, 108, 109, 126n, 202–203

Zeisel, Hans, 180n, 226, 244n, 245n
Zimbardo, Philip G., 14n, 48n, 103n, 149, 153n
Zimmerman, Mrs. C. C., 246n
Zoning regulations, 195